Abbreviations

1 absolute, absolutely	2 adminis-trate, ion	3 advertise	4 America, n	5 amount	6 and	7 approximate, approxi-mately	8 April	9 associate	10 August
11 avenue	12 average	13 boulevard	14 bureau	15 capital, capitol	16 catalog	17 certify, certificate	18 child	19 children	20 Christmas
21 company	22 corporation	23 credit	24 day	25 December	26 department	27 discount	28 doctor	29 East	30 envelope
31 establish	32 February	33 federal	34 feet, foot	35 figure	36 Friday	37 government	38 inch	39 independent	40 intelligent, intelligently, intelligence
41 invoice	42 January	43 July	44 June	45 junior	46 magazine	47 manufacture	48 March	49 maximum	50 May
51 memorandum	52 merchandise	53 mile	54 minimum, minute	55 miscel-laneous	56 Monday	57 month	58 mortgage	59 North	60 November
61 number	62 October	63 ounce	64 page	65 paid	66 pair	67 parcel post	68 percent	69 place	70 popular
71 post office	72 pound	73 president	74 question	75 railroad	76 railway	77 represent, represent-ative	78 room	79 Saturday	80 second, secretary
81 senior	82 September	83 signature	84 South	85 square	86 street	87 subscribe, subscription	88 Sunday	89 superin-tendent	90 telephone
91 Thursday	92 total	93 Tuesday	94 vice-president	95 volume	96 warehouse	97 Wednesday	98 week	99 West	100 year
101	102	103	104	105	106	107	108	109	110

PRINCIPLES OF *Speedwriting*®

LANDMARK SERIES
SECONDARY EDITION

Speedwriting® EDITIONS

LANDMARK SERIES SECONDARY EDITION

PRINCIPLES OF *Speedwriting®*

Speedwriting® WORKBOOK

Speedwriting® DICTATION AND TRANSCRIPTION

Speedwriting® DICTIONARY

PRINCIPLES OF
Speedwriting®

LANDMARK SERIES
SECONDARY EDITION

The *Speedwriting* Division of
The Bobbs-Merrill Company, Inc.

The Bobbs-Merrill Company, Inc.
4300 West 62nd Street
Indianapolis, Indiana 46268

First Edition
Second Printing—1977

Cover photo by Joseph W. McGuire

Library of Congress Catalog Card Number: 76-40756
ISBN 0-672-98001-0

Contents

Acknowledgments

The Publishers wish to acknowledge the efforts of Verleigh Ernest, whose skill, knowledge, and dedication have made this contribution to better education possible.

The Publishers

Introduction

The concepts of the SPEEDWRITING system represent the culmination of fifty years of research, testing, refinement, and practical application. *Principles of SPEEDWRITING* has been written to provide the necessary skills to meet vocational objectives for stenographers, secretaries, and other office professionals.

The SPEEDWRITING system uses the letters of the alphabet and familiar punctuation marks to represent sounds. As a result, taking notes, building speed, and transcribing are accelerated.

OBJECTIVES OF SPEEDWRITING

The objectives of *Principles of SPEEDWRITING* are to:

1. Develop the ability to recognize sounds.
2. Develop the ability to apply the rules of SPEEDWRITING to the sounds.
3. Develop automatic writing of SPEEDWRITING.
4. Develop fluency of reading shorthand notes.
5. Develop the ability to construct new shorthand outlines.
6. Review preferred spelling, grammar and punctuation in preparation for transcription.

ORGANIZATION OF THE SPEEDWRITING TEXT

Principles of SPEEDWRITING consists of twenty chapters, each divided into three lessons. Each chapter contains a statement of new principles, a thorough explanation of the principles, and vocabulary illustrating applications of the principles, followed by shorthand sentences containing these words.

The last lesson of each chapter offers a graphic summary of the new principles introduced in that chapter in a manner that serves as mnemonic aids to learning.

In each succeeding chapter there is a profusion of review material designed to give continuity and to tie new principles to previously learned materials.

The brief forms and standard abbreviations are distributed among the twenty chapters to ease the learning load.

PRINCIPLES OF *Speedwriting*®

LANDMARK SERIES
SECONDARY EDITION

1

1 You are about to study a system of shorthand in which letters of the alphabet and marks of punctuation are written to represent the sounds that make up our language. It is a scientific system composed of rules that can be employed for the writing of **all** words in the English language—words used in business, law, medicine, engineering, the arts—all fall under a shorthand principle. In this course, you will be trained to apply these principles as easily and naturally as you now write longhand.

□ All shorthand systems are based on sounds, so **write what you hear**. The word *know*, for example, is made up of two sounds, "n" + "o." The *k* and *w* are silent letters. The outline for *know* is 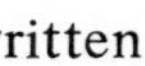 . The word *few* is also made up of two sounds, "f" + "u." The *ew* has the sound "u," so the outline is written . Eliminate the mental picture of the longhand spelling of a word and **listen to its sounds.**

Study these words and practice them:

a~~i~~d	*ad*	v~~i~~ew	*vu*
pa~~y~~	*pa*	di~~e~~	*di*
o~~w~~n	*on*	~~yo~~u	*u*
sno~~w~~	*sno*	I	*i*
se~~e~~	*se*	de~~e~~p	*dep*
o~~we~~	*o*	se~~a~~l	*sel*
si~~g~~n	*sin*	nic~~e~~	*nis*
new	*nu*	go~~a~~l	*gol*

☐ Let's look at the alphabet. Since this system of shorthand uses letters of the alphabet to represent sounds, let's examine some of the features of the alphabet. As you know, the alphabet is divided into two types of letters called **vowels** and **consonants**. The letters we call vowels are *a, e, i, o,* and *u.* All other letters are called consonants.

Each vowel has many sounds. When the sound of the vowel is the same as its alphabetic name, it is called a long vowel. Each word in the previous list contains a long vowel sound. In other words, a long vowel is one that is pronounced as follows:

a as in ape and make

e as in eat and seal

i as in ice and file

o as in oat and hope

u as in unit and fuse

The vowel sound in the words *do, too,* and *tool* is so similar to the one heard in *due* and *tube* that we treat it as a long "u" sound.

These are **all** the sounds of long vowels. A vowel having **any other sound** is referred to as a short vowel.

Pronounce the following groups to become familiar with the differences in the sounds of long and short vowels:

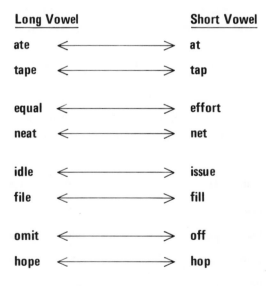

Long Vowel		Short Vowel
ate	⟷	at
tape	⟷	tap
equal	⟷	effort
neat	⟷	net
idle	⟷	issue
file	⟷	fill
omit	⟷	off
hope	⟷	hop

Most of the consonants have only one sound. The sound of "b" in the words *book, about,* and *rib* is the same sound. The sound of "d" in the words *day, edit,* and *bread* is the same sound. A few consonants, however, have more than one sound. For example, the letter *c* has the sound of "s" or "k" in the words *face* and *case; s* has the sound of "s" or "z" in *base* and *rise;* and *g* has the sound of "g" or "j" in *get* and *age*.

How will this be important to you in learning shorthand? Since shorthand is based on **sound**, you will completely disregard the spelling of words and concern yourself only with the sounds that you hear. This is true of all shorthand systems—symbolic as well as alphabetic. **Listen for the sounds!**

☐ A word about writing shorthand. Because this shorthand system is based on precise, clearly defined rules, you will find it an easy system to learn. And since you will be using your **natural** penmanship to a large extent, you will also find it is an easy system to write.

Let's talk for a moment about how to use your natural penmanship to maximum advantage. Observe the handwriting in the following words:

high	*hi*	**race**	*ras*
type	*tip*	**tool**	*tul*
fee	*fe*	**rule**	*rul*
who	*hu*	**safe**	*saf*
do	*du*	**tie**	*ti*
say	*sa*	**file**	*fil*
huge	*huj*	**knew**	*nu*

age	*aj*	**tube**	*tub*
ate	*al*	**robe**	*rob*

The amount of writing has been cut down considerably by not writing silent letters and by eliminating all nonessential strokes. For example, in writing *high* omit the initial stroke on the *h*, omit the dot above the *i*, and omit the two silent letters *g* and *h*: *hi* . You must lift your pen and move it back to dot an *i* or to cross a *t*. This is time-consuming, so the strokes are omitted. In the word *type*, omit the initial stroke on the *t* and do not cross the letter; do not dot the *i*; and omit the silent *e*: *tip* . In the word *huge*, omit the initial stroke on *h*; omit the final stroke on *j* and do not dot the *j*; and omit the silent *e*: *huj* .

You are not expected to radically change your normal handwriting. If you will practice streamlining these letters, you will be able to increase your writing speed.

Write what you hear, omitting all medial short vowels.

Let's examine this rule carefully to see what it means. "Write what you hear" tells you that words will be written according to **sound, not** longhand spelling.

Look at the shorthand words listed on pages 4-5. All these were written according to what is **heard**, and they all contain long vowel sounds.

There are three positions a sound may have in a word: It may be the first sound; it may be the last sound; or it may be somewhere between the first and the last sound. There is a definite name that is given to each of these positions:

Initial refers to the sound at the **beginning** of a word. For example, the *i* in the word *item* and the *b* in the word *book* are initial sounds.

Final refers to the sound at the very **end** of a word. For example, the *o* in *radio* and the *d* in *bad* are final sounds.

Medial refers to any sound that occurs **between** the first and the last sound in a word. For example, the *a* in the word *made* and the *ol* in *hold* are medial sounds.

Now turn your attention to the second part of the rule: "Write what you hear, **omitting all medial short vowels.**" You know that *medial* means middle, so the rule simply tells you that a **short** vowel will **not** be written if it occurs anywhere in the middle of a word. In other words, it is only at the beginning or at the end of a word that a short vowel is to be written.

Compare the words *seal* and *sell.* You have already written *seal* *sel* . What of the word *sell*? In *sell*, the *e* has a short-vowel sound, and it occurs in the middle of the word. According to the rule, you are to drop this **medial short vowel** and write *sell* *sl* . For the same reason *bill* is *bl* .

Study these words and practice them:

said	*sd*	**yet**	*yt*
felt	*flt*	**gone**	*gn*
set	*st*	**bell**	*bl*
bought	*bt*	**tell**	*tl*
let	*lt*	**get**	*gt*
red	*rd*	**rough**	*rf*
build	*bld*	**did**	*dd*

The examples you have seen so far have all been one-syllable words. The omission of medial short vowels also applies to words that contain **more** than one syllable. For example, the word *metal* contains more than one short vowel. Applying the rule to drop **all** medial short vowels, you write *ribbon* rbn ; *happen* hpn.

Study these words and practice them:

bulletin	blln	**ballot**	bll
written	rln	**panel**	pnl
senate	snl	**level**	lvl
knowledge	nlj	**civilian**	svln
citizen	slzn	**deposit**	dpzl
solicit	slsl	**visit**	vzl

You have now covered some words that contain long vowels and some that contain short vowels. There are, of course, many words that contain **both** long and short vowels. For example: *value, item, ready.* To write these words, simply apply the rule that tells you to write long vowels and omit medial short vowels.

Study these words and practice them:

value	vlu	**happy**	hpe
ready	rde	**policy**	plse
follow	flo	**fellow**	flo
heavy	hve	**gallon**	gln
revenue	rvnu	**dozen**	dzn

Remember, it is to **medial** short-vowel sounds only that this rule refers. Short vowels at the beginning or end of a word **will** be written.

Study these words and practice them:

off	*of*	**ahead**	*ahd*
often	*ofn*	**add**	*ad*
us	*us*	**edit**	*edt*
egg	*eg*	**if**	*if*
enough	*enf*	**asset**	*ast*
office	*ofs*	**afar**	*afr*
edifice	*edfs*	**echo**	*eco*

SUMMARY

1. **Write all pronounced consonants and all long vowels.**
2. **Write short vowels only at the beginning or end of a word.**
3. **Disregard spelling and write words according to sound.**

READING EXERCISE

1. *i bt a plse.*
2. *u o a fe.*
3. *i no a fu hu tip.*
4. *gt a hve pnl.*

KEY: (1) I bought a policy. (2) You owe a fee. (3) I know a few who type. (4) Get a heavy panel.

2 What shortcuts have we employed?

1. **No capital letters. We do not use capitals except as applied to certain principles that you will learn later.**
2. **No unnecessary strokes on the first and last letters of each word.**
3. **No crossing of t's or dotting of i's or j's.**

Finally, you should learn to write a streamlined *m* and *w*. Since these are the most time-consuming letters to write, we recommend the use of  for *m*. What we are doing is simply writing a longhand *m* without any up-and-down movement of the pen, like this:  .

Similarly, we are going to write  for *w*. Like the *m*, we have just streamlined the longhand *w*  .

In your shorthand pad, practice writing the streamlined  and  in the following:

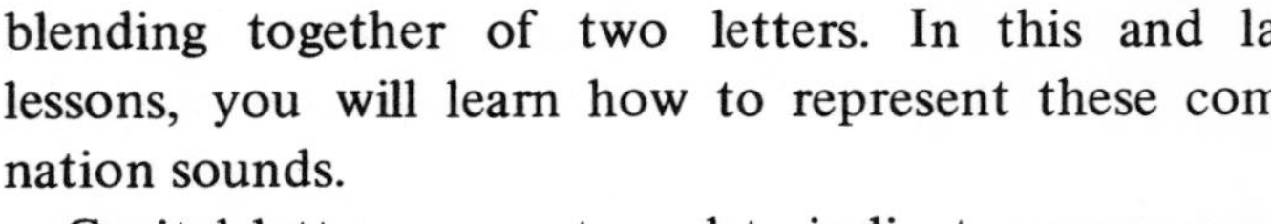

☐ Our language contains certain combination sounds such as "ch," "sh," and "th" that result from the blending together of two letters. In this and later lessons, you will learn how to represent these combination sounds.

Capital letters are not used to indicate proper names. If it is necessary to indicate that a word is to be capitalized, use a wavy line under the first letter of the word Bill (). Be extremely careful, therefore, never to write a capital letter except in the application of rules you will learn in this course.

Write capital C for the sound of "ch."

What does this rule tell you? It simply states that whenever the sound of "ch" is heard in a word, it is represented by writing a capital C. Thus, the word *cheap* is written Cep, the word *much* mC. Notice, in writing the C in *much*, that it is joined to the *m* mC; similarly, *watch* wC.

Study these words and practice them:

match	mC	**reach**	reC
teach	leC	**such**	sC
chief	Cef	**rich**	rC
touch	tC	**each**	eC
attach	alC		

□ Throughout this course, the word *outline* will be used to mean the shorthand representation of a word. Thus, the outline for the word *pay* is pa, and the outline for the word *my* is mi.

Although every word in the English language can be written according to one of our shorthand rules, certain words are used so often in our daily speech that we adopt **special** outlines for them so that they can be written in the shortest time possible. All shorthand systems do this. We call such outlines **Brief Forms.** Fortunately, our list of Brief Forms is not very long; but the words in the list are vital to your success in taking dictation. Since they are not written according to rules, you must study and practice them until you know them thoroughly. Here is the first list of Brief Forms (others will be given in later lessons):

is, his	s	**the**	.
that	la	**to, it**	t
for	f	**will, well**	l
can	c	**we**	e
in, not	n	**are, our, hour**	r

Notice that two or three words are sometimes represented by the same Brief Form outline. You will find that, when read in context, only **one** of the meanings will make proper sense, so there is no confusion. Also notice that the Brief Form for the word *the* is the period—the punctuation mark usually put at the end of a longhand sentence. Since you will have to indicate the end of a sentence in your shorthand notes, you will do so by using a backward slant like this \ **in place of** the period.

Pay the bill. I will pay the bill.

pa . bl \ i l pa . bl \

☐ Certain abbreviations that are used in the business world and in our daily lives are so common that they come to mind automatically. We are going to make use of some of these popular abbreviations. Here are a few. You will study others in later lessons.

company co

and & **(This is called an ampersand.)**

paid pd

president P

vice-president VP

☐ Your goal during the initial stages of this course is not only to learn the rules and their application, but also to acquire the ability to read your shorthand outlines fluently and rapidly. This skill can be acquired only through practice, and we urge you to read and reread each of the **Reading Exercises** you will find in every lesson until you can read them as easily as longhand.

In writing these exercises, we have indicated paragraphs, punctuation, and proper names in the following manner.

1. **Paragraphs: The end of a paragraph is indicated by doubling the last mark of punctuation. For example:** \\ ??
2. **Punctuation marks: Indicated by encircling them within the sentence. For example:** (,) (;)
3. **Proper names: Indicated by placing a wavy line (~) under the word or words that are proper names. For example: Bill and May** bl + ma.

If you have difficulty in reading a particular outline, do not puzzle too long over it. Instead, read on to the end of the sentence to see whether this will give you a clue to the outline that caused you trouble. If you still cannot read the outline, refer to the Key that follows each Reading Exercise.

READING EXERCISE

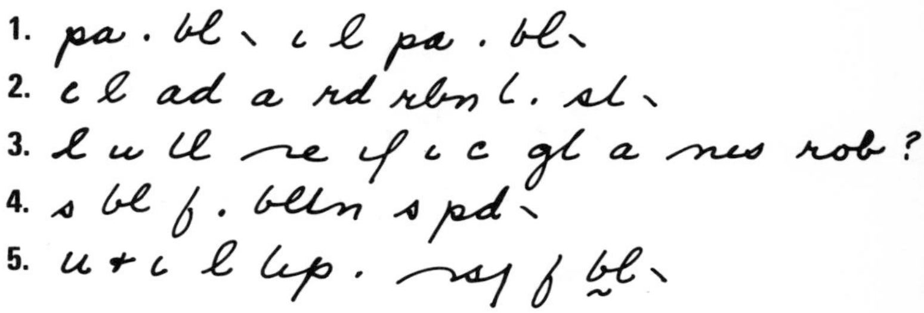

KEY: (1) Pay the bill. I will pay the bill. (6 words) (2) I will add a red ribbon to the set. (7 words) (3) Will you tell me if I can get a nice robe? (9 words) (4) His bill for the bulletin is paid. (6 words) (5) You and I will type the message for Bill. (7 words).

3 As was stated in the introduction, our shorthand system makes use of the alphabet and marks of punctuation to represent sounds. (By a mark of punctuation, we mean any character that is found on the keyboard of a typewriter.) The next rule refers to one of these marks of punctuation—the **underscore.**

When "ing" or "thing" is added to a word, underscore the last sound of the outline.

You know that *reach* is written reC . If the ending "ing" is added to form the word *reaching*, the C will be underscored in compliance with the rule. Thus, *reaching* re<u>C</u> . The word *mailing* is composed of the word *mail* + *ing*. Following the rule, *mailing* is written ma<u>l</u> .

Study these words and practice them:

building	bl<u>d</u>	**weighing**	w<u>a</u>
adding	a<u>d</u>	**watching**	w<u>C</u>

living	lv̲	**soliciting**	slsl̲
running	rn̲	**giving**	gv̲
hoping	hop		

Also use the underscore to indicate the addition of "thing." *Something* is written s̲ and *nothing* is written n̲ .

☐ In shorthand, as in longhand, you are going to build words from the simple to the more complex by starting with a word that is already familiar and adding to it. For example, you know that *for* is written f . Whenever a word contains the sound of "for," write f for the sound.

form	f	**forgive**	fgv
force	fs	**formal**	fml
forget	fgl	**fortune**	fCn
can	C	**into**	nl
cancel	csl	**inform**	nf
canvas	cvs	**involve**	nolv

SUMMARY

j**U**dge jj

A

E

I

O

1. Write what you hear, omitting all medial short vowels.

CHeese C

2. Write capital C for the sound of "ch."

sing ING —

3. When "ing" or "thing" is added to a word, underscore the last sound of the outline.

READING EXERCISE

1. c u du s̲ l ad l . —me ?
2. dd u sa la u r rde l du . lp̲?
3. e r hpe l flo . rul u sl f du̲ . edl̲.
4. i bl a nu rd rob + i l pa f l an.
5. u ra uz . —me i l qv u l pa f . nu rob.
6. e r bl̲ u f . vC̲ lap la e r val̲ l u.
7. f . blln u r lp̲ s rde i l edl l.
8. e r hop̲ a sy l flo l̲l̲ us 'a a nu vC s n . val.
9. e dd n se u dpzl . —me n . ofs saf.
10. c i gl a vll fel l vC . unl n r ofs? ll re no f u sl sC a fel.

KEY: (1) Can you do something to add to the money? (10 words) (2) Did you say that you are ready to do the typing? (9 words) (3) We are happy to follow the rule you set for doing the editing. (13 words) (4) I bought a new red robe and I will pay for it soon. (9 words) (5) You may use the money I will give you to pay for the new robe. (11 words) (6) We are billing you for the matching tape that we are mailing to you. (12 words) (7) If the bulletin you are typing is ready, I will edit it. (12 words) (8) We are hoping a message will follow telling us that a new watch is in the mail. (15 words) (9) We did not see you deposit the money in the office safe. (11 words) (10) Can I get a metal file to match the unit in my office? Let me know if you sell such a file. (18 words)

HOMEWORK Shorthand graduates repeatedly and enthusiastically look back and point to the definite role homework played in their success. It can be of the same distinct importance in *your* success too.

You know it takes study—diligent study—to master any subject. And shorthand is no exception to this rule. If you study diligently, you will learn more easily. If you study in the right way, you will progress more rapidly toward the desirable goal which you have set for yourself.

Here are some helpful hints on how to study in "just the right way"—the way that brings *results*:

First, be sure in your own mind that the *meaning* of each rule is crystal-clear. Think about it. It is the very foundation of your study.

Then go on to the words listed under the rule. These are typical examples of how the rule is applied. Examine each one carefully. Can you see how the rule is applied to produce the shorthand outline? It is imperative that you do in every case.

Now, move to the brief forms and abbreviations. *Memorize* and fix each outline in your mind. Write each brief form and abbreviation several times to help you memorize it. Remember, they are the very backbone of the dictation you will be taking in the future.

Now complete your assignment by reading—and rereading—the shorthand plates which appear in the lesson. It is the practice you get now that will help you when you are ready to transcribe from your own shorthand notes!

Cp 2

1 You have learned to write an underscore to indicate that the sound of "ing" or "thing" has been added to a word. You are now going to learn to write a hyphen to represent another sound.

For the medial and final sound of "nt" or "ment" write a hyphen (-).

Let's start with the sound of "nt" heard at the end of the words *agent* and *want.* The word *age* is aj . If the sound of "nt" is now added to form the word *agent,* simply add a hyphen (-) and write *agent* aj- . The word *want* is made up of the sounds "w" + "nt," so write w- .

Study these words and practice them:

sent	s-	**bent**	b-
event	ev-	**rent**	r-
went	w-	**paint**	pa-
absent	abs-	**resident**	rzd-

What is the sound at the end of the words *doesn't* and *don't?* Do you recognize it as the same sound heard in *went*? Since it is the same sound of "nt," apply the rule to these contractions.

Study these words and practice them:

won't	wo-	**didn't**	dd-
doesn't	dz-	**don't**	do-

The second part of this rule tells you that the hyphen is also written for the medial or final syllable "ment." You know that *pay* is pa ; in the word *payment* you simply add a hyphen for the syllable "ment," pa- .

Study these words and practice them:

settlement	sll-	**management**	mj-
regiment	rj-	**judgment**	jj-

The rule tells you to write a hyphen for the **medial** and **final** sound of "nt" or "ment." In other words, you will also write a hyphen for the sound of "nt" in the middle of a word such as *rental* r-l .

Study these words and practice them:

dental	d-l	**regimental**	rj-l

There are many words that end in the sound of "nt" to which "ing" is added. For example: *hunting* and *wanting.* When writing these words, the hyphen will be handled just as if it were a letter of the alphabet, and the rule to underscore for "ing" will be applied.

hunting	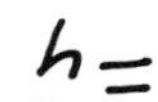	**painting**	
renting	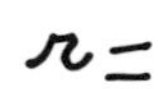	**regimenting**	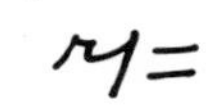

What of the word *meant?* This rule tells you to write a hyphen for the **medial** and **final** sound of "ment" but it does **not** say initial. Therefore, the word *meant* is written  and *mental* .

It is important in writing the hyphen to use a short stroke in order to save time and to facilitate the reading of your notes.

READING EXERCISE

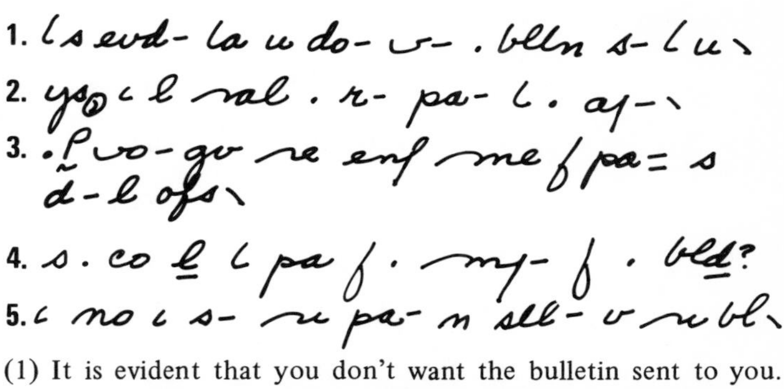

KEY: (1) It is evident that you don't want the bulletin sent to you. (11 words). (2) Yes, I will mail the rent payment to the agent. (9 words) (3) The President won't give me enough money for painting his dental office. (13 words) (4) Is the company willing to pay for the management for the building? (13 words) (5) I know I sent my payment in settlement of my bill. (10 words)

☐ In the word *when* the "wh" combination contains a sound of *h* that is lightly pronounced. Use  for this combination sound.

Study these words and practice them:

when		**which**	
what		**whale**	

Add *s* to form the plural of a shorthand outline that ends in a letter of the alphabet; when an outline ends in a mark of punctuation, form the plural by repeating the mark of punctuation.

The word *net* is written nl . This rule instructs you to add *s* to the outline to indicate the plural. Thus, *nets* nls . Since *piece* is written pes , you will write *pieces* pess .

Study these words and practice them:

units	unls	**offices**	ofss
faces	fass	**lots**	lls
maps		**debts**	dls
hopes	hops	**assets**	asls
companies	cos	**hours**	rs

Some plurals have the sound of "z"; for example, *items* and *jobs.* Through long years of usage, you are accustomed to writing *s* for all plurals regardless of sound. You are going to take advantage of this established habit by doing the same in shorthand, so you add *s* to your outline for either plural sound. Thus, *items* ıtms ; *jobs* jbs ; *dues* dus ; *citizens* stzns .

Although the rule refers to the formation of plurals, you are going to use the same rule to indicate possessives, contractions, and the addition of *s* to verbs.

Study these words and practice them:

pays	pas	**follows**	flos
gives	gvs	**reaches**	reCs
women's	ᴗ—ms	**men's**	—ms
what's	ᴗts	**types**	tps
gets	gts	**tells**	tls
touches	tCs	**sells**	sls
it's	ts	**that's**	tas

In all of the examples given for this rule, you will notice that the pronunciation of the basic word remains unchanged with the addition of *s*. Since this is not true of *says* and *does,* you will recall that these words are written *says* sz and *does* dz .

The second part of the rule refers to outlines that end in a mark of punctuation. For example, *want* ᴗ– . The rule states that in such cases you are to repeat the mark of punctuation to indicate the addition of *s* to the word, so *wants* ᴗ– – . As you know, the outline for the word *paint* is pa- . To write *paints* you simply add another hyphen: *paints* pa- -. Consider the word *buildings.* Since the outline for the word *building* is bld , you add another underscore to your outline: *buildings* bld . Similarly, *payment* is pa- and *payments* pa- - .

Study these words and practice them:

ceilings	sel	**wrappings**	rp
agents	aj- -	**billings**	bl
mailings	mal	**paintings**	pa

READING EXERCISE

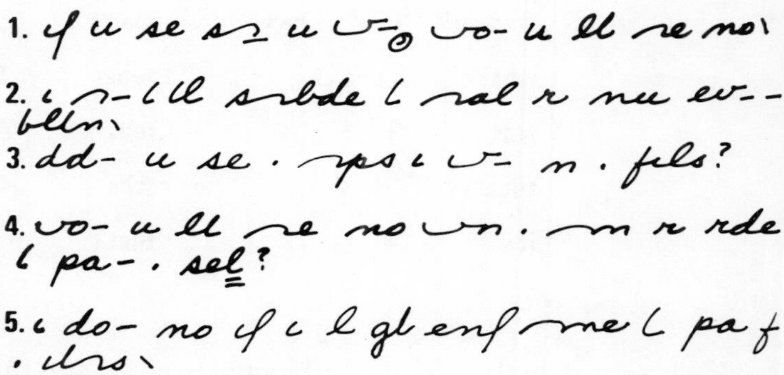

KEY: (1) If you see something you want, won't you let me know. (9 words) (2) I meant to tell somebody to mail you our new events' bulletin. (12 words) (3) Didn't you see the maps I want in the files? (8 words) (4) Won't you let me know when the men are ready to paint the ceilings? (11 words) (5) I don't know if I will get enough money to pay for the items. (12 words)

2 For the sound of "sh" write capital *S* .

In the word *show* you hear the sound of "sh."

Applying the rule that you are to write *S* for this sound, *show* is written *So* . The sound of "sh" is heard in the word *rush*. Following this rule, you write *rush* *rS* .

Study the following words and practice them:

shouldn't	Sd-	**rushes**	rSs
wish	◡S	**issues**	iSus
showing	So̲	**finish**	fnS
sufficient	sfS-	**issuing**	iSu̲
efficient	efS-	**shape**	Sap

Remember, the rule tells you to write *S* for the sound of "sh." You have learned to disregard spelling and to write what you hear. Notice that we did exactly that in the words *sufficient* and *issues* in the last word list.

You have now learned two combination sounds: "ch" and "sh." Remember, *C* for the sound of "ch" and *S* for the sound of "sh."

Study the following words and practice them:

chop	Cp	**shop**	Sp
cheap	Cep	**sheep**	Sep
chill	Cl	**shell**	Sl
patch	pC	**push**	pS

BRIEF FORMS	firm	*F*	this	*th*
	letter	*L*	on	*o*
	would	*d*	have, very, of	*v*

ABBREVIATIONS	catalog	*cal*	month	
	day	*d*	year	*y*
	week			

SUMMARY

plaNT –
MENT

1. Write a hyphen (-) for the medial or final sounds of "nt" or "ment."

WHeelchair 

2. For the combination sound of "wh," write  .

shoeS 

3. Add s to form the plural of a shorthand outline that ends in a letter of the alphabet; repeat the punctuation mark to form the plural of an outline that ends in a mark of punctuation.

fiSH 

4. Write  **for the sound of "sh."**

READING EXERCISE

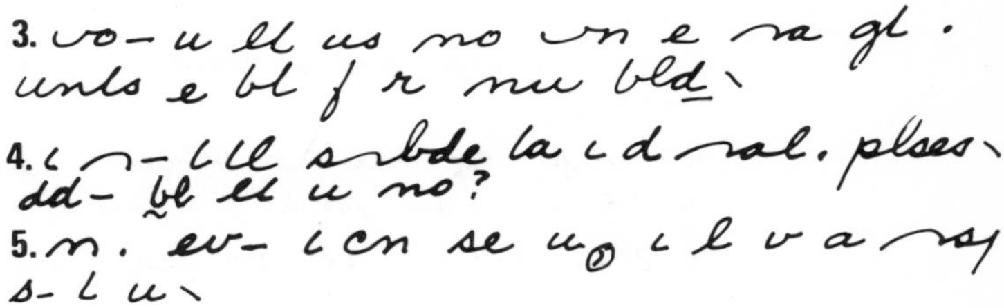

KEY: (1) Fill in and sign the form when it reaches you. Do not delay in doing this. (13 words) (2) Some of the men will visit the showing of the new models that we sell. (13 words) (3) Won't you let us know when we may get the units we bought for our new building. (13 words) (4) I meant to tell somebody that I would not mail the policies. Didn't Bill let you know? (16 words) (5) In the event I cannot see you, I will have a message sent to you. (13 words)

3 WORD DEVELOPMENT

its	ts	haven't	v-
isn't	s-	wouldn't	d-
ours	rs	accompany	aco
having	v	somewhat	s⌣l
into	nl	somebody	s⌣bde

☐ Write the figure to indicate numbers.

someone	s⌣ 1	three policies	3 plses
10 men	10 ⌣n	20 women	20 ⌣⌣n

READING EXERCISE

1. do-fgl la e ⌣- l aco u ⌣n u vzl . nu ofss.
2. d u ll e no ⌣n . ⌣mfnS lip . nal so la i c gl s⌣l l nal . Ls.
3. dz- . Sp sl ⌣ms & ⌣ms Sus?
4. I v r aj-- s- a blln l us nf- us la 5 nu pess r du.
5. f u v- . jb v fl-o fl n . f la e r dlc.

KEY (1) Don't forget that we want to accompany you when you visit the new offices. (15 words) (2) Would you let me know when the women finish typing the mailings so that I can get someone to mail the letters. (20 words) (3) Doesn't the shop sell men's and women's shoes? (7 words) (4) One of our agents sent a bulletin to us informing us that five new pieces are due. (16 words) (5) If you want the job of filing, fill in the form that we are attaching. (17 words)

PEN OR PENCIL?

When you write shorthand, do you:

1. Use a pen?

2. Leave the cap off the pen while you are writing?

3. Carry a sharpened pencil "just in case"?

Experience has proved that a reliable pen is a more efficient writing instrument than a pencil because:

1. Pen-written notes are more legible under artificial light.

2. Pen-written notes do not smudge.

3. Writing with a pen requires less effort, resulting in a minimum of fatigue. You grip a pencil more tightly and press harder when you write.

Cp 3

1 In the word *cat* the letter *c* has the sound of "k"; in the word *city* it has the sound of "s." An analysis of the English language shows that in words that have the sound of "k," this sound is represented by the letter *c* over 90 percent of the time. You need only think of words such as *car, cut, college, coal, coffee, locate, physical, fact,* and *attic* to realize the validity of this figure. Since *k* is one of the most difficult and time-consuming letters to write, and since *c* is the easier and quicker, we represent the sound of "k" in our shorthand system by writing *c* as stated in the next rule.

For the sound of "k" write c .

Study the following words and practice them:

could	cd	**college**	cj
checking	C<u>c</u>	**can't**	c-
copy	cpe	**book**	bc
car	cr	**took**	tc

packages	pcjs	**desk**	dsc
key	ce	**oak**	oc
cabinet	cbnl	**check**	Cc
cases	cass	**talking**	
cash		**cause**	cz
skill	scl	**back**	bc

☐ You have already learned to write the combination sounds of "sh," "ch," and "wh" in previous lessons. Now you are going to learn another combination sound.

For the medial and final sound of "ow" write  .

Let's illustrate this rule with the word *how*. This word is composed of two sound, "h" + "ow." Since you are learning to write  for the sound of "ow," the word *how* will be written  . Similarly, the word *town* contains the sound of "ow" so *town* is written  .

Listen to the **sound** as you say the words *doubt* and *house*. These words also contain the sound of "ow," so *doubt* is 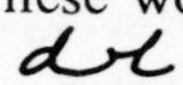 and *house*  .

Study these illustrations:

now		**down**	
allow		**loud**	

READING EXERCISE

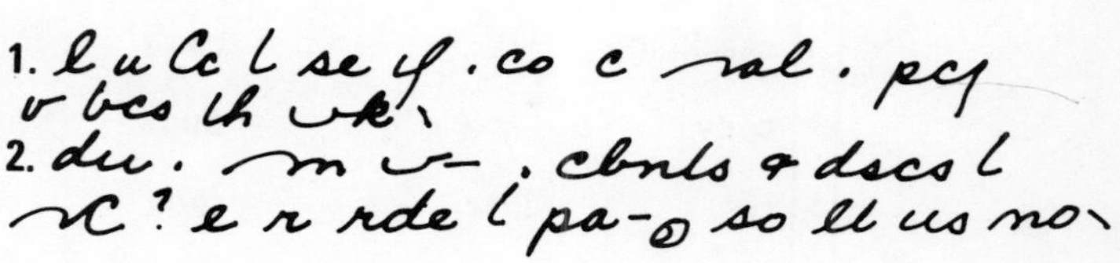

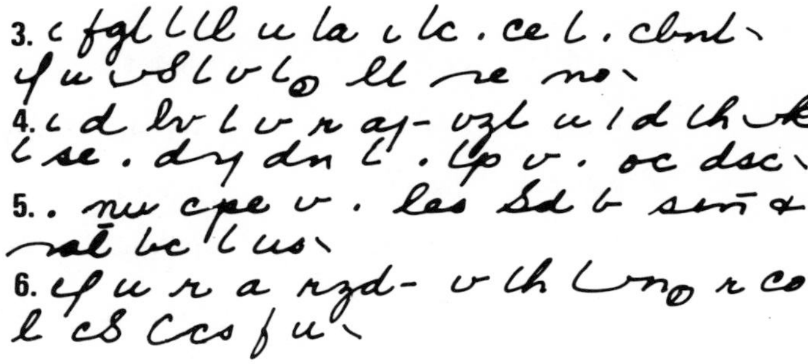

KEY (1) Will you check to see if the company can mail the package of books this week. (13 words) (2) Do the men want the cabinets and desks to match? We are ready to paint, so let us know. (16 words) (3) I forgot to tell you that I took the key to the cabinet. If you wish to have it, let me know. (18 words) (4) I would love to have our agent visit you one day this week to see the damage done to the top of the oak desk. (20 words) (5) The new copy of the lease should be signed and mailed back to us. (11 words) (6) If you are a resident of this town, our company will cash checks for you. (13 words)

2 You have learned that the last letter or mark of punctuation of an outline is underscored to indicate the addition of "ing" or "thing." You are now going to learn to use a mark of punctuation to indicate that the sound of "ed" has been added to a word.

When "ed" is added to a word to form the past tense, overscore the last letter or mark of punctuation of the outline.

For example, the word *file* is written fl ; and when this rule is applied to the word *filed*, you simply overscore the l in the outline and write *filed* f$\bar{l}$. In the same way, the word *reach*, as you know, is written reC ; and *reached* re$\bar{C}$. The word *issue* is iSu ; the word *issued* iS$\bar{u}$.

Study these words and practice them:

used	uz̄	**added**	ad̄
filed	fil̄	**typed**	tip̄
signed	sin̄	**limited**	lt̄
mailed	mal̄	**finished**	fns̄
damaged	dj̄	**listened**	lsn̄

Do you recall that you wrote the word *hunting* h= ? In other words, you treated the hyphen as though it were a letter of the alphabet; and it was underscored to indicate the addition of "ing." Similarly, when an outline ends in a hyphen and "ed" is added to the word, you will **overscore** the hyphen.

Study these words and practice them:

painted	pa=	**rented**	r=
invented	nv=	**wanted**	◡=

You have now had two rules—one dealing with the underscore and one dealing with the overscore. To help separate these rules in your mind, think of the g in ing ; its downward stroke points to the underscore that represents "ing." And think of the d in ed ; its upward stroke points to the overscore that represents "ed."

BRIEF FORMS	**help**	hp	**buy**	b
	like	lc	**by**	b

during	du	**be**	b
why	y	**been**	b
ask	sc	**but**	b

SUMMARY

Cat c

1. Write c for the sound of "k."

mOUse

2. For the medial or final sound of "ow," write .

mailED —

3. To add the sound of "ed" to a word, overscore the last letter or mark of punctuation of the outline.

READING EXERCISE

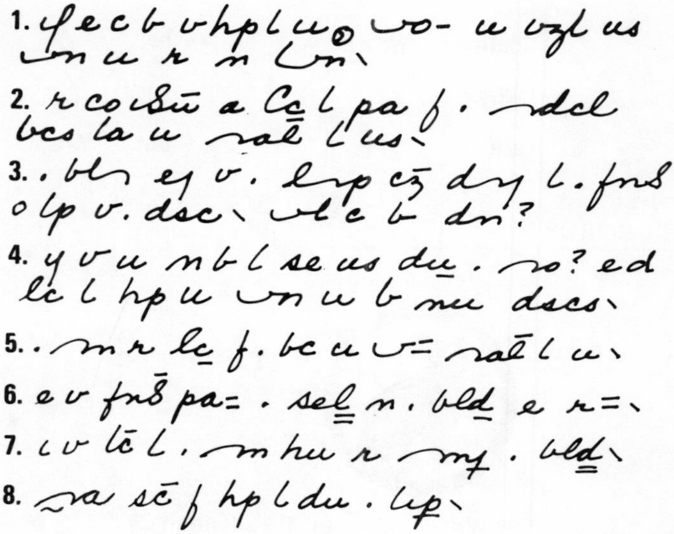

KEY (1) If we can be of help to you, won't you visit us when you are in town. (13 words) (2) Our company issued a check to pay for the medical books that you mailed to us. (15 words) (3) The bottom edge of the lamp caused damage to the finish on top of the desk. What can be done? (17 words) (4) Why have you not been to see us during the month? We would like to help you when you buy new desks. (17 words) (5) The men are looking for the book you wanted mailed to you. (10 words) (6) We have finished painting the ceilings in the building we rented. (11 words) (7) I have talked to the men who are managing the buildings. (10 words) (8) Mae asked for help to do the typing. (6 words)

3 Indicate salutations and complimentary closings as follows:

Dear Sir		**Sincerely yours**	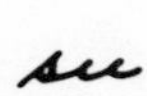
My dear Sir		**Very truly yours**	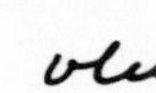
Dear Madam		**Yours truly**	

Gentlemen / **Yours very truly** uvl

Cordially yours cu **Respectfully yours** ru

READING EXERCISE

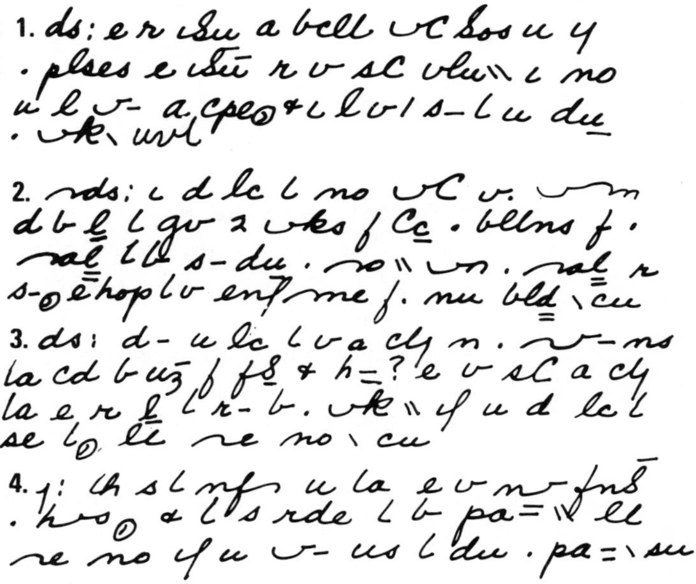

KEY (1) Dear Sir: We are issuing a booklet which shows you why the policies we issue are of such value. (P) I know/ you will want a copy, and I will have one sent to you during the week. Yours very truly, (37 words) (2) My dear Sir: I would like to know which of the women would be willing to give two weeks for checking the bulletins/ for the mailings to be sent during the month. (P) When the mailings are sent, we hope to have enough money for the/ new buildings. Cordially yours, (44 words) (3) Dear Sir: Wouldn't you like to have a cottage in the mountains that could be used for fishing and hunting? We have such/ a cottage that we are willing to rent by the week. (P) If you would like to see it, let me know. Cordially yours, (40 words) (4) Gentlemen: This is to inform you that we have now finished the house, and it is ready to be painted. (P) Let me/ know if you want us to do the painting. Sincerely yours, (30 words)

READING SHORTHAND Have you stopped to consider how the Reading Exercises are helping you to develop shorthand skill?

Each exercise helps you to fix in your mind the new principles that have been presented in the lesson. For example, the preceding Reading Exercise contains 14 words that use the new principles introduced in Chapter Three. The brief forms and standard abbreviations are also reviewed.

All of this repetition is necessary to the mastering of shorthand.

The efficient use of shorthand depends upon easy and rapid reading of outlines. To acquire the skill of reading easily and rapidly, read all the shorthand you can. The more shorthand you read, the more rapidly you will be able to write shorthand.

Cp 4

1 You know that you write *c* for the sound of "ch" and *s* for the sound of "sh." You will now learn how to write another combination sound.

For the sound of "th" write *l* .

This rule states that whenever the sound of "th" is heard in a word, you are to write *l* for that sound.

Study these words and practice them:

them	*lm*	**methods**	*-lds*
health	*hll*	**then**	*ln*
thus	*ls*	**though**	*lo*
than	*ln*	**death**	*dl*

□ For the final sound of "lee" write *l* .

You know that *rapid* is written *rpd* . To write *rapidly* you simply add *l* . Thus, *rapidly* *rpdl* .

Study these words and practice them:

daily	dl	**duly**	dul
yearly	yl	**hourly**	rl
family	fml	**badly**	bdl
efficiently	efs-l	**evidently**	evd-l
readily	rdl	**highly**	hil
easily	ezl	**valley**	vl

Applying the rule to write l for the final sound of "ly," *hilly* will be written hl, the same as *hill* hl. When you are reading your notes, the context will tell you which form of the word to use. So, too, with words such as *chill* Cl and *chilly* Cl.

Although the word *happy* is written hpe, the final *e* becomes a medial short vowel when *ly* is added to the root word. The word *happily* is written hpl and the word *easily* is written ezl.

The word *knowing* is written no̲. When *ly* is added to an outline ending with an underscore, attach the l to the underscore. The word *knowingly* is written no̲l.

READING EXERCISE

1. r fml l lv n. vl n. nu y.
2. e r lkg v rpdl n-.
3. wn l u vzt ls? cd u du th / d th no?

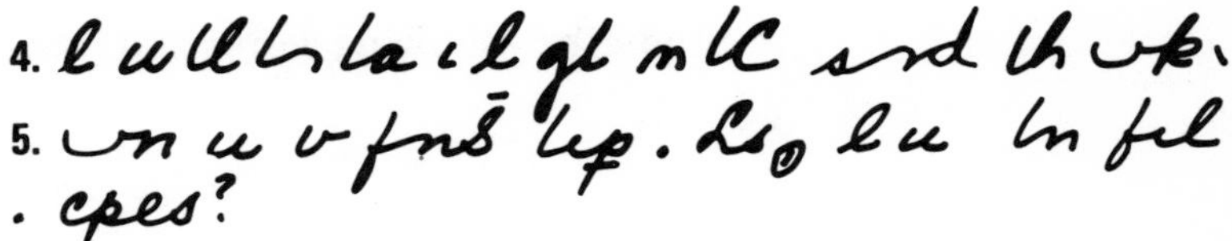

KEY (1) Our family will live in the valley in the new year. (10 words) (2) We are typing very rapidly now. (7 words) (3) When will you visit them? Could you do this one day this month? (10 words) (4) Will you tell them that I will get in touch someday this week. (10 words) (5) When you have finished typing the letters, will you then file the copies? (13 words)

2 As you pronounce the following words, notice that the initial sound in each word is produced by a blending together of two sounds: *bred, cry, drive, from, grant, profit, truck.* It is to this combination sound of an initial letter combined with "r" that the next rule applies.

To indicate the sound of an initial letter that is combined with "r" write a hyphen on the initial letter of the outline.

Thus, at the beginning of a word you write  for "br,"  for "cr," 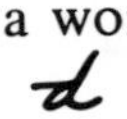 for "dr," 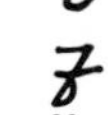 for "fr,"  for "gr,"  for "pr," and  for "tr."

You know that *bed* is written . How would you write *bred?* Since  represents the initial sound of "br," the word *bred* is written 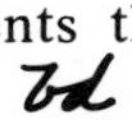. In the same way, you write *beef* 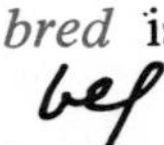 and *brief* .

Write the hyphen first at the point where you begin the letter that follows it. You know that *cash* is written 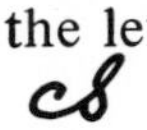. Therefore, *crash* is 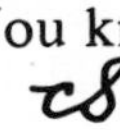.

Applying this same principle, you can see why *grow* is written ; *drop* 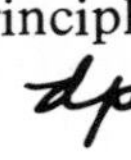; *profit* 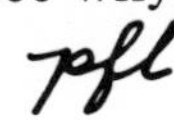; *try* .

Study the following words and practice them:

brown	b⌒n	**broad**	bd
brought	bl	**broke**	boc
cry	ci	**crashed**	cs̄
critical	clcl	**crop**	cp
dry	di	**drag**	dg
free	fe	**from**	f⌒
group	gup	**granted**	g=
growth	gol	**growing**	go_
profits	pfls	**privilege**	pvlj
print	p-	**proud**	p⌒d
proof	puf	**promise**	p⌒s
traffic	tfc	**true**	tu
travel	tvl	**trees**	tes
tried	tī	**trying**	ti_

What of the word *earn?* There is no practical way to attach a hyphen to an *e* written in this manner: e . Therefore, write ε in this instance because it lends itself more easily to the attaching of an initial hyphen. For the sound of initial "er" write Ɛ . The word *earn* will be written Ɛn and *earth* Ɛl . Notice that the word *urge* is written uj although the initial sound is identical with that at the beginning of the word *earn*. This is done as an aid to transcribing.

Note the sound at the beginning of the words *through* and *throw*. You know that you write *t* for the sound of "th." Since "thr" combines this sound with "r," follow the rule and write an initial hyphen on the *t* for the sound of "thr": *through* Tu ; *throw* To ; and *thrill* Tl .

Similarly, for the sound of "shr" in the word *shred* the initial hyphen is added to S ; the word *shred* is written Sd and *shrubs* Sbs .

Study these words and practice them:

urban	ubn	**argue**	agu
article	alcl	**arguments**	agu--
irons	ins	**or**	o
originally	ojnl	**urgent**	uj-
army	ae	**art**	al
air	a	**arch**	aC
erred	Ē	**thrilled**	Tl̄
shredding	Sd̲	**shroud**	Surd

READING EXERCISE

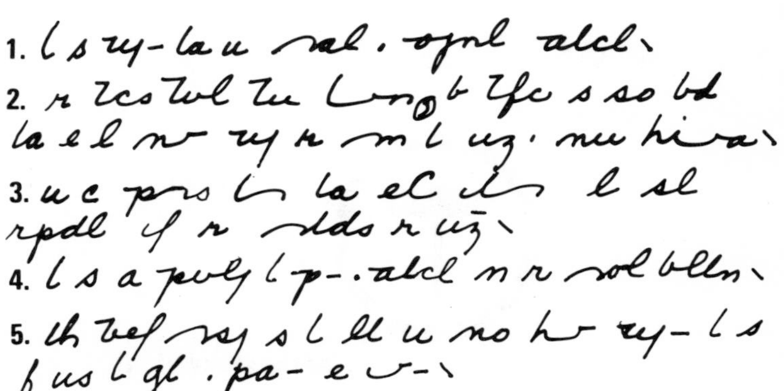

KEY (1) It is urgent that you mail the original article. (11 words) (2) Our trucks travel through town, but traffic is so bad that we will now urge our men to use the new highway. (18 words) (3) You can promise them that each item will sell rapidly if our methods are used. (14 words) (4) It is a privilege to print the article in our monthly bulletin. (13 words) (5) This brief message is to let you know how urgent it is for us to get the paint we want. (16 words)

3

BRIEF FORMS

your	u	price	ps
great	g	woman	wm-
man	m-	as, was	z
their, there	ℓ	were, with	w

ABBREVIATIONS

credit	cr	discount	dis

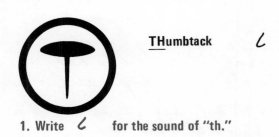

SUMMARY

THumbtack ℓ

1. Write ℓ for the sound of "th."

hoLLY ℓ

2. Write ℓ for the final sound of "lee."

IRon 

3. Write a hyphen on the initial letter of an outline to indicate the sound formed by the initial letter combined with r.

READING EXERCISE

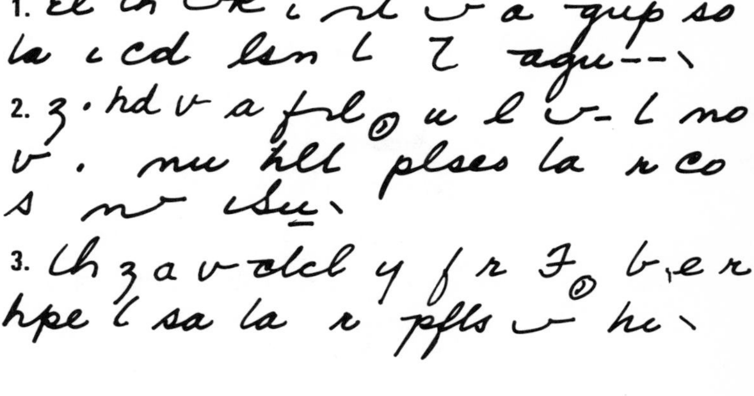

4. ʌC z . cos d lc l du so⊙ e cn dp . ps v a Tol lcls.

5. T r s fils n r Lns hu v b b clys o . beC.

6. ds: a ʌsy Fs r ap-lls us la u hos n . vlz bdl dy̅ " ylh s Tu⊙ a Cc l b s- l pa f . dy. ul

7. ds: yf u c gv us puf v vl u sd n u L⊙ e l ln v a nu ʌn s- n a fu ds. vlu

8. j: r F s go v rpdl⊙ + e Sd b pd v lh gol " lh Tef ʌsy s l ll u la u + u ʌm c b pd v vl u v du l hp us. su

9. ds: e v v hpe l gl u ʌol Cc n . ʌal ld. e l cr u f lh pa- . . alcls u v- l b s- n a d o 2 " b . va⊙ du u no la u c En a dis b sll lh bl ʌn 30 ds? ul

10. ds: e v b Tu f 2 vks l reC u⊙ b u v evd-l b ava fs u

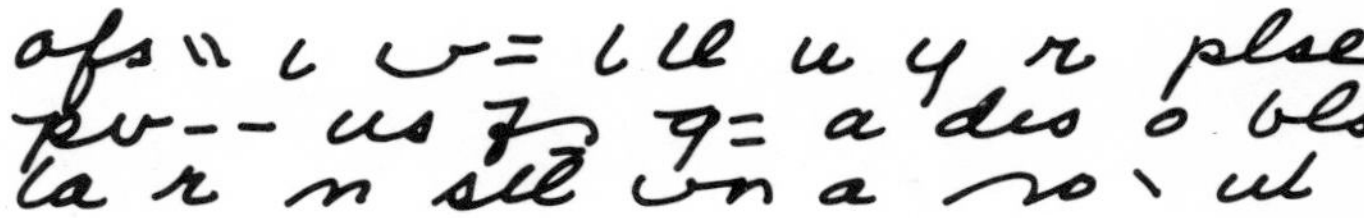

KEY (1) Early this week I met with a group so that I could listen to their arguments. (14 words) (2) As the head of a family, you will want to know of the new health policies that our company is now issuing. (21 words) (3) This was a very critical year for our firm, but we are happy to say that our profits were high. (18 words) (4) Much as the companies would like to do so, we cannot drop the price of air travel tickets. (23 words) (5) There are some families in our town who have been buying cottages on the beach. (14 words) (6) Dear Sir: A message from our agent tells us that your house in the valley was badly damaged. (P) If this is true, a/ check will be sent to pay for the damage. Yours truly, (29 words) (7) Dear Madam: If you can give us proof of what you said in your letter, we will then have a new iron sent in a/ few days. Very truly yours, (25 words) (8) Gentlemen: Our firm is growing very rapidly, and we should be proud of this growth. (P) This brief message is to tell/you that you and your men can be proud of what you have done to help us. Sincerely yours, (35 words) (9) Dear Madam: We were very happy to get your monthly check in the mail today. We will credit you for this payment./ The articles you want will be sent in a day or two. (P) By the way, do you know that you can earn a discount/ by settling this bill within 30 days? Yours truly, (50 words) (10) Dear Sir: We have been trying for two weeks to reach you, but you have evidently been away from your office. (P) I/ wanted to tell you why our policy prevents us from granting a discount on bills that are not settled within/ a month. Yours truly, (42 words)

Cp 5

1 You have learned to write the long-vowel sounds in such words as *mail* ***mal*** ; *seal* ***sel*** ; *type* ***tip*** ; *hope* ***hop*** ; *rule* ***rul*** . Notice that these are all one-syllable words. The following rule deals with long-vowel sounds that occur in words of more than one syllable.

Omit all medial long vowels in words of more than one syllable.

In other words, a long vowel in the middle of a word will be written in a one-syllable word only. For example, you know that the outline for the word *tail* is ***tal*** . The word *retail,* however, has more than one syllable, and the rule in this lesson tells you to omit this medial long vowel. Therefore, *retail* is written ***rtl*** . Look at the word *league.* It is a one-syllable word so you write the long "e" in your outline: *league* ***leg*** . On the other hand, the word *legal* is a word of more than one syllable, so omit the medial long vowel and write *legal* ***lgl*** . As a further example, the words *deep* and *deeply* both contain the sound of "e" but you write this vowel only in the word that has one syllable. Thus, *deep* **dep** ; *deeply* **dpl** .

When words become longer, there are more consonants to be written in the outlines so the vowels are not needed to indicate what the words are.

Study the following words and practice them:

recently	rs-l	**taken**	tcn
machine	mSn	**decide**	dsd
alone	aln	**prevailing**	pvl_
radio	rdo	**proceed**	psd
chosen	Czn	**schedule**	scdl
obtaining	obtn_	**music**	mzc
appeal	apl	**producing**	pds_
reason	rzn	**reduce**	rds
presented	pz=	**prevent**	pv-
hotel	htl	**ordeal**	odl
season	szn_	**local**	lcl
provided	pvd¯	**gasoline**	gsln
region	rjn	**aluminum**	almn
recent	rs-	**coupon**	cpn
remain	rmn	**refuse**	rfz
revised	rvz¯	**proposal**	ppzl
patiently	pS-l	**widely**	wdl

The word *title* is written **ttl**. Notice that for clarity in reading the double *t* is crossed in the outline.

There are a few simple exceptions to this rule which you need to understand in order to apply it correctly.

First, when "ing" or "ed" is added to an outline that contains a long vowel, this vowel is not dropped from the outline. Thus: *hoping* **hop**; *teaching* **leC**; *filed* **fil**.

Second, when the outline of a root word ends in a vowel, that vowel is retained when a suffix is added to it. For example: *high* **he**; *highly* **hel**; *highway* **he-sa**; *true* **tu**; *truly* **tul**; *pay* **pa**; *payroll* **parl**; *payment* **pa-**; *renew* **rnu**; *renewal* **rnul**.

Notice in these examples that the pronunciation of the root word remained unchanged when the suffix was added. But you must remember that in such words as *ready* **rde**, *readily* **rdl**, *happy* **hpe**, and *happily* **hpl** the pronunciation of the basic word changes when the suffix is added, and therefore the vowel is not retained.

Finally, when a long vowel is followed by a mark of punctuation, retain the vowel. For example: *moment* **mo-**; *truant* **tu-**.

READING EXERCISE

1. l se. no rzn y. nSns cn b s-.
2. . nsj sd la u v b Czn l leC nzc ns r lcl cly th szn.
3. e rs-l dsd l obln nu nSns f r rll Sps.
4. e r ndd hpe l no v u rs- fCn.
5. . lcl rdo cspn la u ppz lb v q hp l r cz.

KEY (1) I see no reason why the machines cannot be sent. (9 words) (2) The message said that you have been chosen to teach music in our local college this season. (16 words) (3) We recently decided to obtain new machines for our retail shops. (13 words) (4) We are indeed happy to know of your recent fortune. (9 words) (5) The local radio campaign that you proposed will be of great help to our cause. (14 words)

2 Another sound that is common in our language is the sound of "oi" that is heard in such words as *boy, choice,* and *loyal.*

For the sound of "oi" write *y* .
Study these words and practice them:

oil	*yl*	**appointments**	*apy---*
boys	*bys*	**avoid**	*avyd*
points	*py--*	**choice**	*Cys*
join	*jyn*	**noise**	*nyz*
disappoint*	*dsapy-*	**toys**	*tys*
voice	*vys*	**loyal**	*lyl*

*Remember: when a prefix is added to an outline that begins with a vowel, this vowel is retained.

BRIEF FORMS

feel, fail	*fl*	**field**	*fld*
those	*los*	**busy**	*bz*
she, shall, ship	*S*		

ABBREVIATIONS

doctor	dr	number	no
secretary, second	sec		

☐ The months of the year are written as follows:

January	ja	July	jl
February	fb	August	ag
March	mr	September	sp
April	ap	October	oc
May	ma	November	nv
June	jn	December	dc

READING EXERCISE

1. 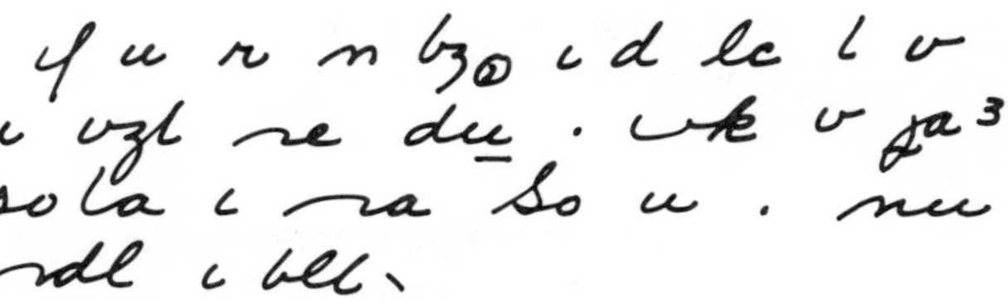

2. 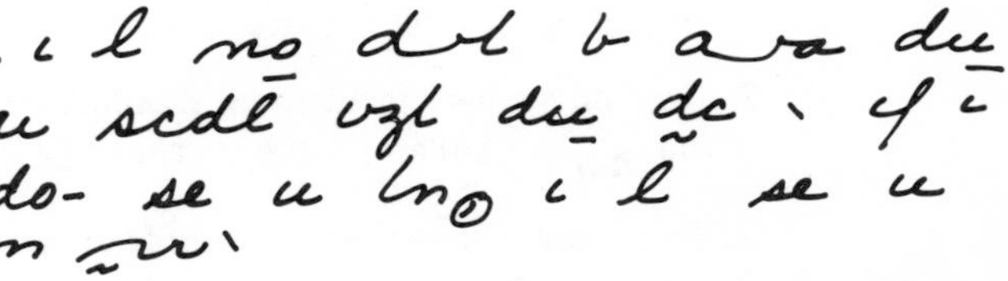

3. 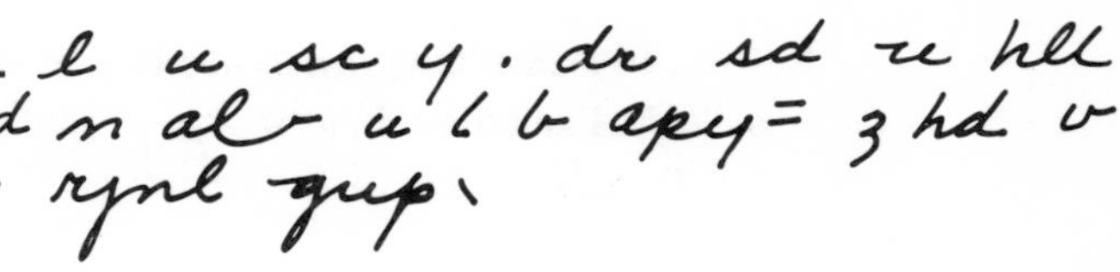

4. 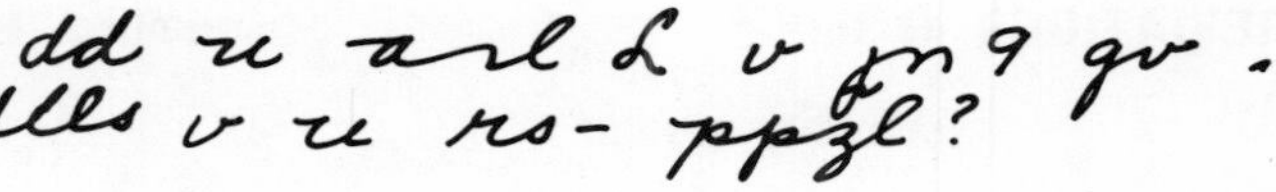

5. 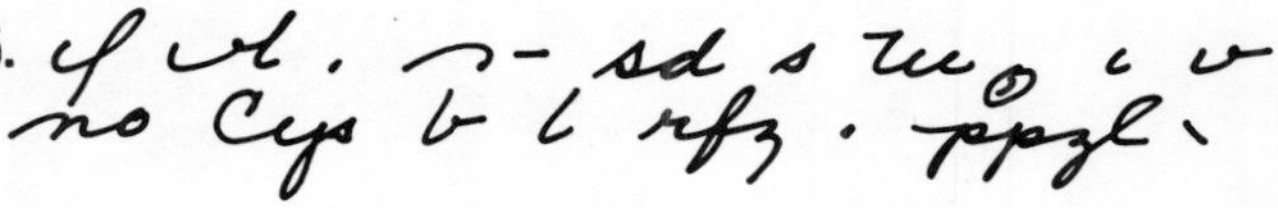

KEY (1) If you are not busy, I would like to have you visit me during the week of January 3 so that I/ may show you the new model I built. (26 words) (2) I will no doubt be away during your scheduled visit during December. If I don't see you then, I will see/ you in March. (22 words) (3) Will you ask why the doctor said your health would not allow you to be appointed as head of the regional group. (20 words) (4) Did your airmail letter of June 9 give the details of your recent proposal? (14 words) (5) If what the man said is true, I have no choice but to refuse the proposal. (13 words)

3 Let's summarize what has been covered in the rules regarding the writing or omission of long and short vowels.

1. **Write vowels—long or short—at the beginning and end of a word. Examples:** each *eC* ; value *vlu* ; add *ad* ; data *dta* ; yellow *ylo* ; review *rvu* .
2. **Omit all medial short vowels. Examples:** bit *bt* ; rug *rg* ; bulletin *bltn* ; ahead *ahd*.
3. **Write medial long vowels in words of one syllable. Examples:** reach *reC* ; shape *Sap* ; tool *tul* .
4. **Omit all medial long vowels in words of more than one syllable. Examples:** suppose *spz* ; aside *asd* ; retain *rtn* .

☐ Study these words and practice them:

base	bas	**basic**	bsc
basis	bss	**lease**	les
release	rls	**brief**	ef
briefly	fl	**belief**	blf
relief	rlf	**broke**	oc
broken	cn	**safe**	saf
safely	sfl	**tails**	lals
retails	rlls	**details**	dlls
mail	—al	**airmail**	a—l
recognized	rcgnz̄	**proposed**	ppz̄
yellow	ylo	**ahead**	ahd
data	dla	**amazing**	a—z
retained	rln̄	**preceding**	psd̲

SUMMARY

h<u>I</u>ghw<u>A</u>y hwa

1. Omit all medial long vowels in words of more than one syllable.

t<u>OY</u> y

2. For the sound of "oi" write y .

READING EXERCISE

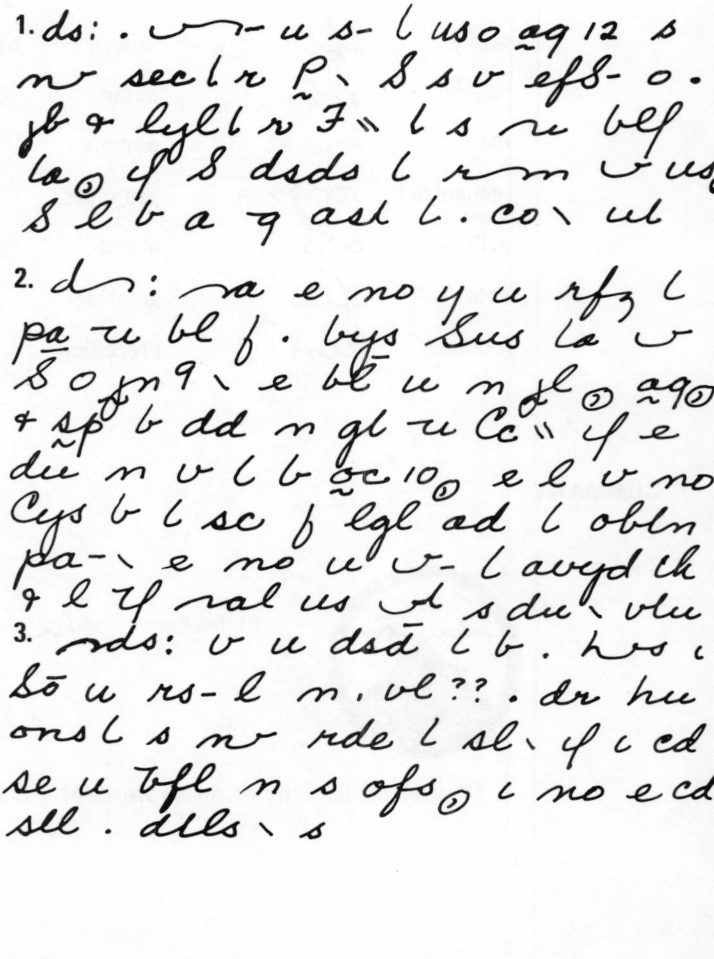

4. ~ds: e r hpe l nfr u la e c nr pvd. al~ns cass la v Czn b. P". cass r vdl uz b a ~no v Is⊙ + e no u l lc L, ul

5. ds: Lh s l lt u no la. pa-o u hll plse z du o ap 19" i no la u rcgnz. vlu v Lh plse + la u l v u pa-n. ~al n a d o 2, su

6. ds: du ~u lc v u sec El Lh ~k⊙ i z nfr la u v n fl l + d n b n. ofs f a no v ~os" if l s s~ ~a n ~C i c b v hp⊙ i hop u l n fl l gl n LC v ~e, ul

7. ~ds: e no la Lh s a v bz szn v. y n u Sp, u v no dbl fgln la pa- s du f. S- la z s- o ja 4, u Cc Sd v b ~al b. sec v. ~o⊙ b zu no⊙ l dd n reC us" Lh L s l sc la u Cc b s- ~n a fu ds, uvl

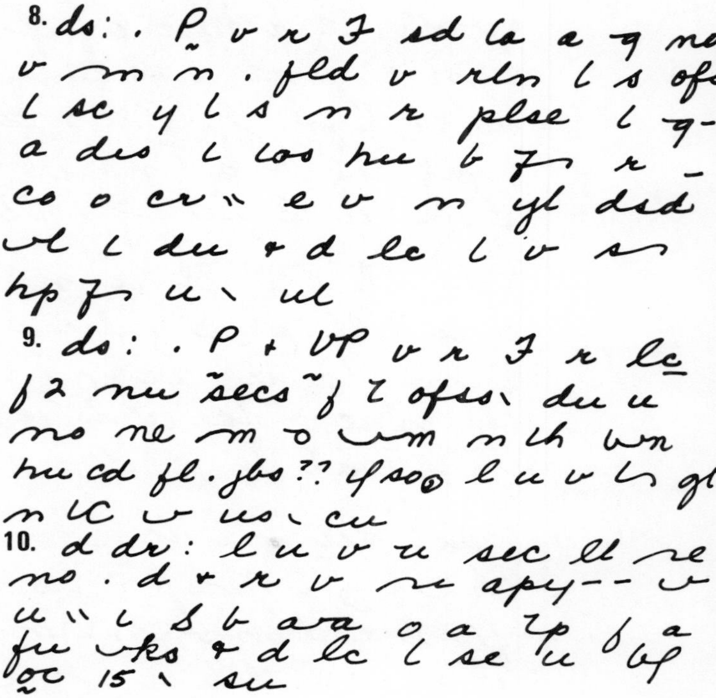

KEY (1) Dear Sir: The woman you sent to us on August 12 is now secretary to our President. She is very/ efficient on the job and loyal to our firm. (P) It is my belief that, if she decides to remain with us, she/ will be a great asset to the company. Yours truly, (50 words) (2) Dear Madam: May we know why you refuse to pay your bill for the boy's shoes that were shipped on June 9. We billed you in/ July, August, and September but did not get your check. (P) If we do not have it by October 10, we will have/ no choice but to ask for legal aid to obtain payment. We know you want to avoid this and will therefore mail us/ what is due. Very truly yours, (62 words) (3) My dear Sir: Have you decided to buy the house I showed you recently in the valley? (P) The doctor who owns it/ is now ready to sell. If I could see you briefly in his office, I know we could settle the details. Sincerely,/ (40 words) (4) My dear Sir: We are happy to inform you that we can now provide the aluminum cases that were chosen/ by the President. (P) The cases are widely used by a number of firms, and we know you will like them. Yours/ truly, (41 words) (5) Dear Sir: This is to let you know that the payment on your health policy was due on April 19. (P) I know/ that you recognize the value of this policy and that you will have your payment in the mail in a/ day or two. Sincerely yours, (42 words) (6) Dear Sir: During my talk with your secretary early this week, I was informed that you were not/ feeling well and would not be in the office for a number of months. (P) If there is some way in which I can be of help, I hope you/ will not fail to get in touch with me. Yours truly, (48 words) (7) My dear Sir: We know that this is a very busy season of the year in your shop. You have no doubt forgotten/ that payment is due for the shipment that was sent on January 4. Your check should have been mailed by the second of the/ month, but as you know, it did not reach us. (P) This letter is to ask that your check be sent within a few days. / Yours very truly, (63 words) (8) Dear Sir: The President of our firm said that a great number of men in the field have written to his office to/ ask why it is not our policy to grant a discount to those who buy from our company on credit. (P) We have/ not yet decided what to do and would like to have some help from you. Yours truly, (54 words) (9) Dear Sir: The President and Vice-President of our firm are looking for two new secretaries for their offices./ Do you know any men or women in this town who could fill the jobs? (P) If so, will you have them get in touch/ with us. Cordially yours, (44 words) (10) Dear Doctor: Will you have your secretary let me know the day and hour of my appointment with you. (P) I shall be away/ on a trip for a few weeks and would like to see you before October 15. Sincerely yours, (38 words)

6

1 Before learning the next rule, let's review one that you have been using from the beginning—the rule that states, "Write what you hear, omitting all medial short vowels." It is according to this rule that the following words are written: *rage* 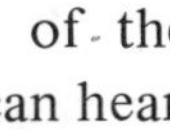 ; *seal* 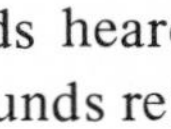 ; *twice* 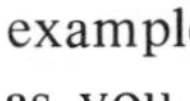 ; cheap 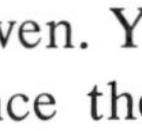 ; *shape* 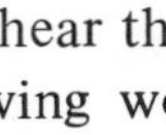 ; *coal* 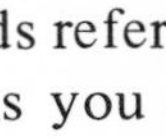 .

In these outlines you wrote all long vowels and all pronounced consonants. You are now going to learn about a group of words that contain a sound that is quite different from any of the sounds heard in the examples just given. You can hear the sounds referred to as you pronounce the following words. As you do so, notice that each word ends in the sound of a long vowel + "t": *rate, meet, write, vote, shoot, mute.*

It is to these final sounds of "ate," "eet," "ite," "ote," "ute" that this next rule refers.

For the final sound of a long vowel and "t," omit the *t* and end the outline with the long vowel.

Let's examine the word *rate*. This word is made up of the sound of "r" + "ate." Since the rule tells you to write *a* for this final sound of "ate," you write *rate* ra .

Study the following words and practice them:

fate	fa	**gate**	ga
date	da	**wait**	ua
late	la	**hesitate**	hzla
indicate	ndca	**locate**	lca
weight	ua	**freight**	Fa

Look at another example: the word *meet* contains the final sound of "eet," and since the rule tells you to write *e* for this final sound, you write *meet* me .

Study the following words and practice them:

sheet	Se	**heat**	he
beat	be	**wheat**	ue
receipt	rse	**cheat**	Ce
repeat	rpe	**seat**	se

What of the word *write*? Again referring to the rule, you write *i* for the final sound of "ite," therefore, *write* is written ri .

Study the following words and practice them:

sight	si	**light**	li
might	mi	**night**	ni

delight	dle	**invite**	nve
height	he	**fight**	fe

In the same way, you write *o* for the final sound of "ote," so *vote* is vo .

Study the following words and practice them:

wrote	ro	**promote**	pro
coat	co	**boat**	bo
vote	vo	**devote**	dvo

Finally, you write *u* for the final sound of "ute." Since this is the sound at the end of the words *suit* and *shoot,* you write *suit* su and *shoot* Su .

Study the following words and practice them:

boot	bu	**mute**	mu
route	ru	**fruit**	fu
lute	lu	**root**	ru

Remember, the rule states that you are to write *a* for the sound of "ate" at the end of a word. That is, you are to drop *t* after a **long** vowel. The word *fat* does not contain a long vowel so this rule does **not** apply: *fat* ft . Similarly, since the word *seat* contains the final sound of "eet," you write *seat* se ; but you write *set* sl . Don't forget that *t* is dropped at the end of a word **only** when it follows a **long** vowel. The rule will **not** be applied when the long vowel and *t* is a medial sound. For example: *vital* vll ; *futile* fll ; *title* ttl

Study these words and practice them:

cheat	Ce	**cheap**	Cep
chief	Cef	**wife**	wf
white	wi	**wit**	wl
tight	ti	**type**	tip
tile	til	**lit**	ll
wrote	ro	**role**	rol
bit	bl	**bright**	bi
beat	be	**beak**	bec

□ Let's pause for a moment to consider something that will be important in the application of this and future rules; namely, the meaning of the term "root word." In its simplest form, "root word" is defined as a word to which a prefix or suffix can be added.

A prefix is something put before or in front of, such as: *type*write, *a*wait, *en*joy, *en*roll, and *re*lease.

A suffix is something added to the end, such as: wait*ed*, writ*ing*, clear*ly*, and consum*er*.

For example, *light* is the root word of *lights, lighting,* and *lightly*. See how you build your outlines by adding suffixes and prefixes to a root word: *light* li ; *lights* lis ; *lighting* li̲ ; *lightly* lil .

Note that the basic outline of *li* for *light* is maintained in all these words. From *indicate* *ndca* you derive *indicates* *ndcas*; *indicating* *ndca̲*; and *indicated* *ndcā*.

See how the outline for the root word has been retained in each of the following examples: *meetings* *me̳* ; *eliminated* *elmā*; *nightly* *nil* ; *voting* *vo̲* ; *treats* *Tes* ; *treated* *Tē* ; *treatment* *Te-* .

Study these words and practice them:

lately	lal	**receipts**	rses
rates	ras	**calculated**	clclā
awaiting	awa̲	**designated**	dzgnā
dates	das	**dated**	dā
meets	mes	**invited**	nvī
typewriting	Tpri̲	**voted**	vō
devoted	dvō	**routes**	rus
located	lcā	**related**	rlā
waiting	wa̲	**meetings**	me̳
suits	sus	**sheets**	Ses
devoting	dvo̲	**writing**	ri̲

READING EXERCISE

1. l v ru L n wC u ndcā la. wr Ses l bl l b S̄ o ja 4 \

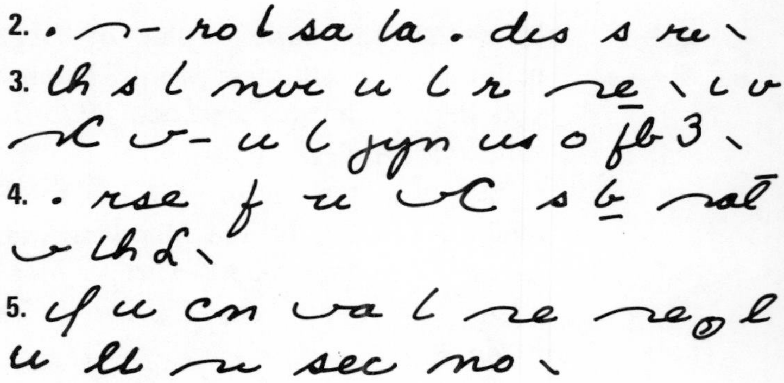

KEY (1) I have your letter in which you indicated that the white sheets I bought will be shipped on Jan. 4. (17 words) (2) The man wrote to say that the discount is right. (8 words) (3) This is to invite you to our meeting. I very much want you to join us on Feb. 3. (16 words) (4) The receipt for your watch is being mailed with this letter. (10 words) (5) If you cannot wait to meet me, will you let my secretary know. (12 words)

2 Now that you have learned the rule that has just been presented, you will have no difficulty with the next rule because it simply states that you are going to treat words that end in a long vowel + "v" in the same way as those ending in a long vowel + "t."

For the final sound of a long vowel and "v," drop the *v* and end the outline with the long vowel.

Let's illustrate this rule with the word *gave*. The rule tells you to drop *v* when it follows a long vowel; therefore, write *gave* ga . Similarly, you write *e* for the sound "eve" that is heard in the word *leave,* and write *leave* le . The word *drive* ends in the sound of "ive"; thus, *drive* is written de ; *drove* do ; *grove* go .

Study these words and practice them:

arrived	arv̄	**arrival**	arvl
achieve	aCe	**achievement**	aCe-
receive	rse	**leaving**	le̲
pave	pa	**driving**	dv̲
believed	blē	**brave**	b̄a
cove	co	**deceive**	dse

For the sound of "kw" (qu) write q.

The sound of "kw" is always associated with the letter *q* in longhand and, as you can see, you are going to take advantage of this association in this rule.

Study these words and practice them:

quite	qi	**equipped**	eqp̄
quickly	qcl	**quote**	qo
equal	eql	**frequently**	f̄q-l
acquainted	aqa=	**quit**	qt

Note that in the outline for the word *acquainted* you are using the rule that instructed you to write the long vowel if it is followed by a sound that is represented by a mark of punctuation.

BRIEF FORMS

charge	Cg	**purchase**	pC
keep	cp	**too**	to

an, at *a* | am, many 

he, had, him *h*

ABBREVIATIONS percent *pc* | amount *ad*

READING EXERCISE

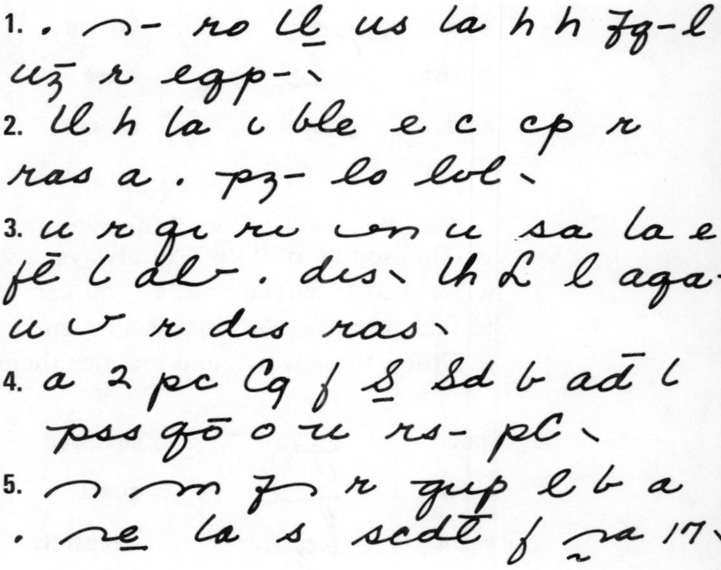

KEY (1) The man wrote telling us that he had frequently used our equipment. (12 words) (2) Tell him that I believe we can keep our rates at the present low level. (13 words) (3) You are quite right when you say that we failed to allow the discount. This letter will acquaint you with our discount rates. (20 words) (4) A 2-percent charge for shipping should be added to prices quoted on your recent purchase. (17 words) (5) Many men from our group will be at the meeting that is scheduled for May 17. (15 words)

3 Salutations containing proper names are written as follows:

My dear Mr. Gray: 

Dear Mrs. Price: 

Dear Doctor: 

Dear Bill: 

Note: When *Mr.* or *Mrs.* appears within the body of a letter, the form 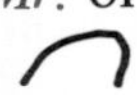 and  will also be used. Example: . . . a letter from Mr. Brown.

☐ The joining of words is known as phrasing, and such phrasing can be an aid to speed building. For example, the joining of *you can* 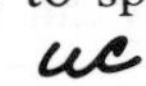 or *I will* 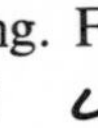 is faster to write and therefore advisable. However, excessive phrasing (the joining of more than two words) is to be avoided because it results in outlines that are usually difficult to read. In the matter of phrasing, it is best to be guided by your own personal experience. If the joining of words comes naturally to you, by all means follow through with it; but if you find it unnatural, you would be wise to avoid it.

In the exercises that follow, some phrasing has been done in such words as *you can* 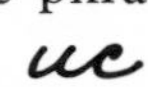 ; *to reach* 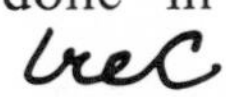 ; *it will*  . Keep this in mind as you read your shorthand plates.

SUMMARY

bOAT	o
ATE	a
ETE	e
ITE	i
UTE	u

1. For words ending in the final sound of a long vowel and t, drop the t and end the outline with the long vowel.

dIVE	i
AVE	a
EVE	e
OVE	o
UVE	u

2. For words ending in the final sound of a long vowel and v, drop the v and end the outline with the long vowel.

QUarter q

3. Write q for the sound of "kw."

READING EXERCISE 1.

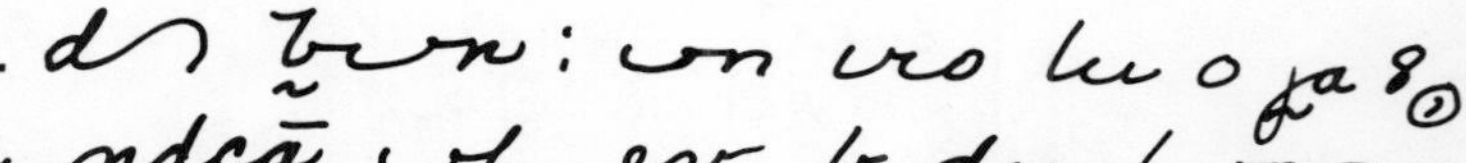

. bld v a nu hra" 3 a
rzd- n Ch bn ⊙ ul nodl
gcl se h sC a hra d
hp elma hve 7fc la rnstu
. sdl v Ln a . he v . rSr"
n nve u lad us n aCe r
gol b vo f . psj v . bl la s nr
bf . snl \ ul

2. ds: n n rse v u al L dā
fb 3 \ . le eqp-u v- l le r Coo
fb 14 + Sd are b fb 18 \ 7a Cgs v
b ad L . opnl pC ps + lbndcā o
u bl \ vlu

3. dn Z- : fgv re f n re lu bf
Ch la da \ cno la eh a apy-- o fl
29⊙ + c Tē lreC u lsa la cz lo sc lcp
L \ cdd lcl ss1 n u ofs⊙ + h ga
re s prs la h d rpe ru rsj
lu" cf ur Ze o aq4⊙ cd b v hpe
L de u lse . bld w lcā f u nu
ofss \ . r- b gō s eql L vl ue
nv pa \ s

4. sds: . alC Se Sd b ad L . cal
u rsē El Ch so" L Sos . n nu
cls er sl + ndcas . ras lb Cq
f r Lpre eqp- \ ul

5. 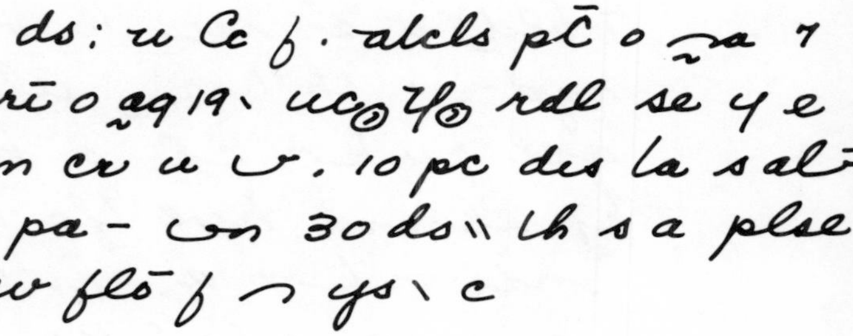

KEY (1) Dear Mr. Brown: When I wrote to you on January 8, I indicated what we have been doing to promote/ the building of a new highway. (P) As a resident in this town, you will no doubt quickly see/ how such a highway would help to eliminate the heavy traffic that runs through the middle of town at the height of the/ rush hour. (P) I am inviting you to aid us in achieving our goal by voting for the passage of the bill that/ is now before the Senate. Yours truly, (87 words) (2) Dear Sir: I am in receipt of your airmail letter dated February 3. (P) The lighting equipment you want/ will leave our company on February 14 and should arrive by February 18. Freight charges/ have been added to the original purchase price and will be indicated on your bill. Very truly yours, (58 words) (3) Dear Mr. Front: Forgive me for not writing to you before this late date. I know that we had an appointment on/ July 29, and I tried to reach you to say that I was too sick to keep it. I did talk to someone/ in your office, and he gave me his promise that he would repeat my message to you. (P) If you are free on August 4,/ I would be very happy to drive you to see the building I have located for your new offices. The rent/ being quoted is equal to what you are now paying. Sincerely, (92 words) (4) My dear Sir: The attached sheet should be added to the catalog you received early this month. (P) It shows the/ many new items we are selling and indicates the rates to be charged for our typewriting equipment. Yours truly,/ (40 words) (5) Dear Sir: Your check for the articles purchased on May 7 arrived on August 19. You can, therefore, readily/ see why we cannot credit you with the 10 percent discount that is allowed for payment within 30 days./ (P) This is a policy we have followed for many years. Cordially, (52 words)

Cp 7

1 Write ol for "old."

This is a rule that requires very little explanation. It simply tells you that whenever the sound of "old" occurs in a word, you are to write *ol.* Thus, the words *old* ol ; *sold* sol ; *told* tol ; *holding* hol .

Study these words and practice them:

gold	gol	**hold**	hol
cold	col	**household**	hshol
fold	fol	**golden**	goln

Note the word *golden.* It is a two-syllable word, but you cannot omit the medial long *o* because ol is needed to represent the sound of "old."

For the sound of medial and final "tiv" write v .

Study these words and practice them:

effective	efcv	**defective**	dfcv
relatively	rlvl	**tentative**	t-v
active	acv	**positive**	pzv

READING EXERCISE

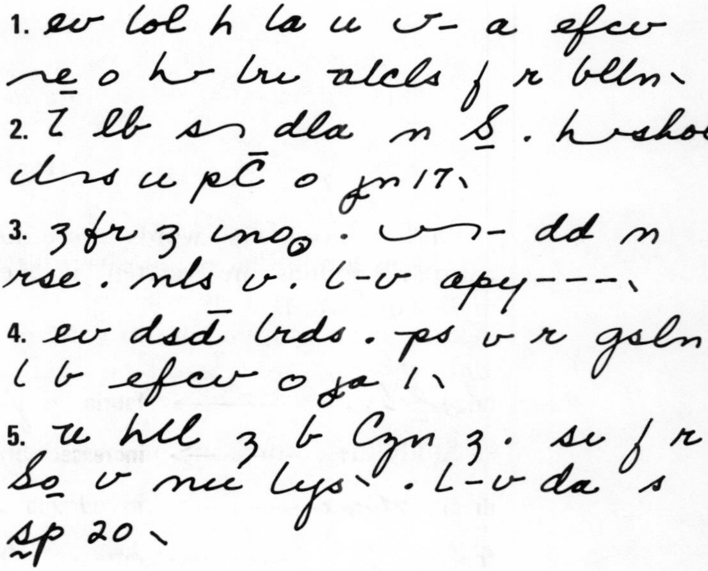

KEY (1) We have told him that you want an effective meeting on how to write articles for our bulletin. (18 words) (2) There will be some delay in shipping the household items you purchased on June 17. (16 words) (3) As far as I know, the woman did not receive the notice of the tentative appointments. (16 words) (4) We have decided to reduce the price of our gasoline to be effective on January 1. (19 words) (5) Your hotel was chosen as the site for our showing of new toys. The tentative date is September 20. (20 words)

2 You have learned how to handle "combination-r" sounds at the beginning of words such as *bright* ; *cry* ; and *from* . These sounds are also heard in the middle of words such as *fabric, afraid,* and *program.* It is to these medial "combination-r" sounds that this next rule refers.

To express a medial "combination-r" sound, capitalize the letter that precedes *r* and omit the *r* from the outline.

In other words, in the **middle** of a word write for "br"; for "cr"; for "dr"; for "fr"; for "gr"; for "pr"; for "tr."

Study the following words to see how these "combination-r" sounds are written at the beginning and middle of a word.

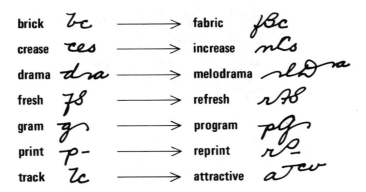

brick	⟶	**fabric**	
crease	⟶	**increase**	
drama	⟶	**melodrama**	
fresh	⟶	**refresh**	
gram	⟶	**program**	
print	⟶	**reprint**	
track	⟶	**attractive**	

Note that the capital letters are written in a manner that eliminates the need for raising the pen any more than necessary. Pay particular attention to the capital *f* in the word *refresh.* By continuing the *r* to form the first stroke of the capital *f,* you have not lifted your pen. The same is true for the capital *t* in the word *attractive.* By continuing the *a* to form the first stroke of the capital *t*, you have not lifted your pen.

Note the outline for *melodrama.* This outline may be written  or  , but it saves time to continue the outline from the top of the *d.*

Practice writing these capital letters. As you write these words, you will surely be aware of the fact that these capital letters in the middle of the word can be written fluently and without difficulty.

Study these words and practice them:

abroad		**afraid**	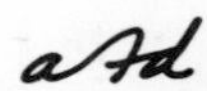
telegram	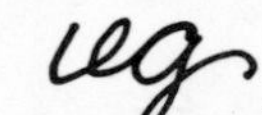	**decrease**	
prescribed	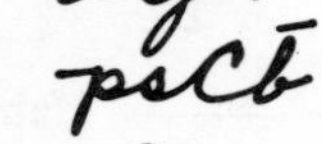	**agreements**	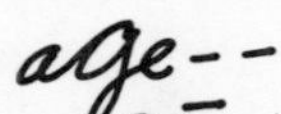
refrain	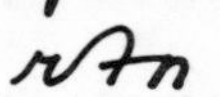	**approached**	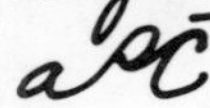
increasing		**degree**	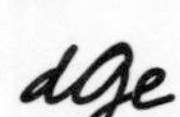
regret	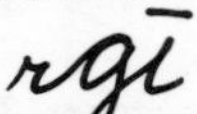	**programs**	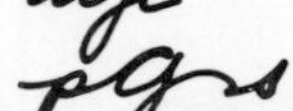
electric	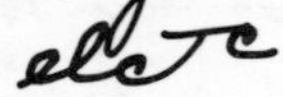	**electrical**	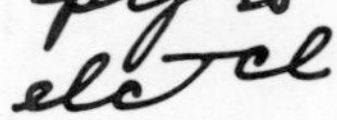
patronage	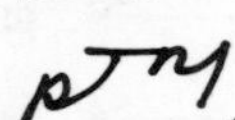	**patronize**	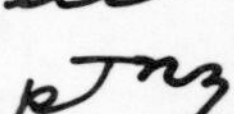
introduce	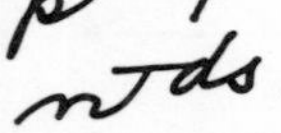	**introducing**	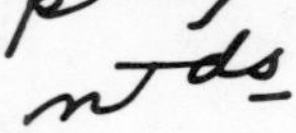

READING EXERCISE 1.

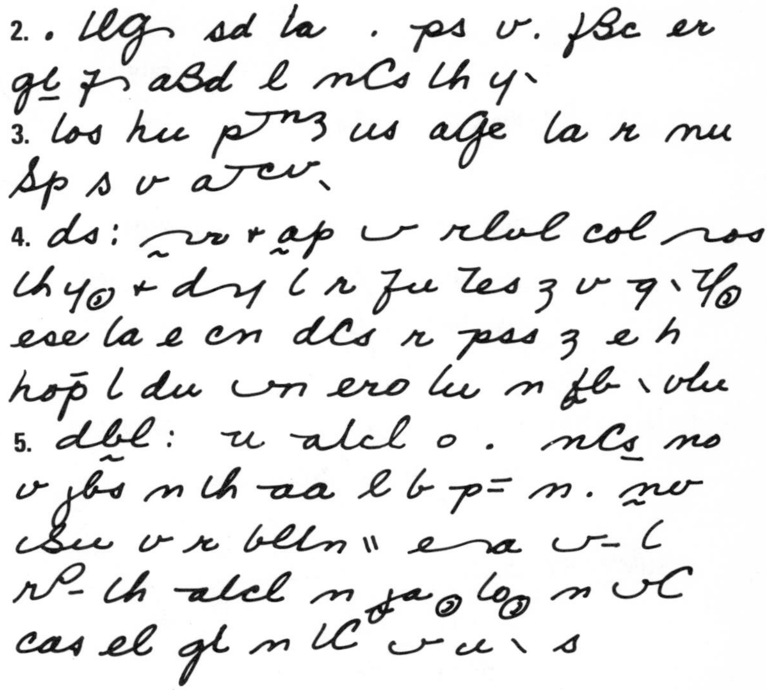

KEY (1) We are afraid that you will regret that you did not agree to his program. (14 words) (2) The telegram said that the price of the fabric we are getting from abroad will increase this year. (17 words) (3) Those who patronize us agree that our new shop is very attractive. (13 words) (4) Dear Sir: March and April were relatively cold months this year, and damage to our fruit trees was very great. Therefore,/ we see that we cannot decrease our prices as we had hoped to do when we wrote to you in February. Very/ truly yours, (42 words) (5) Dear Bill: Your article on the increasing number of jobs in this area will be printed in the/ November issue of our bulletin. (P) We may want to reprint this article in January, too, in which case/ we will get in touch with you. Sincerely, (47 words)

3

BRIEF FORMS	they	ty	easy	ez
	kind	ci	held	hl
	given	gv	line	li
	appreciate	ap	little	ll
	put, up	p	go, good	g
	fine, find	fi		
ABBREVIATIONS	room	rm	telephone	tel
	department	dpt		

SUMMARY

cOLD ol

1. For the sound of "old" write ol .

detecTIVE v

2. For the medial or final sound of "tiv" write v .

coBRa — B

3. For the medial "combination-r" sound capitalize the letter that precedes r and omit the r from the outline.

READING EXERCISE

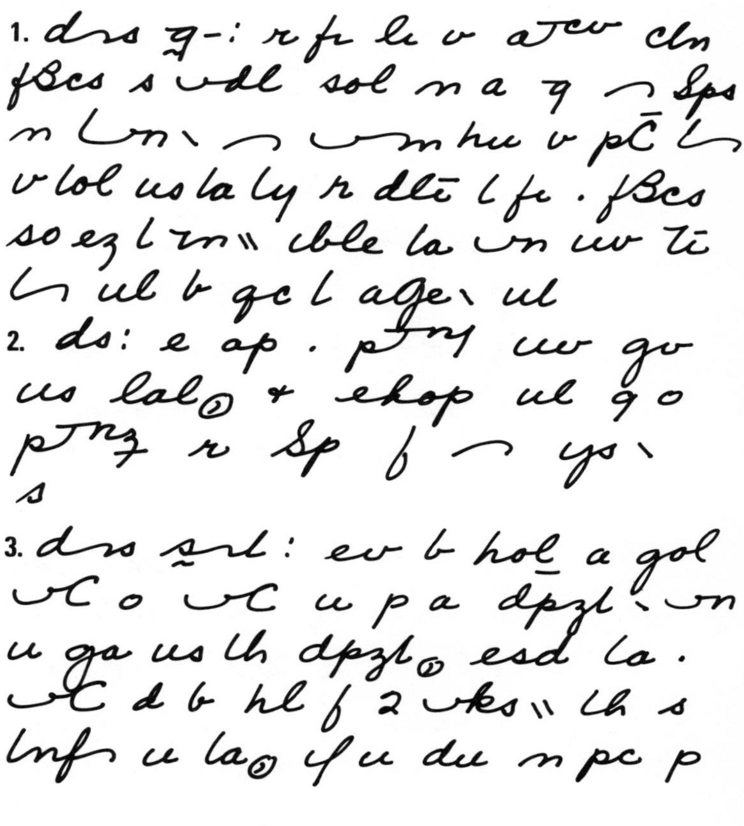

. ᴗC ᴗnad o 2⊙ e fl
fe lsl u ᴗC + rln .
dpzl \ d u cel ll us
no ᴗl u ᴗ- us ldu \
ul

4. ds: ᴗ. aPC ᴗ. nu y⊙
i ᴗS l ll u h— C cap. hp
uv gv us du. ol y \ ffl la
r pg d nvbso efcv ᴗ
l r f u efls n r bhf \
s

5. ds: ev sl fl 3 z a l-v da
f r rol re ᴗ. hds v los
cos hu v b sl r li v elcl
eqp- n lh aa \ lh lb r fel
re ᴗ. y" cd lc lv u + u
sec fyn us o la da \ c

6. ds: fu ᴗS lq aBd lh y⊙
r Tol dpl s rde lhp u ᴗ.
dlls v u Tp" y n lel r ofs +
ll | v r aj-- ll u h— ez lo
l Tol b a o bo f rlvl ll
me \ vlu

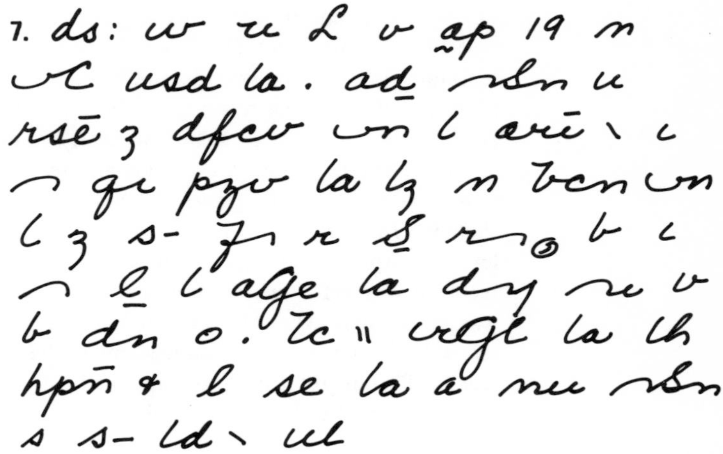

KEY (1) Dear Mrs. Grant: Our fine line of attractive cotton fabrics is widely sold in a great many shops in town. Many/ women who have purchased them have told us that they are delighted to find the fabrics so easy to iron./ (P) I believe that when you have tried them you will be quick to agree. Yours truly, (53 words) (2) Dear Sir: We appreciate the patronage you have given us lately, and we hope you will go on patronizing/ our shop for many years. Sincerely, (27 words) (3) Dear Mrs. Smith: We have been holding a gold watch on which you put a deposit. When you gave us this deposit,/ we said that the watch would be held for two weeks. (P) This is to inform you that, if you do not pick up the watch within/ a day or two, we feel free to sell your watch and retain the deposit. (P) Would you kindly let us know what you/ want us to do. Yours truly, (65 words) (4) My dear Sir: With the approach of the new year, I wish to tell you how much I appreciate the help you have given/ us during the old year. I feel that our program would not have been so effective were it not for your efforts/ in our behalf. Sincerely, (45 words) (5) Dear Sir: We have set July 3 as a tentative date for our monthly meeting with the heads of those companies/ who have been selling our line of electrical equipment in this area. This will be our final meeting/ of the year. (P) I would like to have you and your secretary join us on that date. Cordially, (56 words) (6) Dear Madam: If you wish to go abroad this year, our Travel Department is ready to help you with the details/ of your trip. (P) Why not telephone our office and let one of our agents tell you how easy it is to travel/ by air or boat for relatively little money. Very truly yours, (54 words) (7) Dear Sir: I have your letter of April 19 in which you said that the adding machine you received was defective/ when it arrived. I am quite positive that it was not broken when it was sent from our shipping room, but I/ am willing to agree that damage might have been done on the truck. (P) I regret that this happened and will see that a/ new machine is sent today. Yours truly, (67 words)

Cp 8

1 Many shorthand rules include the vowel in the sound affected. For example, for the sound of "old," write *ol*. The next rule is similar in that it applies to the sound of "ake," which includes the vowel in the sound. For the medial and final sound of "ake" write *c*.

Study these words and practice them:

make	*mc*	**lake**	*lc*
making	*mc̲*	**break**	*bc*
sake	*sc*	**take**	*tc*
fake	*fc*	**brake**	*bc*

This is a simple rule if you remember that it applies only to the sound of "ake." It does **not** apply to the sounds formed with any other vowel such as *seek* *sec*; *broke* *boc*; *hike* *hic*.

For the sound of medial or final "shun," vowel plus "shun," and "nshun" write *1* .

The sound of "shun" to which this rule refers may be spelled in various ways in longhand and may also have slight variations in pronunciation. For example: na*tion,* fa*shion,* discu*ssion,* physi*cian,* occa*sion.* It is to the sounds in these words this rule applies.

Let's start with the word *addition.* You know that *add* is *ad* . Thus, for the word *addition*, you simply write *ad1* ; and the word *provisions* is *pvjs*. Since the rule states that *1* is also written for the medial sound of "shun," you apply this rule to the words *national* *n1l* ; and *occasionally* *oc1l* . Note that only one *l* is used for *lly.*

Although these sounds all contain the sound of "sh," the rule that takes precedence is the one that applies to the larger portion of the word. Since "shun" is a larger portion of the word than "sh," apply the new rule for writing *1* rather than writing *S* for "sh" and adding *n*.

Study these words and practice them:

solution	*sl1*	**division**	*dv1*
position	*pz1*	**election**	*elc1*
production	*pdc1*	**nation**	*n1*
vacation	*vc1*	**protection**	*ptc1*
qualifications	*qlfcjs*	**introduction**	*ntdc1*
decisions	*dsjs*	**education**	*edc1*
television	*tlv1*	**relation**	*rl1*
actions	*acjs*	**deduction**	*ddc1*

session		**locations**	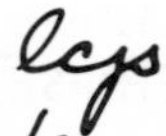
occasion		**fashion**	
additional		**motion**	
reduction		**section**	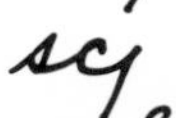
selection	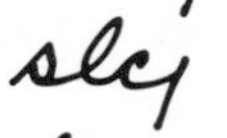	**professional**	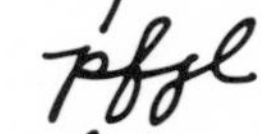
discussion		**dedication**	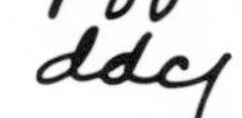
promotion		**invitation**	

This rule also instructs you to write for the entire sound of "nshun." Thus *mention* .

Study these words and practice them:

mentioned		**prevention**	
attention		**dimensions**	
intention		**mentioning**	

What of a word such as *reaction*? You previously learned that the first and last letter of a root word do not change when a prefix or suffix is added. Therefore, you retain this initial vowel from the root word and write *reaction* 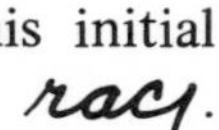.

You have learned that the word *value* is written . *Valuation* is written 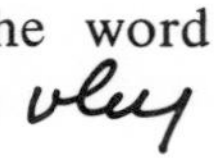 and *evaluation* is written 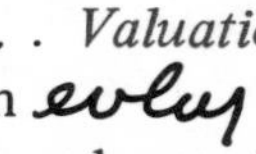.

This rule applies to **medial** and **final** sounds only; *ocean* is written 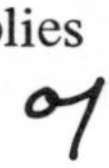.

READING EXERCISE

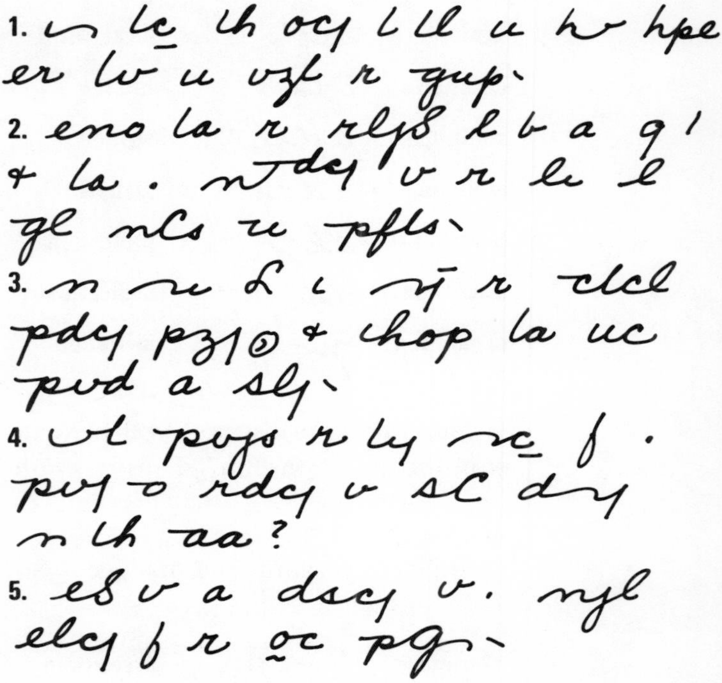

KEY (1) I am taking this occasion to tell you how happy we are to have you visit our group. (16 words) (2) We know that our relationship will be a good one and that the introduction of our line will greatly increase/ your profits. (22 words) (3) In my letter I mentioned our critical production position, and I hope that you can provide a solution. (20 words) (4) What provisions are they making for the prevention or reduction of such damage in this area? (19 words) (5) We shall have a discussion of the national election for our October program. (16 words)

2 The next rule is very similar to the one in which you learned to attach a hyphen to the initial letter of a word to indicate the "combination-r" sound. For example: *front* 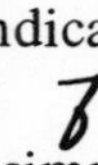 ; *bright* 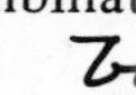 ; *true* 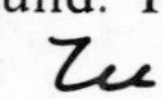 . The next rule simply explains what's to be done to indicate that the initial letter of a word is combined in sound with the "l" that follows it as in such words as *album, blue, closely,* and *flood.*

When the initial letter of a word is combined with the sound of "l," indicate the resulting sound by writing a dash (——) on the initial letter of the outline.

You can see how similar this rule is to the one you have previously learned. In the word *album* the initial letter is pronounced with "l," and the rule states that this sound of "al" is indicated by writing a dash on the *a* Thus, *album* is written  . The dash is distinguished from the hyphen by its length, so you can see why the initial stroke on the word *album* is longer than the hyphen used to indicate the sound "ar" at the beginning of the word *arm*  . To avoid any confusion, be sure to form the habit of making your dash at least twice as long as the hyphen.

Let's look at the word *blue.* The first letter of this word is combined with "l," and for the resulting sound of "bl," you write  . Therefore, *blue* 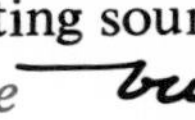 . What of the word *closely*? Since you write  for the initial sound of "cl," *closely* is written  .

You will recall that in writing the word *earth* you use this  because it is easier to attach an initial hyphen  . For the same reason, you will use this same form of  when you indicate the sound of initial "el"  . Thus, *else*  . Now see how the rule has been applied to the following words.

Study these words and practice them:

black		**ill**	
clients		**planned**	

club	cb	play	pa
element	E-	slow	so
flight	fi	slight	si
flood	fd	ultimate	ultd
gladly	gdl	alibi	ab
clothe	col	fleet	fe
clothing	col	plants	p--
pleasant	pz-	ailment	a-
aisle	i	slip	sp
classroom	csr	clinic	cnc

Note the word *clothe.* You have learned that when a word ends in the sound of a long vowel and *t* you write the vowel and drop the *t. Clothe,* however, ends in the sound of a long vowel and "th" so this rule does not apply. Write c for the sound of "cl," o for the medial long vowel in a one-syllable word, and l for the sound of "th."

Before continuing, let's pause for a moment to call your attention to a fact that is essential to your understanding of the rules governing the use of the initial hyphen and dash. To illustrate, let's consider the words *arm* and *album.* Notice that in these words the sounds of the first two letters are blended together into a single sound. On the other hand, in the words *arise* and *alone,* there is not the combination of two sounds into one. You must bear in mind, therefore, that it is **only** when the initial letter is **combined with** the sound of "l" or "r" that these two rules are applied. In view of this, you can understand why *arise* is written arz and *election* elcj.

When the medial sound of "combination-l" occurs in a word, omit the *l* and write the letter that precedes it. Following this rule, *problems* is written pb-s. Study these words and practice them:

obliged	obj̄	**obligation**	obgj
include	ncd	**inclusion**	ncj
legislation	ljsj	**legislative**	ljsv
apply	api	**application**	apcj
supplement	sp-	**supply**	spi
reply	rpi	**inflation**	nfj

READING EXERCISE

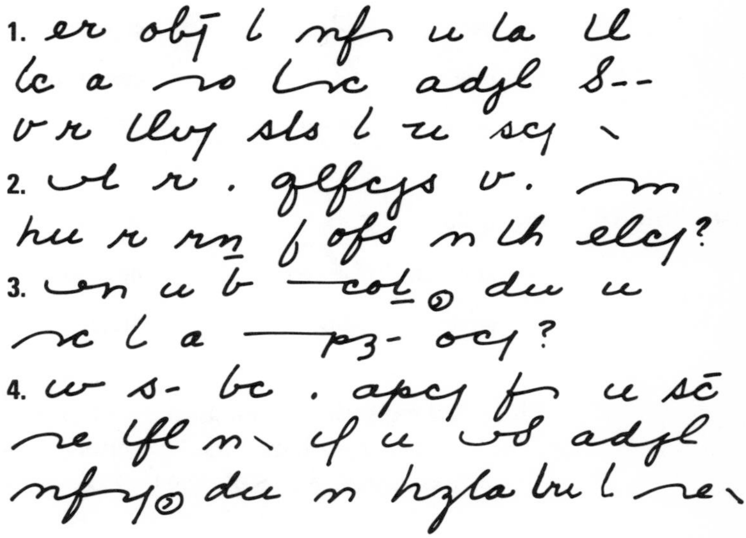

5. f . gs u pC du n arv wn a fu ds. ll me no + l dpca . S-\

KEY (1) We are obliged to inform you that it will take a month to make additional shipments of our television/ sets to your section. (24 words) (2) What are the qualifications of the men who are running for office in this election? (16 words) (3) When you buy clothing, do you make it a pleasant occasion? (11 words) (4) I have sent back the application form you asked me to fill in. If you wish additional information, do/ not hesitate to write to me. (26 words) (5) If the goods you purchased do not arrive within a few days, let me know and I will duplicate the shipment. (20 words)

3

BRIEF FORMS

about	ab	**customer**	K
has	as	**came**	k
over	O	**come**	k
order	$\bar{O}$	**committee**	k
please	-p		

ABBREVIATIONS

child	ch	**avenue**	ave
children	chn	**boulevard**	blvd
street	st	**place**	pl

☐ To express an even amount of dollars or cents write:
dollar, dollars d ; cents c .
Examples: $5 5d ; $1 1d ; 45 cents 45c ;

$2 2d.

To express an uneven amount of money write:

$33.62 33^{62}; $98.75 98^{75}; $7.29 7^{29}.

SUMMARY

rAKE c

1. Write c for the medial or final sound of "ake."

televISION 1
ASHUN
ESHUN
ISHUN
OSHUN
USHUN
NSHUN

2. Write 1 for the medial or final sounds of "shun," vowel and "shun," and "nshun."

PLant —p

3. Write a dash on the initial letter of an outline to indicate the initial "combination-l" sound.

airPLane p

4. When the "combination-l" sound occurs in the middle of the word, omit the l and write the letter that precedes it.

READING EXERCISE

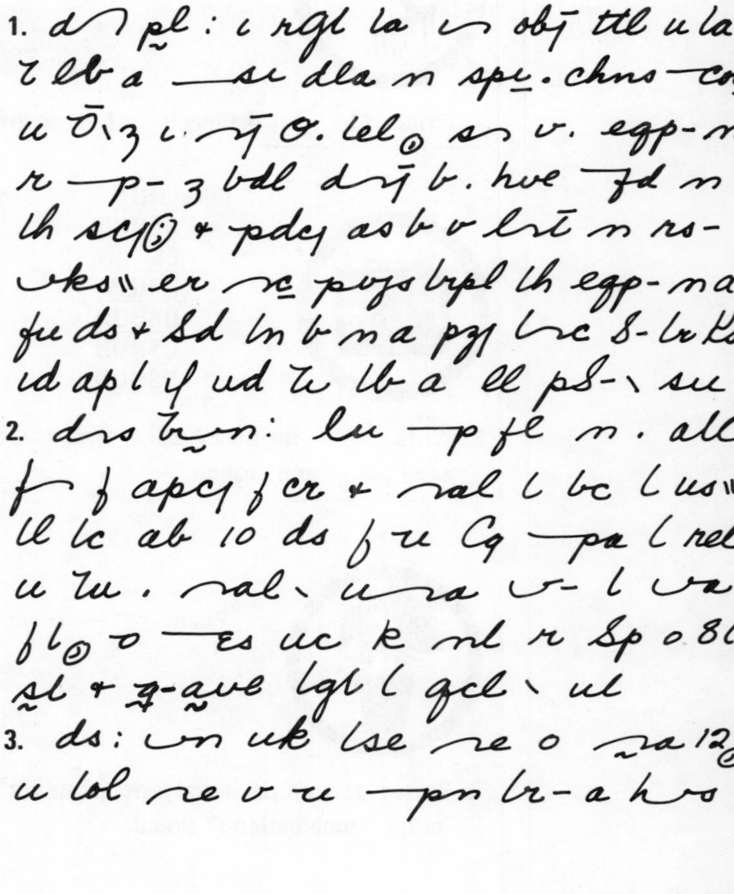

o . lc f u k vcy" lh s lll u
no la w lcā a —pz- 5 r cly
la cd lc u lse . l r-- f 150d a
ro + lh ps ncds . us v a fe
nu bo . uno ul fe lh cly l
sū f u vf + ch" ufu vS l re
re . vS b —gd l lc u lse l . ul

4. dK: lh s n rpe l u L v r 7" .
sp- er sal lu Sd b ad l . cal e s-
n fb . l Sos r le v —abrs + gos .
ps v el cl" —p du n fgl la
ufu O s O50d . S Cgs lb ncd
n . pC ps . ul

5. d: s ros aq a k 3 f lle
nl . nyl pbrs v edcy . hd v .
qup as alge lk lr —cb re l ll
us ab . fu v . k . ncd n s lc
lb a dscy v . lysv acy b
—pn lhp los chn hu v- lql
cly b du n v sfS- me ldu so"
3 a v- v 2 chn uno ul
pfl 7 s lc . v sal lh noly
n . hop la ul v- lb pz- o . ne
v ap 19 . pl Czn f . re s . q- hel
o — blod . uvl

KEY (1) Dear Mr. Place: I regret that I am obliged to tell you that there will be a slight delay in supplying the/ children's clothing you ordered. As I mentioned over the telephone, some of the equipment in our plant was badly/ damaged by the heavy flood in this section; and production has been very limited in recent weeks. (P) We/ are making provisions to replace this equipment in a few days and should then be in a position to/ make shipment to our customers. (P) I would appreciate it if you would try to be a little patient./ Sincerely yours, (102 words) (2) Dear Mrs. Brown: Will you please fill in the attached form for application for credit and mail it back to us. (P) It/ will take about ten days for your charge plate to reach you through the mail. You may want to wait for it, or else you can come/ into our shop on Eighth Street and Grant Avenue to get it quickly. Yours truly, (54 words) (3) Dear Sir: When you came to see me on May 12, you told me of your plan to rent a house on the lake for your coming/ vacation. (P) This is to let you know that I have located a pleasant five-room cottage that I would like you to/ see. It rents for $150 a month, and this price includes the use of a fine new boat. I know you/ will find this cottage well suited for your wife and child. (P) If you wish to meet me, I shall be glad to take you to see/ it. Yours truly, (82 words) (4) Dear Customer: This is in reply to your letter of March 7. (P) The supplement we are mailing to you should/ be added to the catalog we sent in February. It shows our line of albums and gives the price of each /item. (P) Please do not forget that, if your order is over $50, shipping charges will be included/ in the purchase price. Yours truly, (65 words) (5) Dear Madam: Some months ago, a committee was formed to look into the national problems of education./ The head of the group has agreed to come to our club meeting to tell us about the findings of the committee. /Included in his talk will be a discussion of the legislative action being planned to help those children/ who want to go to college but do not have sufficient money to do so. (P) As a woman with two children, I/ know you will profit from his talk. I am mailing this invitation in the hope that you will want to be present/ on the night of April 19. The place chosen for this meeting is the Grant Hotel on Elm Boulevard. Yours very/ truly, (123 words)

9

1 You have learned that the initial sound of "er" is written E. The next principle refers to this sound at the end of a word.

For the final sound of "er" or "ter" write a joined slant.

Before explaining the rule, let's first define what is meant by the "joined slant." Simply stated, a joined slant is a long upward stroke attached to the letter that precedes it. The following letters illustrate the addition of a joined slant:

a/ b/ c/ d/ e/ f/ g/

Now with this made clear, let's discuss the final sound of "er," which the rule tells you to indicate by a joined slant. Let's start with the word *bigger*. You know that *big* is written bg; therefore, *bigger* is bg/; *color* cl/; *richer* rC/. The word also ends in the sound of "er," so write *cover* cv/.

Study these words and practice them:

manager mj/ **summer** s/

manner	mn	**builder**	bld
officer	ofs	**earlier**	El
rubber	rb	**owner**	on
washer	wS	**older**	ol
retailer	rll	**power**	pw
her	h	**paper**	pp
picture	pcC	**procedure**	psj
similar	sml	**newspaper**	nzpp
professor	pfs	**favor**	fv
occur	oc	**dinner**	dn
error	E	**familiar**	fml
pressure	pS	**wider**	wd
offer	of	**refer**	rf
chamber	Cmb	**prior**	pi
honor	on	**nature**	nC
major	mj	**neighbor**	nb

You will recall that you double the mark of punctuation at the end of a word to indicate the addition of *s*. Thus, *wants* w-- ; *buildings* bld . You will apply this same principle when adding *s* to words ending in a joined slant.

Study these words and practice them:

covers	cv//	**pictures**	pcC//

offers	of//	**dollars**	dl//
shoppers	Sp//	**officers**	ofs//
papers	pp//	**errors**	E//
features	fC//	**owners**	on//

You have learned that d is used to express an even amount of dollars such as 5d or 18d. When no number is written before the words *dollar* or *dollars,* use dl/ or dl//.

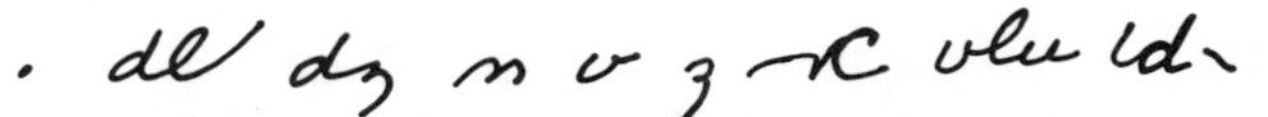

The dollar does not have as much value today.

Let's now consider those words in which the sound of "er" follows a sound that is represented by a mark of punctuation, such as *hunter.* As you know, *hunt* is h- . Therefore, *hunter* h-/ and *hunters* h-//; *winter* w-/ and *winters* w-//; *center* s-/ and *centers* s-//.

Now, how will you handle root words that end in "er" or "ter" to which "ing" and "ed" are added? Simply follow the rule you have previously learned for the use of the underscore and overscore.

Study these words and practice them:

offering	of/_	**covered**	cv/‾
featuring	fC/_	**offered**	of/‾
covering	cv/_	**occurred**	oc/‾
referring	rf/_	**referred**	rf/‾
occurring	oc/_	**preferred**	pf/‾

There is one point that must be stressed in order for you to fully understand the application of this rule. You learned that, when the outline of a root word ends in a vowel, the vowel is retained when a suffix is added to it. For example: *truly* Tul ; *highway* hwa ; *payment* pa- . Thus, although *truly* and *highway* are words of more than one syllable, the long vowel is not omitted because it occurs **at the end** of the root-word outline.

You have learned that **medial** vowels are dropped in words of more than one syllable. The one-syllable word *broke* is boc and the two-syllable word *broken* is bcn. Since *broker* is a word of more than one syllable, you write bc/ . In the same way, you write *safe* saf , but *safely* sfl and *safer* sf/

Study these words and practice them:

brief	bef	⟶	**briefer**	bf/
cheap	Cep	⟶	**cheaper**	Cp/
teach	leC	⟶	**teacher**	lC/

But what of the word bolder? You learned to write *ol* for "old" in words of one or more syllables. Applying this rule, *bolder* is written bol/ ; *folder* fol/ ; *policyholder* plsehol/; *folders* fol//; and *holders* hol//.

The following words show you how "er" is added to a root word by simply adding a joined slant to the root-word outline.

Study these words and practice them:

few	fly
fewer	flier
low	high
lower	higher
late	elevate
later	elevator
write	neat
writer	neater
heat	typewrite
heater	typewriter
grave	believe
graver	believer
purchaser	buyer

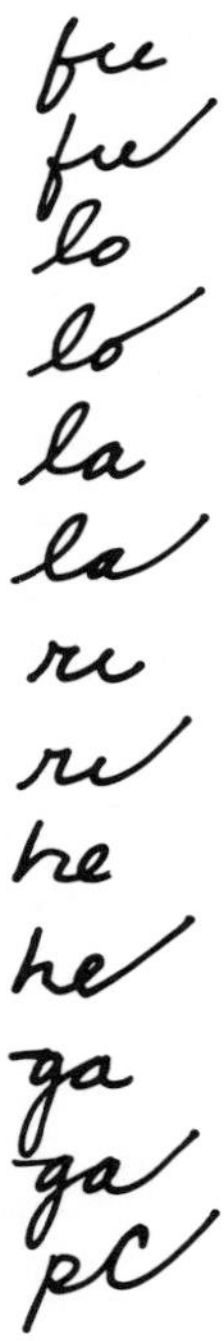

The rule also states that a joined slant will be used to represent the final sound of "ter."

Study these words and practice them:

matter	after
factors	water
latter	better
matters	editor
chapter	meter

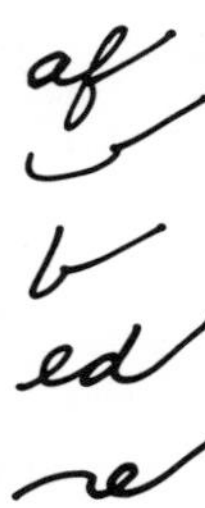

Remember, long vowel sounds are written before punctuation marks so the long *e* is written in *meter* .

Finally, before leaving this rule, let's stress one further aspect of it. Namely, this rule is to be applied **only** at the end of a word. That is, except for an underscore, overscore, or a second slant to indicate the addition of *s*, you will **not** write the joined slant for "er" or "ter" in the middle of an outline. These medial sounds will be covered in a later lesson.

READING EXERCISE

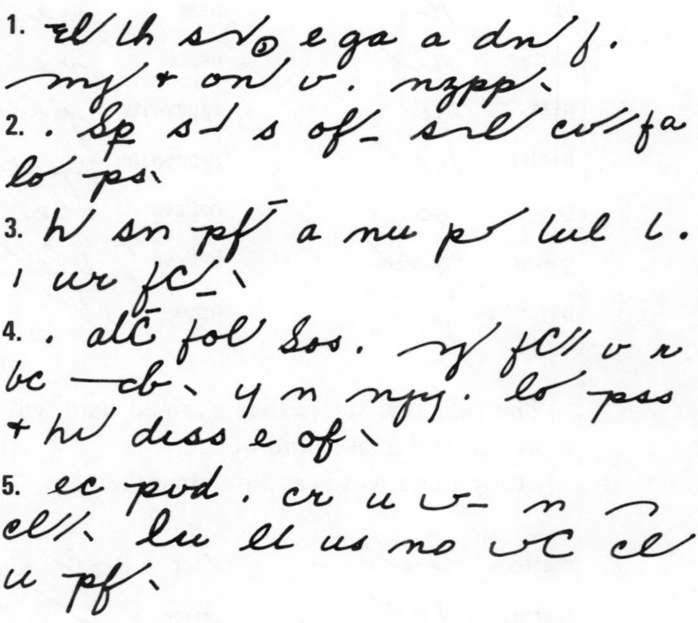

KEY (1) Earlier this summer, we gave a dinner for the manager and owner of the newspaper. (17 words) (2) The shopping center is offering similar covers for a lower price. (19 words) (3) Her son preferred a new power tool to the one you are featuring. (12 words) (4) The attached folder shows the major features of our book club. Why not enjoy the lower prices and higher/ discounts we offer. (23 words) (5) We can provide the car you want in many colors. Will you let us know which color you prefer. (17 words)

2 For the initial and final sound of "aw" write a .

You learned that the initial "combination-1" sound is indicated by writing a dash on the initial letter of the outline. For example, *alley,* the *a* is a short vowel sound —ae ; in the word *ale,* the *a* is a long vowel sound —a . In this rule the sound is "aw."

Study these words and practice them:

all	al	**law**	la
although	allo	**saw**	sa
draw	da	**alter**	al/
drawer	da/	**laws**	las

Here, again, it is important to understand that the rule refers to the sound of "aw" **only** at the **beginning** and **end** of words. Remember that the rule is **not** to be applied to the medial sound of "aw." For example: *cause* cz ; *lawn* ln ; *bought* bl ; *brought* bl ; *caught* cl ; *talk* lc ; *taught* tt .

For the final sound of "all" write al .

Study these words and practice them:

fall	fal	**crawl**	cal

hall	hal	**tall**	lal
wall	val	**ball**	bal

Though this is a simple rule, there is a point about its application that must be clarified and stressed so that you will be sure to use it correctly. Notice that you are instructed to write *al* for the **final** sound of "all." What of such words as *fault* or *walnut?* Since the sound of "all" is **not final** in these words, you can understand why this rule does not affect them; so you write *fault* fll ; *walnut* vlnl ; *false* fls ; *ballroom* blr ; *falsely* flsl ; *halt* hll .

READING EXERCISE

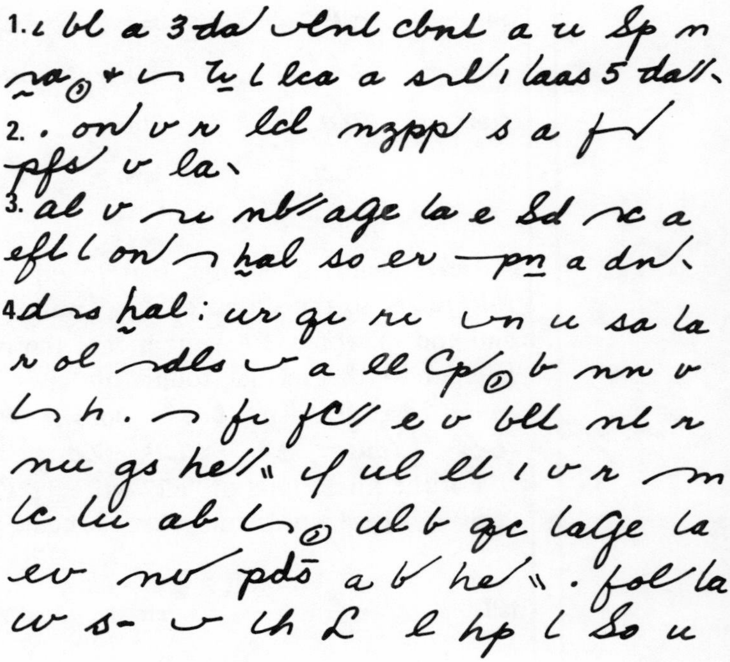

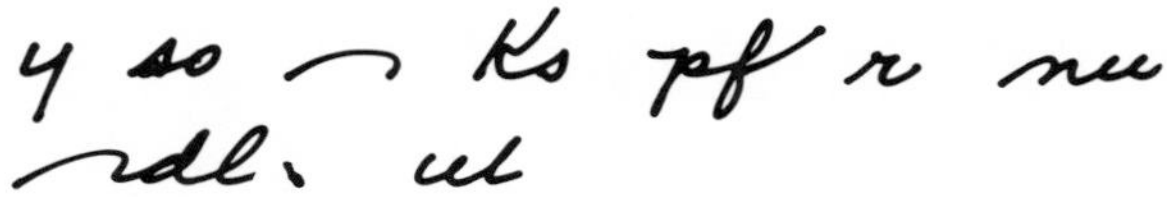

KEY (1) I bought a three-drawer walnut cabinet at your shop in May, and I am trying to locate a similar/ one that has five drawers. (24 words) (2) The owner of our local newspaper is a former professor of law. (14 words) (3) All of my neighbors agree that we should make an effort to honor Mr. Hall so we are planning a dinner. (20 words) (4) Dear Mrs. Hall: You are quite right when you say that our old models were a little cheaper, but none of them had the/ many fine features we have built into our new gas heaters. (P) If you will let one of our men talk to you about/ them, you will be quick to agree that we have never produced a better heater. (P) The folder that I have sent with/ this letter will help to show you why so many customers prefer our new model. Yours truly, (77 words)

3

BRIEF FORMS

again, against		**business**	
where		**advantage**	
sale*	S	**out**	
save		**member**	
future			

*Note that this word is represented by a printed *s*. Any other letter in the alphabet may be written or printed in an outline except *s*.

ABBREVIATIONS **envelope**  **invoice**

SUMMARY

doll<u>AR</u> dl/

1. Write a joined slant to indicate the final sounds of "er" and "ter."

b<u>ALL</u> al

2. Write al for the final sound of "all."

s<u>AW</u> a

3. Write a for the initial or final sound of "aw."

READING EXERCISE

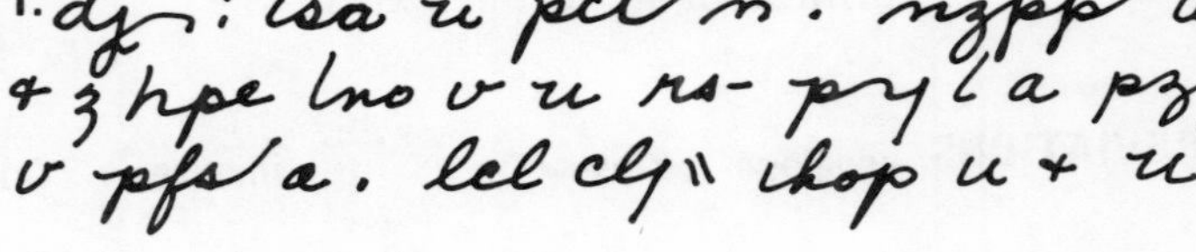

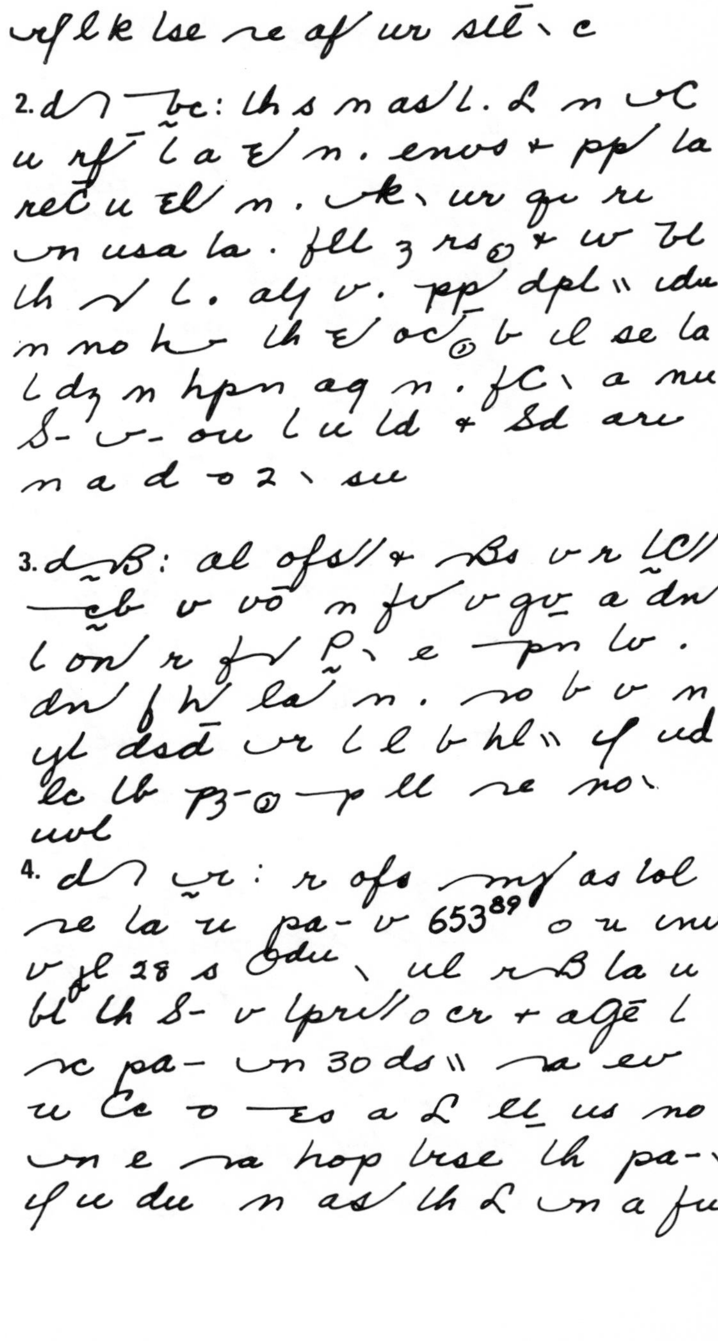

ds⊙ eS fl obj̄ ttc lgl acy
aqu\ su

5. ⌒ds: z. on/ v a rll Sp⊙ u
no dvl ⌒S lse u bs go n fC
ys⊙ + u ⌒- l nCs. no v Ks
hu pC z dl spes z, u\\ .
alC fol/ l So u h⌒ lh c b
dn\ l oules s⌒ v. psy// la
v b flō b a q ⌒ rll// + lls
h⌒ u⊙lo⊙ c nCs u ss du.
y\\ af uv rd. fol/⊙ chop ul
al⌒ 1 v r ay-- lqO. dlls ⌒ u\ ul

6. dro ga: n Cc r fels⊙ e se
la u v n uz u Cq ⌒pa f⌒
⌒ros\ Z/⊙ u⌒a n b fel/ ⌒.
nu Sp s⌒ ev bll lrpl r ol
1\ ⌒a e nvl u l dp n
lse us\ ul fc la⊙ allo r Sp
s bq/+ b ln lz n fv/ ys⊙
e of/ lo/ pss + g/ diss ln
uc gl ⌒Esvz\\ y n lc avy
v. huy s er n⌒ v a ⌒C
er fC/_ fal + ⌒/ cos\ ev
nv bl/ pvd r Ks ⌒ a ⌒d
Cys v cl//⊙ + ev nv/ h sC a

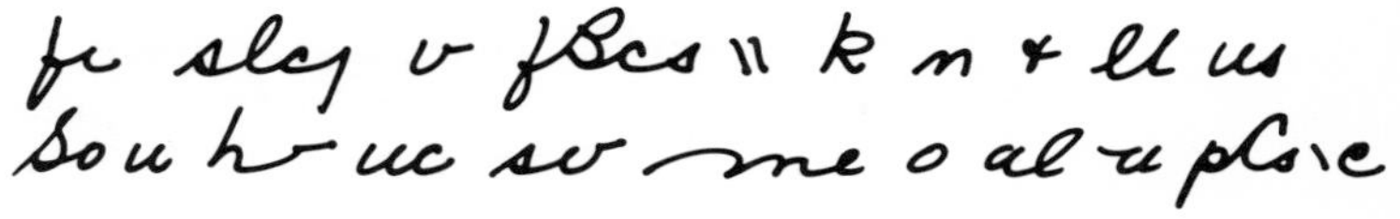

KEY (1) Dear Jim: I saw your picture in the newspaper today and was happy to know of your recent promotion to/ a position of professor at the local college. (P) I hope you and your wife will come to see me after you/ are settled. Cordially, (44 words) (2) Dear Mr. Black: This is in answer to the letter in which you referred to an error in the envelopes and/ paper that reached you earlier in the week. You are quite right when you say that the fault was ours, and I have brought this/ matter to the attention of the proper department. (P) I do not know how this error occurred, but I will see/ that it does not happen again in the future. A new shipment went out to you today and should arrive in a day or/ two. Sincerely yours, (85 words) (3) Dear Member: All officers and members of our Teachers Club have voted in favor of giving a dinner to/ honor our former President. We plan to have the dinner for her later in the month but have not yet decided/ where it will be held. (P) If you would like to be present, please let me know. Very truly yours, (56 words) (4) Dear Mr. White: Our Office Manager has told me that your payment of $653.89/ on your invoice of July 28 is overdue. You will remember that you bought this shipment/ of typewriters on credit and agreed to make payment within 30 days. (P) May we have your check or else a letter/ letting us know when we may hope to receive this payment. If you do not answer this letter within a few/ days, we shall feel obliged to take legal action against you. Sincerely yours, (93 words) (5) My dear Sir: As the owner of a retail shop, you no doubt wish to see your business grow in future years; and you/ want to increase the number of customers who purchase their daily supplies from you. (P) The attached folder will show/ you how this can be done. It outlines some of the procedures that have been followed by a great many retailers/ and tells how you, too, can increase your sales during the year. (P) After you have read the folder, I hope you will allow/ one of our agents to go over the details with you. Yours truly, (92 words) (6) Dear Mrs. Gray: In checking our files, we see that you have not used your charge plate for many months. Therefore, you may not/ be familiar with the new shopping center we have built to replace our old one. (P) May we invite you to drop in/ to see us. You will find that, although our shop is bigger and better than it was in former years, we offer lower/ prices and greater discounts than you can get elsewhere. (P) Why not take advantage of the huge sale we are now having/ at which we are featuring fall and winter coats. We have never before provided our customers with a/ wider choice of colors, and we have never had such a fine selection of fabrics. (P) Come in and let us show you/ how you can save money on all your purchases. Cordially, (130 words)

Cp 10

1 Let's stop for a moment to review some of the rules you have learned about the way a long vowel is handled.

1. **In words of one syllable, write what you hear—writing all long vowels and all pronounced consonants. Examples:** rage *raj*; cheap *Cep*; sign *sin*; hope *hop*; broke *boc*; seek *sec*.

2. **For the sound of a long vowel and "t" or "v," write the long vowel only. Examples:** mate *ma*; neat *ne*; write *ri*; vote *vo*; boot *bu*; gave *ga*; leave *le*; drive *di*; drove *do*; groove *gu*.

You are now going to learn another rule for handling long vowels in the medial and final sounds with "d" or "z."

For the medial and final sounds of "ade," "ede," "ide," "ode," "ude" write *d*; for the medial and final sounds of "aze," "eze," "ize," "oze," "uze" write *3*.

Let's separate the two parts of this rule and examine them individually.

In this principle you learn to omit the long vowel and write *d* for the sounds heard in words such as m*ade*, n*eed*, w*ide*, r*oad*, and f*eud*.

Study these words and practice them:

made	md	**traded**	td̄
needs	nds	**reading**	rd̲
wide	wd	**sides**	sds
code	cd	**rude**	rd
food	fd	**leading**	ld̲

The second part of this rule instructs you to write *z* for the sound of a long vowel + "z."

Study these words and practice them:

raise	rz	**these**	tz
size	sz	**chose**	Cz
whose	hz	**choose**	Cz
rising	rz̲	**seized**	sz̄

In the following sentence, the word *close* is pronounced in two different ways. If you are close to the drawer, will you close it? Notice that in writing this sentence in shorthand, the word *close* is written according to its pronunciation, not its spelling.

Study the following words to see the application of the various rules:

WRITING LONG VOWELS AND CONSONANTS

rails	rals	sign	sin
robe	rob	cheek	Cec

WRITING LONG VOWELS ONLY

rates	ras	raves	ras
sight	se	drive	de
wrote	ro	rove	ro
cheat	Ce	achieve	aCe
root	ru	grooves	gus

DROPPING OF LONG VOWELS

raids	rds	raises	rzs
grade	gd	size	sz
road	rd	rose	rz
feeding	fd	cheese	Cz
rude	rd	cruise	cz
rake	rc	sake	sc

READING EXERCISE

1. du u v- l -p- lz Tes & -Sbs o. sd v. rd ld l u h-s?

2. e lc q pd n. nly la r Ks Td v us. ly no e sl hu gd ds a lo pss.

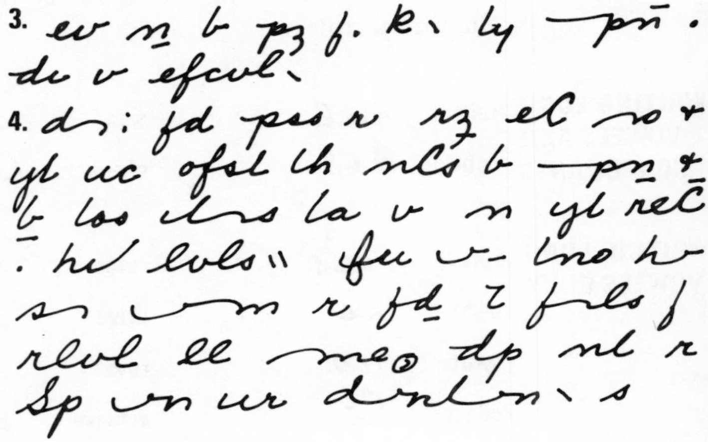

KEY (1) Do you want to plant these trees and shrubs on the side of the road leading to your house? (14 words) (2) We take great pride in the knowledge that our customers trade with us. They know we sell high-grade items at low prices. (20 words) (3) We have nothing but praise for the committee. They planned the drive very effectively. (15 words) (4) Dear Madam: Food prices are rising each month and yet you can offset this increase by planning and buying those items/ that have not yet reached the higher levels. (P) If you want to know how some women are feeding their families/ for relatively little money, drop into our shop when you are downtown. Sincerely, (55 words)

2 Write a dash (——) for the sound of "nd."

In this rule, you are learning to write a dash whenever the sound of "nd" appears in a word.

In comparing the following words, notice how important it is to make the dash at least twice as long as the hypen that is used for "nt" or "ment." Be sure to form the habit of writing a short stroke for the hyphen and a long stroke for the dash.

Study these words and practice them:

send	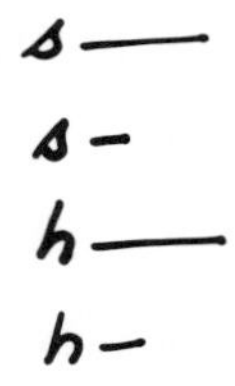	**grand**	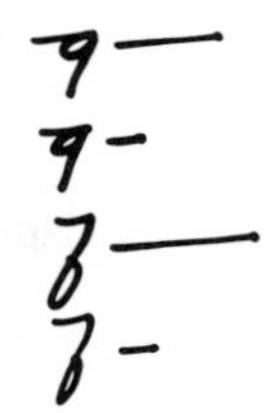
sent		**grant**	
hand		**friend**	
hint		**front**	

Study these words and practice them:

demand	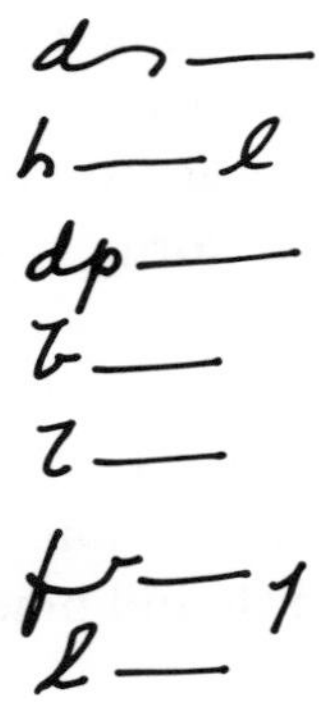	**found**	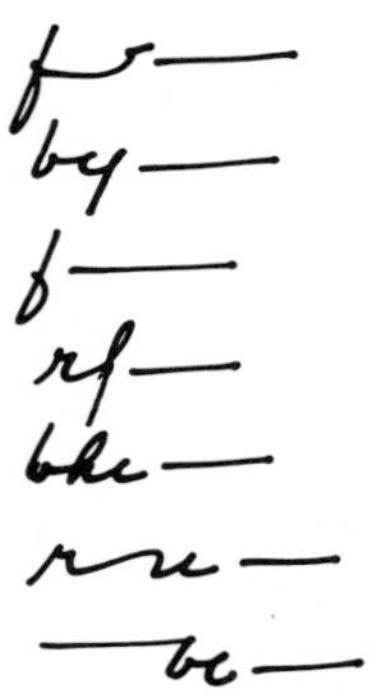
handle		**beyond**	
depend		**fund**	
brand		**refund**	
trend		**behind**	
foundation		**remind**	
lend		**blind**	

Remember, write a long vowel sound before a punctuation mark as in *behind* 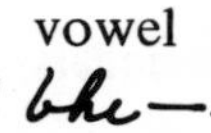.

Some words contain both the sound of "nd" and "ment" or "nd" and "nt," which simply means that both rules will be applied in their proper places. For example: *amendment* 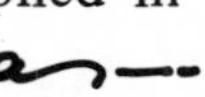 .What of the plural of these words? You follow the rule you have already had to double the last mark of punctuation: *amendments* 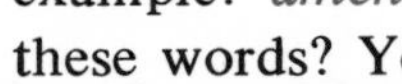

As with all outlines that end in marks of punctuation, you underscore the dash when "ing" is added; and you overscore when "ed" is added. Thus, *sending* 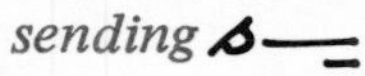 .

Study these words and practice them:

dependent	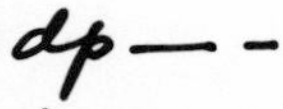	**demanded**	
dependents		**bonds**	
attends		**funds**	
branding		**reminded**	

Remember, in writing a hyphen for "nt" or "ment" be sure to use a short stroke; in writing a dash for "nd," be sure to use a longer stroke.

There are many words in which the sound of "nd" is followed by "er." For example: *calendar* or *wonder.* In writing the outlines for these and similar words, you simply treat the dash as you did the hyphen in *winter* 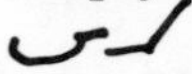 and you write a joined slant.

Study these words and practice them:

wonder		**reminders**	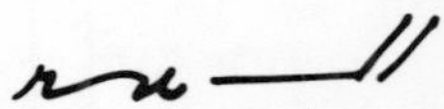
calendars		**binder**	

READING EXERCISE

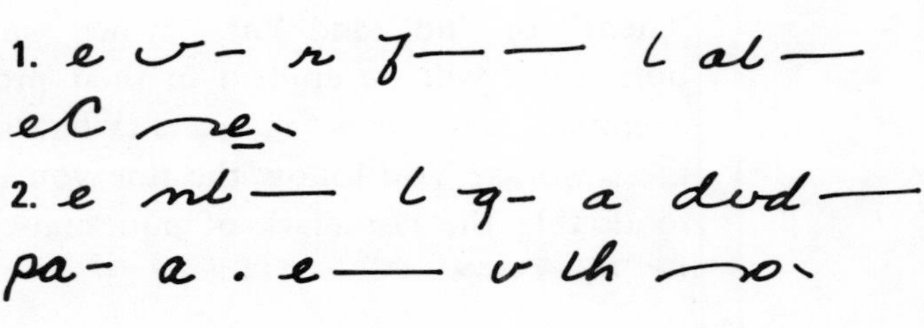

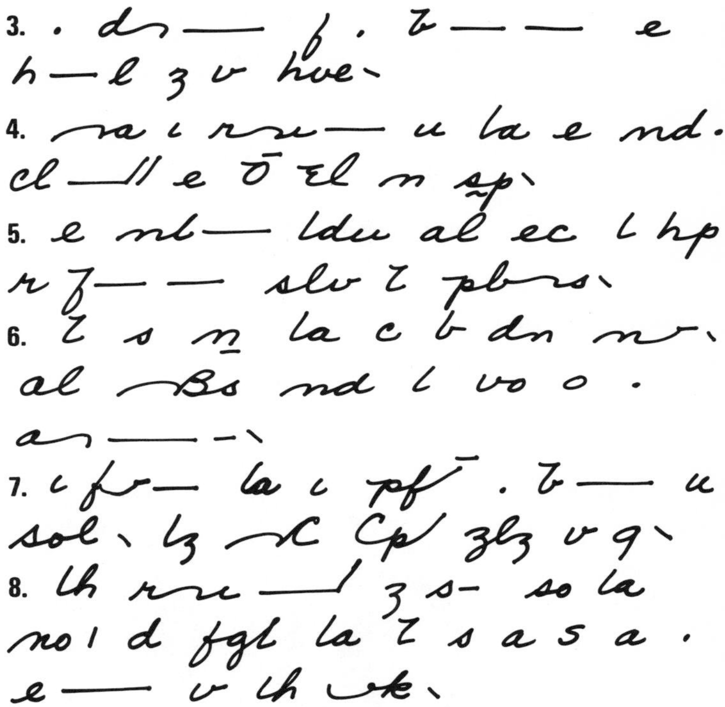

KEY (1) We want our friends to attend each meeting. (7 words) (2) We intend to grant a dividend payment at the end of this month. (12 words) (3) The demand for the brands we handle was very heavy. (10 words) (4) May I remind you that we need the calendars we ordered early in September. (15 words) (5) We intend to do all we can to help our friends solve their problems. (11 words) (6) There is nothing that can be done now. All members need to vote on the amendment. (14 words) (7) I found that I preferred the brand you sold. It was much cheaper as well as very good. (16 words) (8) This reminder was sent so that no one would forget that there is a sale at the end of this week. (17 words)

3

BRIEF FORMS

school	scl	because	cs
until	ul	other	T
only	nl	every, ever	E
begin, began	bg		

ABBREVIATIONS

popular	pop	merchandise	‿dse
absolute, absolutely	abs	intelligent, intelligence, intelligently	inl

SUMMARY

spADE
EED
IDE
ODE
UDE

d

1. For medial and final sounds of a long vowel and d, omit the vowel and write d.

chEESE
AZE
IZE
OZE
UZE

z

2. For medial and final sounds of a long vowel and z, omit the vowel and write z.

caNDle ———

3. Write the dash (——) for the sound of "nd."

READING EXERCISE

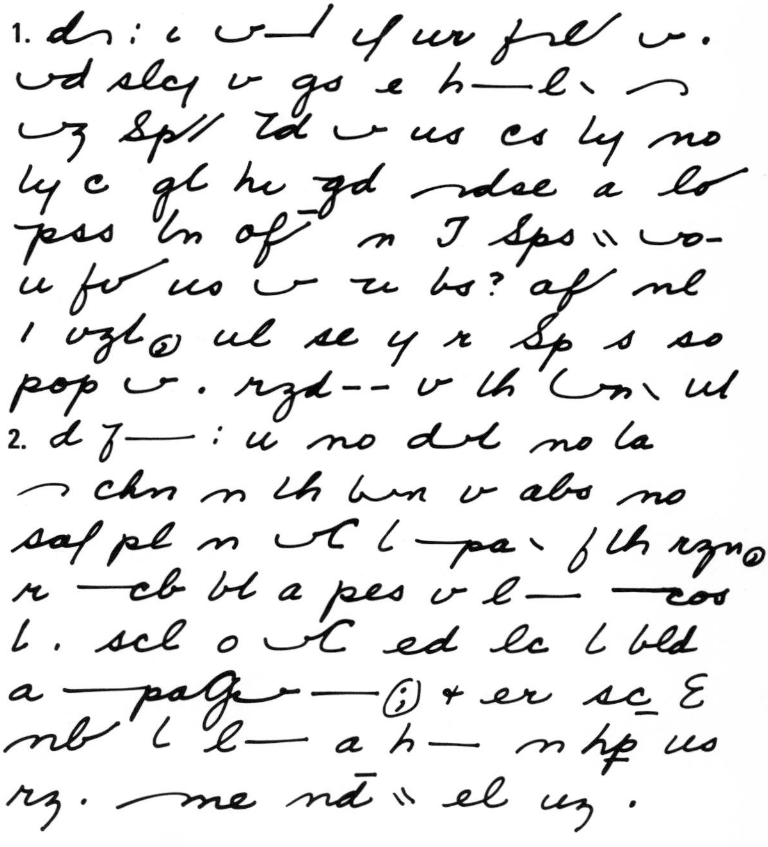

f— — tpa f eqp-⊙ + ehop
l fe a inl ⌒-o ⌣⌒-hu l
lc Cq v sl p a pfs f lz chn"
cf ud lc l jyn us n lh f—
rz di⊙ —p fl ze l gl n lC
⌣ re. ec uz al. hp ec gl. s

3. d⌒ El: lh s l ll u h⌣
—p̄ ⌣ ⌣. ⌒ol blln u
iSu. w b rd l f a q ⌒ ys⊙
+ uz l z ⌒u nl gd⊙ w pC⌒
b— — la v b s⌣— + v pd
⌒re v hi ras" cfl la E1
hu uzs lh blln z a f⌣—1
f. pC v b— — l b gcl
aGe ⌣ ⌒re. c

4. drs El: u ⌒a n no
la T s a bqs b hl a r Sp
o q- ave + goln blod. w ul
. e— v lh ⌣k lk n f l"
lc so ⌒ I Ks⊙ ul ap r v
fe li v ⌒dse. ul b —p̄⊙ lo⊙
⌣. ⌒me uc sv o E pC.
u ⌒a lc aiy v r ez pa-

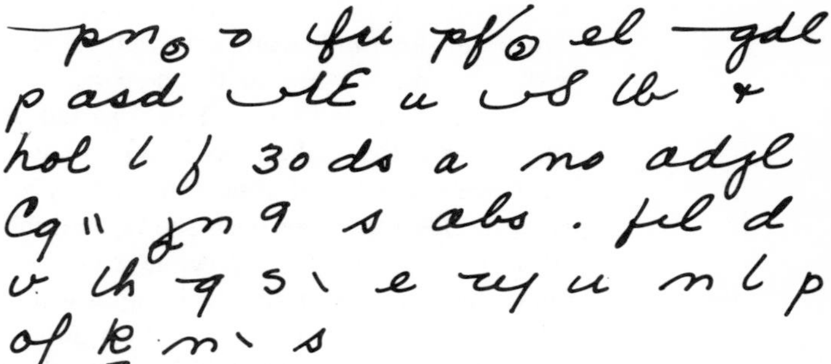

5.

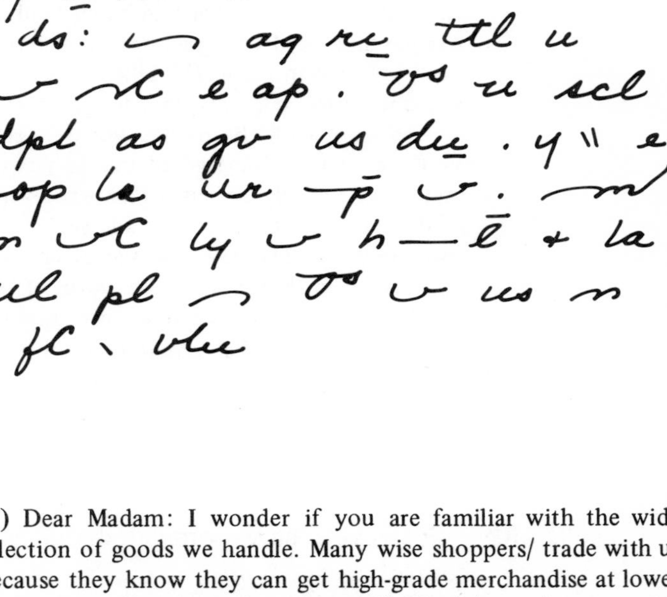

KEY (1) Dear Madam: I wonder if you are familiar with the wide selection of goods we handle. Many wise shoppers/ trade with us because they know they can get high-grade merchandise at lower prices than offered in other shops. (P) Won't/ you favor us with your business? After only one visit, you will see why our shop is so popular with the/ residents of this town. Yours truly, (66 words) (2) Dear Friend: You no doubt know that many children in this town have absolutely no safe place in which to play./ For this reason, our club bought a piece of land close to the school on which we would like to build a playground; and we are/ asking every neighbor to lend a hand in helping us raise the money needed. (P) We will use the funds to pay/ for equipment, and we hope to find an intelligent man or woman who will take charge of setting up a/ program for these children. (P) If you would like to join us in this fund-raising drive, please feel free to get in touch with me./ We can use all the help we can get. Sincerely, (108 words) (3) Dear Mr. Early: This is to tell you how pleased I am with the monthly bulletin you issue. I have been reading/ it for a great many years, and using it as my only guide, I have purchased many bonds that have been sound/ and have paid me very high rates. (P) I feel that everyone who uses this bulletin as a foundation for the/ purchase of bonds will be quick to agree with me. Cordially, (71 words) (4) Dear Mrs. Early: You may not know that there is a big sale being held at our shop on Grant Avenue and Golden/ Boulevard. You have until the end of this week to come in for it. (P) Like so many other customers, you/ will appreciate our very fine line of merchandise. You will be pleased, too, with the money you can save on/ every purchase. You may take advantage of our easy-payment plan, or if you prefer, we will gladly put aside/ whatever you wish to buy and hold it for 30 days at no additional charge. (P) June 9 is absolutely/ the final day of this great sale. We urge you not to put off coming in. Sincerely, (115 words) (5) Dear Sir: I am again writing to tell you how much we appreciate the orders your school department has given/ us during the year. (P) We hope that you are pleased with the manner in which they were handled and that you will place many/ orders with us in the future. Very truly yours, (50 words)

PLATEAUS

Now you have completed one-half of your theory course!

You have probably not been fully aware of the process of automatization to which you have been exposed. Literally hundreds of words are now an instinctive part of your shorthand vocabulary.

The learning process, however, does not always seem to be a continuous one. You, no doubt, feel as if you are "marking time." You feel that your progress has stopped.

Don't be alarmed or discouraged! This is a characteristic of all learning. You have simply reached a plateau in the learning process. What do you do about it? Be patient, diligent, and determined. Try to take every bit of dictation you can get. It will not be long before you are once again aware of making progress!

11

1 In the next rule, you are again writing what you hear. The *e* is silent in most words beginning with *en* and *em*. When the *e* is silent in words beginning with *en* or *em*, all you hear is "n" or "m."

For the sound of "em," write  ; for the sound of "en," write  .

Study these words and practice them:

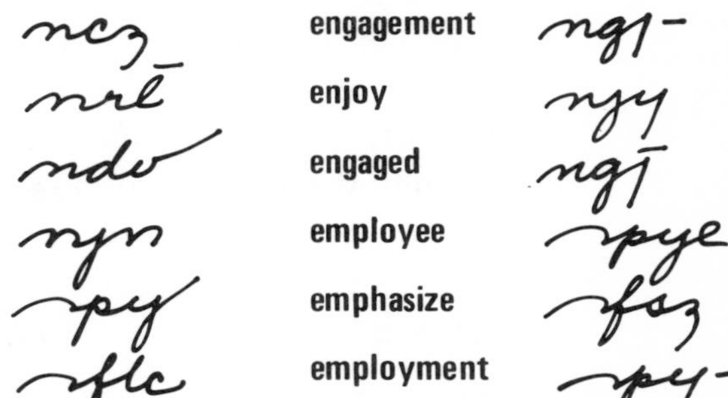

enclose	**engagement**
enrolled	**enjoy**
endeavor	**engaged**
engine	**employee**
employer	**emphasize**
emphatic	**employment**

Notice that this rule states that  is to be written for the **sound** of "en." Listen to the sound at the beginning of the word *any*. Since this word begins with the sound referred to in the rule, you write *any* ne ; *anything* ne ; *anyone* ne1 .

For the sounds of "com," "con," and "coun," write k .

The first sound to which this rule refers is the sound of "com" as in the word *complete*. Since you are already writing *k* for the brief form *come*, it will be natural to write *k* for this sound in a word.

Study these words and practice them:

complete	kpe	**comfort**	kft
comply	kpi	**competent**	kpt-
accomplish	akp8	**combination**	kbnj
complain	kpn	**computer**	kpu/
completion	kpj	**competition**	kptj

The sound of "com" is also heard in *commission* (the second *m* is silent), so you write *commission* kj . Remember, a vowel + "shun" is represented by j . Similarly, *accommodations* akdjs .

Study these words and practice them:

comments	k--	**communicate**	knca
recommends	rk— —	**accommodate**	akda
commitments	kt--	**common**	kn
recommendations	rk—js	**commissioner**	kj/

This rule also instructs you to write k for the sound of "con." For example, *conclusive* kcsv. See how the rule to write k for "con" is applied in the following words.

Study these words and practice them:

convention	kvj	**congratulate**	kgla
contributions	k-bjs	**convenient**	kvn-
consent	ks-	**consequently**	ksq-l
containing	kln	**confident**	kfd-
contents	kl--	**economic**	ekc
connections	kcjs	**control**	k-l

What of the word *confine*? You know that the Brief Form for the word *fine* is f, therefore, *confine* is written kf.

Finally, this rule states that k is also used to represent the sound of "coun" that is heard in *council* and *account*.

Study these words and practice them:

council	ksl	**account**	akl
counsel	ksl	**accountant**	akl-
counselor	ksl/	**counters**	kl//
count	kl	**councilman**	kslm-

READING EXERCISE

1. . ncz bcll Sos . akdjs la e ndv l pvd f . kfl v

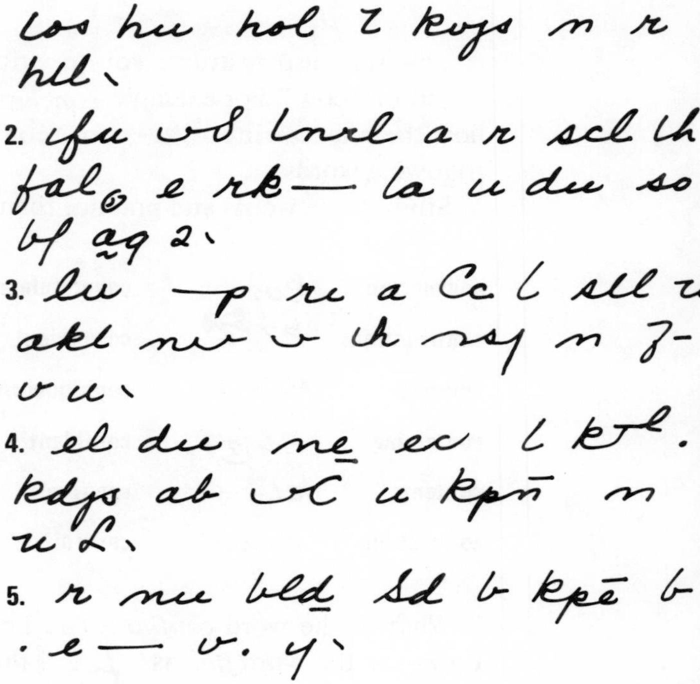

KEY (1) The enclosed booklet shows the accommodations that we endeavor to provide for the comfort of those who hold/ their conventions in our hotel. (26 words) (2) If you wish to enroll at our school this fall, we recommend that you do so before August 2. (17 words) (3) Will you please write a check to settle your account now with this message in front of you. (15 words) (4) We will do anything we can to control the conditions about which you complained in your letter (18 words) (5) Our new building should be completed by the end of the year. (11 words)

2 You are now going to learn about a printed letter that will be used to represent a sound. (Writers who normally print their shorthand will reverse the process and indicate the sound referred to in this rule with a script capital letter.)

In Chapter Nine you learned to use the small printed *s* (**s**) for the brief form for *sale.* You were told at that time that *s* is the only letter in the alphabet that represents different words or sounds when printed and when written.

This new principle makes use of the capital printed *s* (S).

For the sounds of "str," "star," "ster," and "stor," write a *printed* capital S .

Study these examples:

strike
instruments
startle
demonstration
stern
faster
sister
store
storm
instructions
distribution
storage
construction
destroyed
start
starve
straight
registered
yesterday
history
instructors
distribute
industry
semester
illustrates
registration

This rule takes precedence over all others. Learn to be alert to these sounds, especially in the middle and at the end of words. For example, note the "str" in *demonstration*  and the "ster" in *faster* 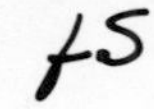 .

READING EXERCISE

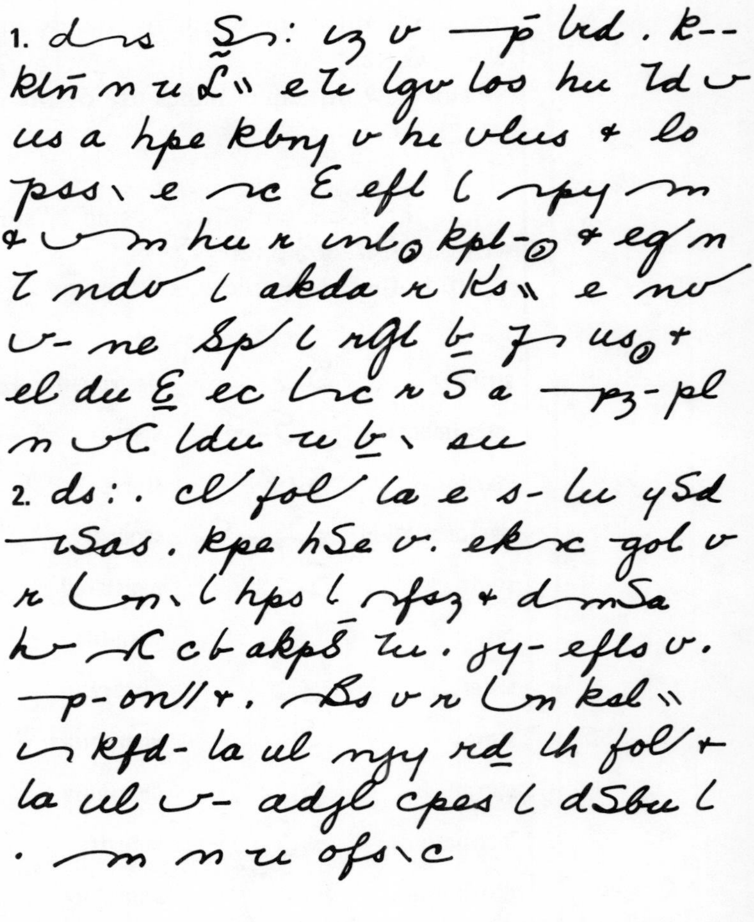

KEY (1) Dear Mrs. Storm: I was very pleased to read the comments contained in your letter. (P) We try to give those who trade with/ us a happy combination of high values and low prices. We make every effort to employ men and/ women who are intelligent, competent, and eager in their endeavor to accommodate our customers./ (P) We never want any shopper to regret buying from us, and we will do everything we can to make our/ store a pleasant place in which to do your buying. Sincerely yours, (91 words) (2) Dear Sir: The color folder that we sent to you yesterday illustrates the complete history of the/ economic growth of our town. It helps to emphasize and demonstrate how much can be accomplished through the joint efforts of the/ plant owners and the members of our town council. (P) I am confident that you will enjoy reading this/ folder and that you will want additional copies to distribute to the men in your office. Cordially, (78 words)

3 BRIEF FORMS

opportunity *opl*

while *ul*

continue *ku*

fire *fr*

several *sv*

necessary, necessarily *nec*

satisfy, satisfaction, satisfactory *sal*

deal, deliver, delivery *dl*

SUMMARY

EMbrace 

1. **Write**  **for the sound of "em."**

<u>EN</u>gine n

2. Write n for the sound of "en."

<u>COM</u>pass k
<u>CON</u>
<u>COUN</u>

3. Write k for the sounds of "con," "com," and "coun."

<u>STAR</u> S
<u>STER</u>
<u>STOR</u>
<u>STR</u>

4. Write S for the sounds of "str," "star," "ster," and "stor."

READING EXERCISE

1. 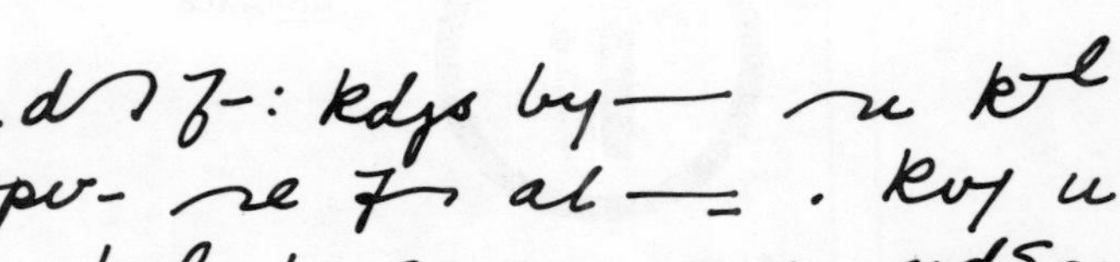

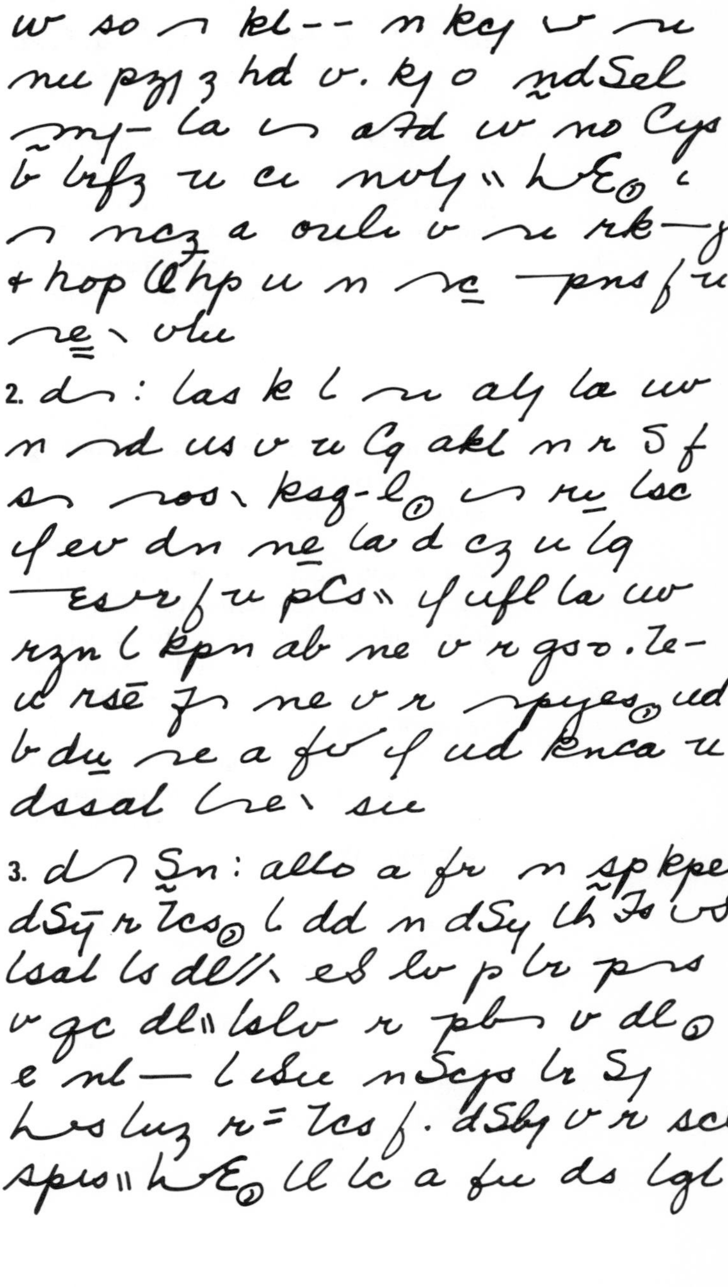

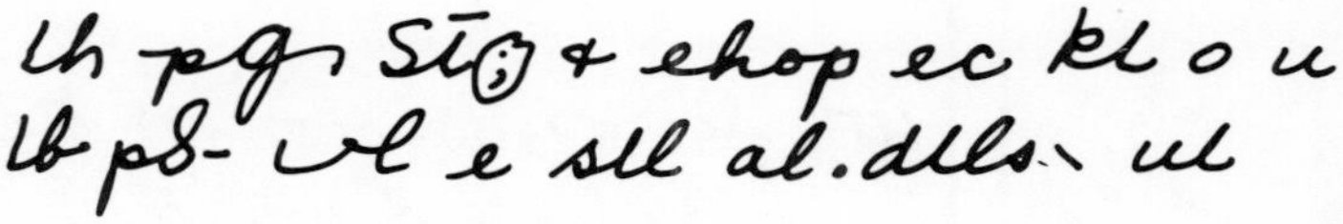

KEY (1) Dear Mr. Front: Conditions beyond my control prevent me from attending the convention you are holding for/ the salesmen in your industry. I have so many commitments in connection with my new position as head/ of the Commission on Industrial Management that I am afraid I have no choice but to refuse your kind/ invitation. (P) However, I am enclosing an outline of my recommendations and hope it will help you/ in making plans for your meetings. Very truly yours, (89 words) (2) Dear Madam: It has come to my attention that you have not made use of your charge account in our store for some months./ Consequently, I am writing to ask if we have done anything that would cause you to go elsewhere for your/ purchases. (P) If you feel that you have reason to complain about any of our goods or the treatment you received from/ any of our employees, you would be doing me a favor if you would communicate your dissatisfaction/ to me. Sincerely yours, (85 words) (3) Dear Mr. Stern: Although a fire in September completely destroyed our trucks, it did not destroy this firm's wish to/ satisfy its dealers. We shall live up to our promise of quick delivery. (P) To solve our problem of/ delivery, we intend to issue instructions to our storage house to use rented trucks for the distribution of/ our school supplies. (P) However, it will take a few days to get this program started; and we hope we can count on you/ to be patient while we settle all the details. Yours truly, (90 words)

Cp 12

1 You have learned to write a hyphen on the *e* for the initial sound of "er" in words such as *earth* El and *earn* En. You have also learned to write the joined slant for the final sound of "er" in words such as *cover* cv and *greater* g/. Now you are going to learn how this and similar sounds are handled in the middle of a word.

For the sound of a medial vowel and *r,* capitalize the letter of the outline that precedes this sound.

Notice in the following words that each contains the sound of a medial vowel and "r"; b*ar*k, b*ar*on, lib*er*al, we*ir*d, b*or*n, p*ir*ate.

This rule instructs you to capitalize the letter of the outline that precedes these sounds. Therefore, the words given above are written: *bark* Bc ; *baron* Bn ; *liberal* lBl ; *weird* Ud ; *born* Bn ; *pirate* pl .

Study these words and practice them:

bargain Bgn **liberally** lBl

burden	*Bdn*	**birth**	*Bl*

Remember, when a root word ends in *l,* do not add the second *l* in the outline for the suffix *ly*. *Liberally* has just one *l* at the end of the outline *lBl* .

The sounds of medial "ar," "er," and "or" are also heard in the following words: p*ar*cel, p*er*son, rep*or*t. This time the sounds are preceded by the letter *p.* Since the rule states that this preceding letter is to be capitalized, you write *P* for the sounds of "par," "per," and "por." Thus: *parcel* *Psl* ; *person* *Psn* ; *report* *rPl* ; *supervisors* *sPvz//* .

Study these words and practice them:

part	*Pl*	**purpose**	*Pps*
personal	*Psnl*	**permit**	*Pml*
operation	*oPj*	**support**	*sPl*
cooperate	*coPa*	**parking**	*Pc̲*

Note the outline for the word *cooperate.* When a prefix or a suffix is added, the outline for the root word is retained. *Operate* is the root word and it is written *oPa* . The addition of the prefix *co* will not change the root word, even though the word contains more than one syllable, *coPa* .

Here is a further illustration of this rule: *card* *Cd* ; *current* *C-* ; *course* *Cs* ; *accordingly* *aCd̲l* . You can see how the rule is applied and *C* is written for the sounds of "kar," "ker," and "kor." Note the joining of *l* to the underscore in the word *accordingly*.

Study these words and practice them:

carton	Cln	**courses**	Css
curb	Cb	**carbon**	Cbn
courtesy	Clse	**record**	rCd
according	aCd̲	**curve**	Cv

See how the letter that precedes the sounds of "ar," "er," and "or" is capitalized in the following list of words.

Study these words and practice them:

dark	Dc	**certainly**	Slnl
modern	⌒Dn	**circular**	Scl/
farm	F⌒	**source**	So
farmer	F/	**research**	rSC
furniture	FnC/	**survey**	Sva
guard	Gd	**assortment**	aSt-
guaranteed	G-ē	**surprise**	SPz
regard	rGd	**turn**	Tn
heard	Hd	**determine**	dT⌒
hardly	Hdl	**returned**	rTn̄
larger	Lj/	**patterns**	pTns
learned	Ln̄	**terminate**	T⌒a
margin	⌒jn	**returning**	rTn̲

market		**alterations**	
merit		**termination**	
normal		**governors**	
normally		**conversation**	
portion		**toward**	
separate		**working**	
tomorrow		**worthy**	
quarter		**yard**	
service		**reserved**	
concerned		**hazards**	

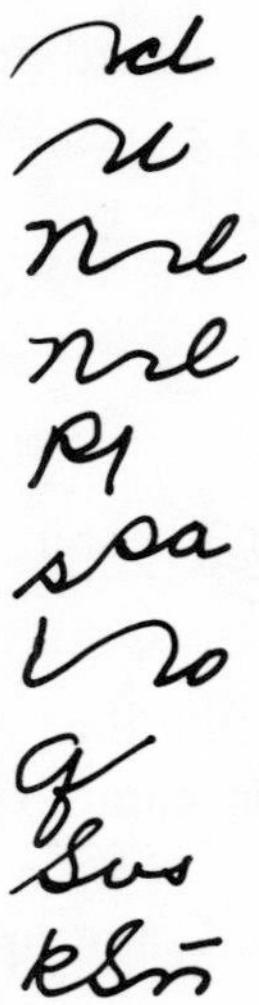

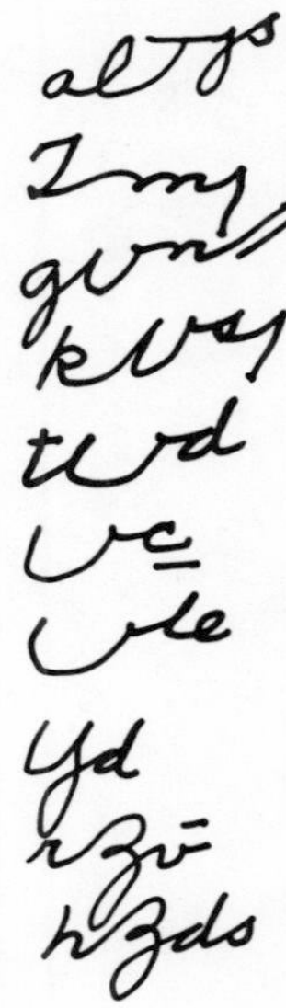

Examine the word *commerce*. For the sound of "comm," you write . This sound is followed by the sound of "er." To indicate a medial sound of "er," you capitalize the letter of the outline that precedes the sound. For "commer" you will write so *commerce* is .

You will recall that when the rule for the writing of a joined slant for the **final** sound of "er" and "ter" was presented, you learned that the joined slant is to be followed only by an underscore, overscore, or a second slant to indicate the addition of *s*. Then what of the word *different*? You know that *differ* is written ; *differs* ; *differed* ; *differing* . However, you will write *different* ; *differently* . Similarly, you will write *proper* ; but *properly* ; *former* ; *formerly* ; *cover* ; *coverage* ; *quarter* q/ ; *quarterly* ql. The words *differ, proper, former, cover,* and *quarter* contain a **final** sound of "er," but the words *different, properly, formerly, coverage,* and *quarterly* contain a medial sound of "er."

Now let's consider such words as *clerk* and *flourish.* As you know, you write ‾c for the initial sound of "cl." Therefore, since this rule tells you to capitalize the sound that precedes the sound of "er," you write ‾C for the resulting sound of "cler." Thus, *clerk* ‾Cc. Similarly, you write ‾F for the sound of initial "fler" and write *flourish* ‾Fs. Make a jog at the end of the dash to indicate that a dash is connected to the F.

Let's review the rules you have had concerning the sound of "r."

Study these words and practice them:

Initial "combination-r"

bread	bd	**crease**	ces
dry	di	**fresh**	Fs
gray	ga	**print**	p-
tread	Td	**arm**	an
earn	En	**iron**	in
or	o	**urn**	un

Medial "combination-r"

abroad	aBd	**increase**	nCs
hydrogen	hDjn	**refresh**	rFs

agree	aGe	approval	asvl
retread	rTd	shrill	Sl

Final "er" and "ter"

lumber	lmb/	occur	oc/
ladder	ld/	refer	rf/
bigger	bg/	paper	pp/
after	af/	chapter	Cp/

Medial vowel + "r"

liberal	lBl	curb	Cb
modern	mDn	fertile	Ftl
garden	Gdn	support	sPt
turn	Tn	certain	Stn

READING EXERCISE

1. e q-e l Tn8 a Lj Scl/ So r mDn TnC.
2. uz SPz l Ln la u aTne dd n kt u uGs.
3. er Stn la . Gls l mTn . Cln v bcs.
4. w Hd la a Sva md ySd ndcas la ss r hv ln los v fr/ ys.

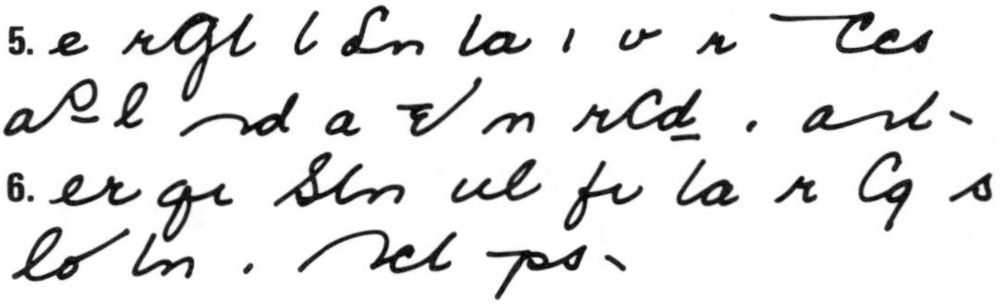

KEY (1) We guarantee to furnish a large circular showing our modern furniture. (14 words) (2) I was surprised to learn that your attorney did not confirm my telegram. (14 words) (3) We are certain that the girls will return the carton of books. (11 words) (4) I have heard that a survey made yesterday indicates that sales are higher than those of former years. (18 words) (5) We regret to learn that one of our clerks apparently made an error in recording the amount. (18 words) (6) We are quite certain you will find that our charge is lower than the market price. (14 words)

2 For the final *ss* and *ness,* write an apostrophe ('); for the final *ssness,* write a quotation mark (").

Notice, in the following words, that an apostrophe (') is written for the final *ss* and *ness* and that the plural is formed by doubling the mark of punctuation.

less		**address**	
class		**classes**	
miss		**missing**	
regardless	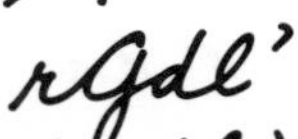	**progress**	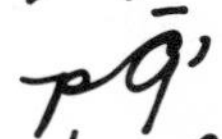
doubtless		**helpless**	
hopeless*		**passing**	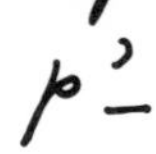
happiness		**illness**	

*Retain *o* in *hopeless* to avoid conflict with *helples*

The rule states that you are to write an apostrophe for the **final** *ss—not* for the medial *ss*. Therefore, *message* msj ; *passage* psj .

The second part of this rule says that a quotation mark (") will be used to represent the **final** *ssness*. Thus, *hopelessness* hopl" ; *helplessness* hpl" .

BRIEF FORMS

above	bv	both	bo
also	lso	call	cl
under	U	full, fully	fu
public, publish	pb		

ABBREVIATIONS

subscribe, subscription	sub	average	av
magazine	mag	maximum	max
minimum	min	question	q

READING EXERCISE

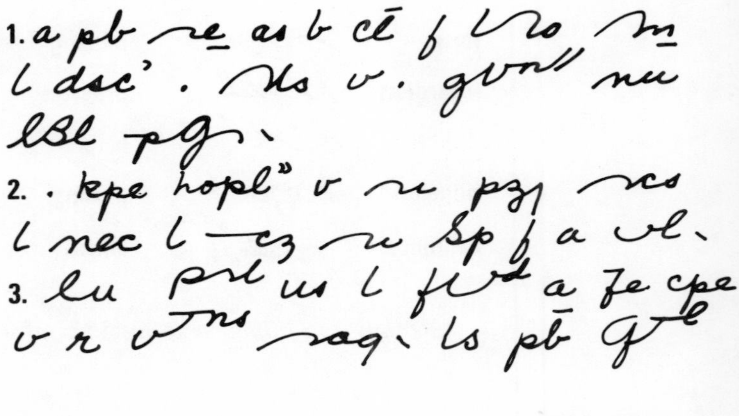

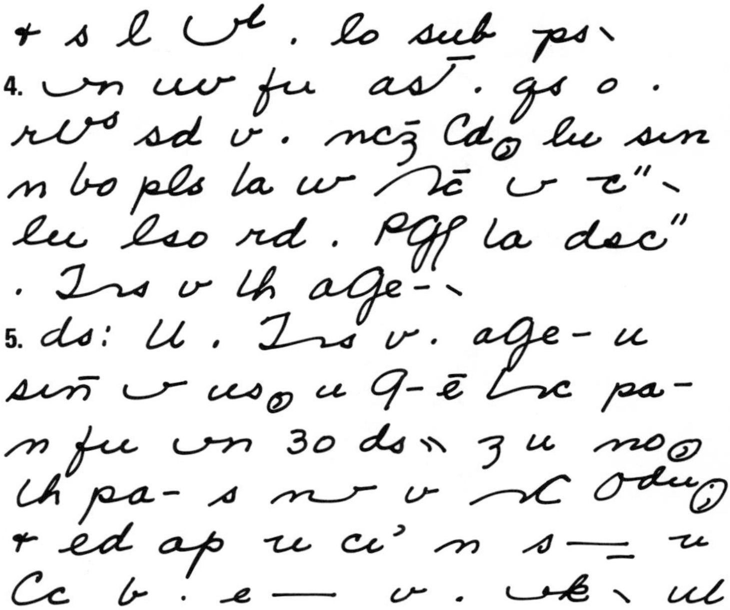

KEY (1) A public meeting has been called for tomorrow morning to discuss the merits of the Governor's new liberal/ program. (21 words) (2) The complete hopelessness of my position makes it necessary to close my shop for a while. (17 words) (3) Will you permit us to forward a free copy of our veteran's magazine. It is published quarterly and/ is well worth the low subscription price. (26 words) (4) When you have fully answered the questions on the reverse side of the enclosed card, will you sign in both places that/ I have marked with crosses. Will you also read the paragraph that discusses the terms of this agreement. (39 words) (5) Dear Sir: Under the terms of the agreement you signed with us, you guaranteed to make payment in full within/ 30 days. (P) As you know, this payment is now very much overdue; and we would appreciate your kindness in sending/ your check by the end of the week. Yours truly, (48 words)

3 DAYS OF THE WEEK

Monday	m	Friday	fr
Tuesday	tu	Saturday	st
Wednesday	wd	Sunday	sn
Thursday	th		

SUMMARY

PIRate P

1. To indicate the medial sound of a vowel and r, capitalize the letter of the outline that precedes this sound.

croSS
NESS '

2. Write an apostrophe (') for the final ss and ness.

careleSSNESS "

3. Write a quotation mark for the final ssness.

READING EXERCISE

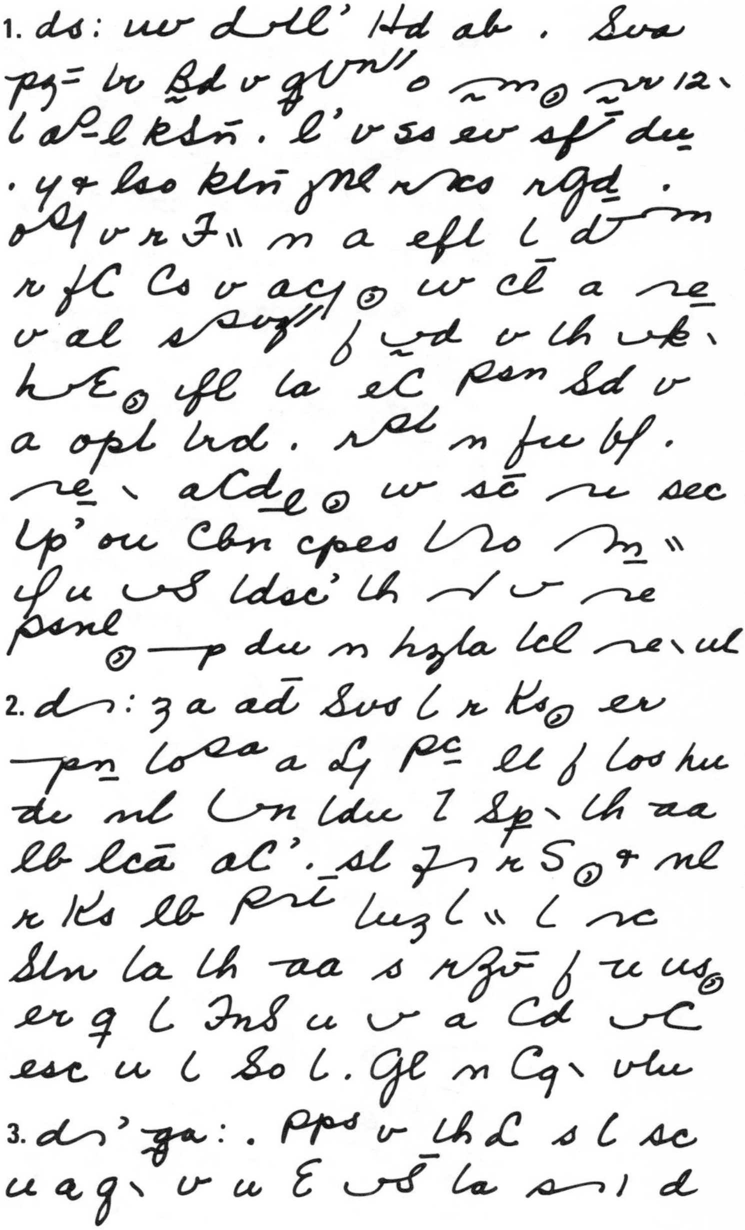

pb a -rag dvō l ng + nfy
ab r ndSe? v-u ofn v=lDn
v. rSC v^c b dn l nv- nu
fBcs f cos + d" ?? f u as l
los qs s ys ln u vo- v-l
r' se. nu -rag la s k of
. p'o -m" l ntdo u l Lh
-rag er q l s— u a Fe cpe
e Q-e la vn uv rd l ul
v-l sub f al fC iBus rB
Lh pby s f. Zd nl + l n b
sol l. fNl pb s

4. ds: -n lc Lh opl laD' Lh L
lu cs -n kSn ab u sns
rCd v —so pQ' n r scl"
uno h lb a by hu s bv av n
unl + yl. v^c h as In n l s
nScll dy n k p l. -un lvl
v aCe-e al icble la. bys
—i' a. bq v. In akls f s lo
-rcs +. pS v lu lcp p v
s—c" s evd-l lo q" cd lc l
dsc' Lh -v fu v bv u + u

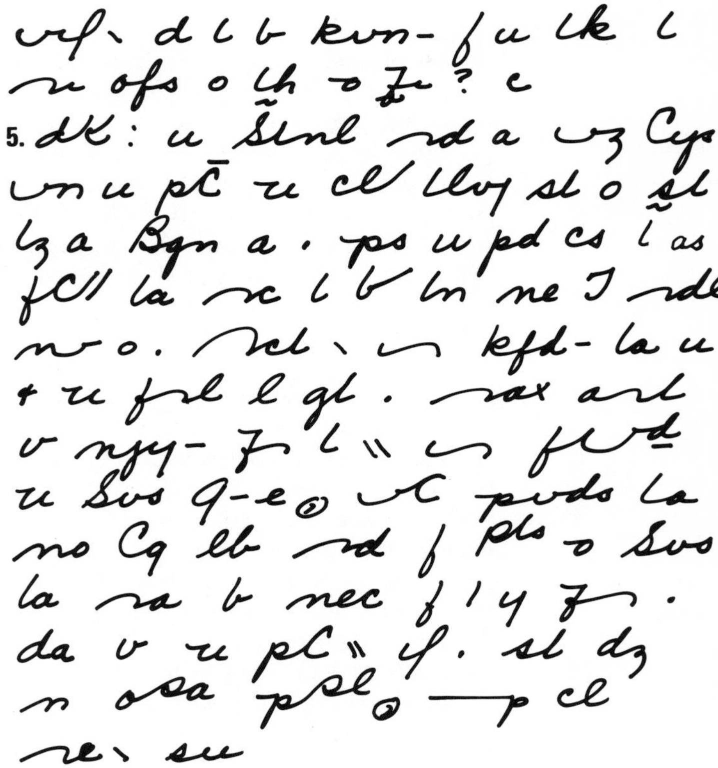

5.

KEY (1) Dear Sir: You have doubtless heard about the survey presented to our Board of Governors on Monday, March 12. It/ apparently concerned the loss of sales we have suffered during the year and also contained general remarks/ regarding the operation of our firm. (P) In an effort to determine our future course of action, I have/ called a meeting of all supervisors for Wednesday of this week. However, I feel that each person should have an/ opportunity to read the report in full before the meeting. Accordingly, I have asked my secretary/ to pass out carbon copies tomorrow morning. (P) If you wish to discuss this matter with me personally,/ please do not hesitate to call me. Yours truly, (128 words) (2) Dear Madam: As an added service to our customers, we are planning to operate a large parking lot for/ those who drive into town to do their shopping. This area will be located across the street from our store, and/ only our customers will be permitted to use it. (P) To make certain that this area is reserved for your/ use, we are going to furnish you with a card which we ask you to show to the girl in charge. Very truly yours,/ (80 words) (3) Dear Miss Gray: The purpose of this letter is to ask you a question. Have you ever wished that someone would publish/ a magazine devoted to news and information about our industry? Haven't you often wanted to/ learn of the research work being done to invent new fabrics for coats and dresses? (P) If your answer to those questions/ is yes, then you won't want to miss seeing the new magazine that is coming off the press on Monday. (P) To/ introduce you to this magazine, we are going to send you a free copy. We guarantee that, when you have read/ it, you will want to subscribe for all future issues. Remember, this publication is for the trade only and/ will not be sold to the general public. Sincerely, (130 words) (4) Dear Sir: I am taking this opportunity to address this letter to you because I am concerned about/ your son's record of slow progress in our school. (P) I know him to be a boy who is above average in/ intelligence, and yet the work he has turned in to his instructors does not come up to the minimum level of/ achievement we allow. I believe that the boy's illness at the beginning of the term accounts for his low marks, and/ the pressure of trying to keep up with his classes is evidently too great. (P) I would like to discuss this matter/ fully with both you and your wife. Would it be convenient for you to come to my office on Thursday or Friday?/ Cordially, (122 words) (5) Dear Customer: You certainly made a wise choice when you purchased your color television set on Saturday./ It was a bargain at the price you paid because it has features that make it better than any other model/ now on the market. I am confident that you and your family will get the maximum amount of enjoyment/ from it. (P) I am forwarding your service guarantee, which provides that no charge will be made for parts or service/ that may be necessary for one year from the date of your purchase. (P) If the set does not operate properly,/ please call me. Sincerely yours, (105 words)

Cp 13

1 The next rule uses the letter *x* to represent certain sounds. This letter can be too time consuming to write unless you learn to write it properly. Before you go any farther, take a few minutes to practice this letter, following these suggestions.

At the **beginning** of a word, write the cross stroke **first** / and then write the final stroke x. Doing this permits you to continue smoothly and quickly with the next letter without an interruption. Practice the word *explain* xpn using this method.

In the middle or at the end of a word, simply write an upward stroke on the letter that precedes the *x* and then go back and cross this upward stroke. Practice these words: *tax* tx and *fixes* fxs.

For the sounds of "aks," "eks," "iks," "oks," and "uks," write x.

Note that the sound of *s* is included in each of these sounds so the *s* is not written in the outline for these sounds.

Study these words and practice them:

tax	*tx*	**extent**	*xt–*
box	*bx*	**fix**	*fx*
deluxe	*dlx*	**examine**	*xm*

What of the sound in the word *accident?* Since the first sound in this word is "aks," and the rule instructs you to write *x* for this sound, you write *accident* *xd–*.

Study the following words and practice them:

accidental	*xd–l*	**index**	*ndx*
express	*xp'*	**expand**	*xp—*
expenditures	*xp—C//*	**oxygen**	*xjn*
experts	*xpts*	**expansion**	*xpj*
exhibit	*xbt*	**exceptionally**	*xpjl*
excessive	*xsv*	**exceed**	*xd*
excellent	*xl–*	**explanation**	*xpnj*

You have learned that the addition of *s* does not change the way in which the root word is written. Thus, *shoes* is written *Sus*. In the same way, the word *back* is written *bc* and the plural *backs* *bcs*. Do **not** apply the present rule when *s* is added to a root word that ends in *k*. For example: *tack* *tc*; *tacks* *tcs*; *box* *bx*; *boxes* *bxs*; *fix* *fx*; *fixes* *fxs*.

Before going on to the next rule let us first remind you of two rules that you had in a previous lesson. You have learned that when a long vowel is followed by the sound of "t" or "v," the long vowel is written to represent the resulting sound. Thus, *wait*  ; *weave*  ; *coat*  ; *cave*  .

You are now going to learn another group of words in which the long vowel is used in the same way.

For the **final** sound of a long vowel and "m," write the long vowel to represent the resulting sound.

You can see how similar this rule is to the ones just reviewed. This rule states that you will write *a* for the final sound of "ame," *e* for the sound of "eem," *i* for the sound of "ime," *o* for the sound of "ome," and *u* for the sound of "ume."

The word *name* is composed of the sounds "n" + "ame," and since you are learning to write *a* for the final sound of "ame," you write *name*  . Similarly, *seem* is made up of the sounds of "s" + "eem." Therefore, since you write *e* for the final sound of "eem," *seem* is  .

Study these words and practice them:

same		**timely**	
claim		**sometime**	
team		**home**	
extremely		**consumer**	
time		**assume**	

READING EXERCISE

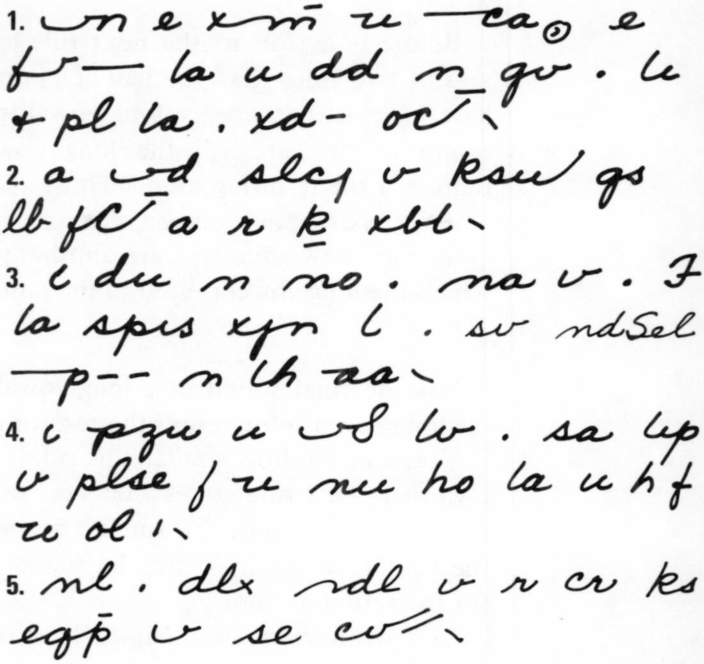

KEY (1) When we examined your claim, we found that you did not give the time and place that the accident occurred. (18 words) (2) A wide selection of consumer goods will be featured at our coming exhibit. (15 words) (3) I do not know the name of the firm that supplies oxygen to the several industrial plants in this/ area. (21 words) (4) I presume you wish to have the same type of policy for your new home that you had for your old one. (19 words) (5) Only the deluxe model of our car comes equipped with seat covers. (13 words)

2 In Chapter Nine you learned to write the joined slant for the **final** sounds of "er" and "ter." This rule does not include the final sound of "ther."

You have learned to indicate the initial and medial sounds of "ther" with a capital *t* as in *thorough*  ; *therapy*  ; and *authorize*  . In these words you used *t* for the sound of "th" and capitalized the *t* to indicate the sounds of "ar," "er," and "or."

With this basic understanding, you should have no difficulty with this next rule.

For the final sound of "ther" write  .

Study these words and practice them:

author		**neither**	
whether		**together**	
mothers		**further**	
either		**farther**	
rather		**brothers**	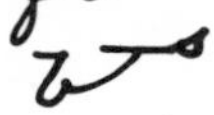
bothered	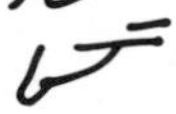	**authors**	
gathering		**weather**	

Note the words *farther* and *further. Farther* is derived from the root word *far,* so you write  for *far* and add "ther." *Further,* however, is not drived from *fur,* so you capitalize *f* for the vowel-r which follows and add "ther."

BRIEF FORMS

note		**direct**	
contract, correct		**benefit**	

even	vn	consider	ks
evening	vn̲	upon	pn

ABBREVIATIONS

Christmas	Xrs	advertise	adv
certificate, certify	cerl		

READING EXERCISE

1. u Sd ks Tol . xl- bnfs ul gl fr adv̲ u lys & gas n . Xrs sSn v r raq.

2. . Dl v r scl vBs re l ll E rT & fT ab r xp— pG.

3. w aT3 mu aTne ldsc' . Trs v mu Kc v u.

4. dr bl: . dlx bx v lrls u O o oc 15 3 S D l u ho b a xP o oc 16. l Sd reC u sr h ld" vn l ks mP xm . kl-- l dT mT o n ne s m fr . sl. if ev n Hd fr u n a fu ds el asu la . sl s kpe & l bl u aCd br opnl Kc" ra

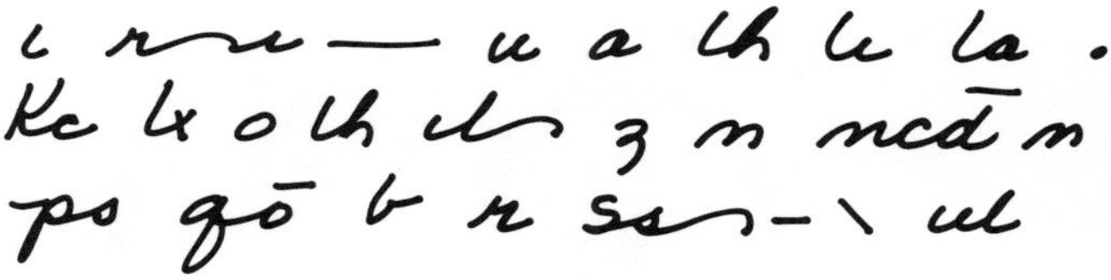

KEY (1) You should consider thoroughly the excellent benefits you will get from advertising your toys and games in/ the Christmas issue of our magazine (27 words) (2) The Director of our school wishes me to tell every mother and father about our expanding program. (20 words) (3) I have authorized my attorney to discuss the terms of my contract with you. (15 words) (4) Dear Mr. Billings: The deluxe box of tools you ordered on October 15 was shipped direct to your home/ by air express on October 16. It should reach you some time today. (P) When it comes, please examine the contents to/ determine whether or not anything is missing from the set. If we have not heard from you in a few days, we/ will assume that the set is complete and will bill you according to our original contract. (P) May I remind/ you at this time that the correct tax on this item was not included in the price quoted by our salesman. Yours truly,/ (100 words)

3 SUMMARY

bOX 
AKS
EKS
IKS
UKS

1. **Write**  **for the sounds of "aks," "eks," "iks," "oks," and "uks."**

flAME a
EEM e
IME i
OME o
UME u

2. When a word ends in the sounds of "ame," "eem," "ime," "ome," or "ume," end the outline with the vowel, dropping the m.

faTHER 
moTHER
broTHER

3. Write  for the final sound of "ther."

READING EXERCISE

1. 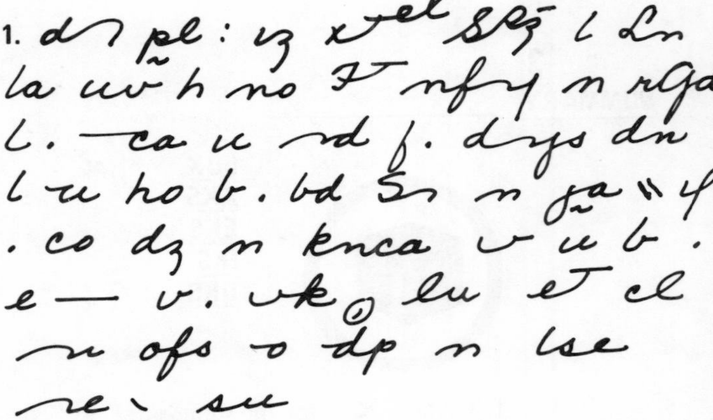

2. d) sno: u vef nl arv
y5d, i qT f, vl u sd la
ur nv nc xl-pq' + se
rT Sln la uc fnd. jb b ap 19"
cl b Tol Tu u Lno vd vn
+ v— cf ec gl lqT f a
ll vl l lc ab. xbl
b — pn f na 10, vlu

3. d) cp: lu — p fl n u
na + aD' o. alC Cd + nl
l bc l us, o. sa d la e
rse l el s— u. bcll la
xpns.) xl- hll + xd-
plses er nv of-" er Kfd-
la E T + fT l gcl se.
avgs v lz plses + l v-
adjl nfy ab L, a lel
cl lr ofs l s— 1 v r
ay-- l u ho l xpn T.
plcy q-e b lh nu lup
v clt, c

4. ds: bf u t lfx rc ol ad_
Sn⊙ Sd ap u lt_ re
no. xl- v. dys +. ps
ul Cq lp l nl pp/ lc_
O" cfl la f. asl xds
30d⊙ ld b l rc ol
lpC aT Sn. ul.

5. d) r: ul fc ncz a
cpe v. Kc u sn o fb 14.
lh Ke gvs u. xcsv rc l
h—l r fc lc v ksu gs
n u aa⊙ + F q-es la
ul nyy. sa bnfs z r
xl— l J aTz dl/"
—p r B la r Ly lc v
xpls s rde + l_ lhp u sl
p u adv_ pq f. k_ Xs
szn. uvl

6. ds' by: lh s l nfs u la
r Bd v D/ as aTz re
l of u a pzy n r vn_
scl. u glfcys se lb

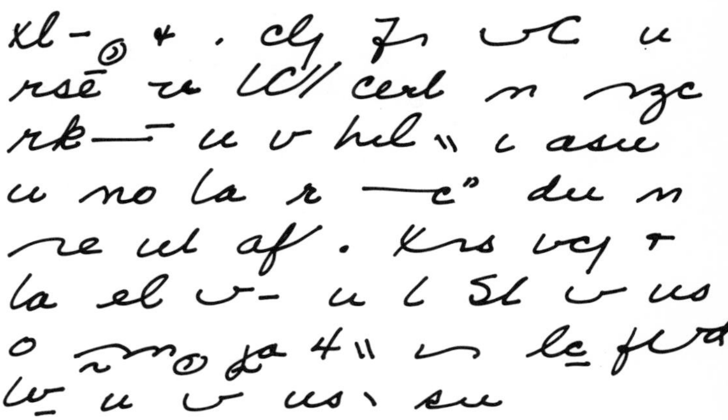

KEY (1) Dear Mr. Place: I was extremely surprised to learn that you have had no further information in regard to/ the claim you made for the damages done to your home by the bad storm in January. (P) If the company does/ not communicate with you by the end of the week, will you either call my office or drop in to see me./ Sincerely yours, (62 words) (2) Dear Mr. Snow: Your brief note arrived yesterday. I gather from what you said that you are now making excellent/ progress and seem rather certain that you can finish the job by April 19. (P) I will be traveling through your/ town on Wednesday evening and wonder if we can get together for a little while to talk about the/ exhibit being planned for May 10. Very truly yours, (69 words) (3) Dear Mr. Camp: Will you please fill in your name and address on the attached card and mail it back to us. On the same/ day that we receive it, we will send you the booklet that explains the many excellent health and accident/ policies we are now offering. (P) We are confident that every mother and father will quickly see the/ advantages of these policies and will want additional information about them. A telephone call to/ our office will send one of our agents to your home to explain further the protection guaranteed by this new/ type of coverage. Cordially, (105 words) (4) Dear Sir: Before you try to fix my old adding machine, I should appreciate your letting me know the extent/ of the damages and the price you will charge to put it into proper working order. (P) I feel that if the amount/ exceeds $30, it would be worth my while to purchase another machine. Yours truly, (57 words) (5) Dear Mr. White: You will find enclosed a copy of the contract you signed on February 14. This contract/ gives you the exclusive right to handle our fine line of consumer goods in your area, and further guarantees/ that you will enjoy the same benefits as are extended to other authorized dealers. (P) Please remember/ that our large team of experts is ready and willing to help you set up your advertising program for the coming/ Christmas season. Yours very truly, (87 words) (6) Dear Miss Bridge: This is to inform you that our Board of Directors has authorized me to offer you a position/ in our evening school. Your qualifications seem to be excellent, and the college from which you received/ your teacher's certificate in music recommended you very highly. (P) I assume you know that our classes/ do not meet until after the Christmas vacation and that we will want you to start with us on Monday, January/ 4. (P) I am looking forward to having you with us. Sincerely yours, (93 words)

TAKE INVENTORY NOW OF THE SKILLS YOU NEED FOR TRANSCRIPTION

Highly paid secretaries have many skills that make them assets to their employers. They take dictation rapidly. They read their notes easily and accurately. In addition, they transcribe their notes into mailable letters quickly and correctly.

Because transcription is a fusion of many skills and knowledge, the wise students at this point will take inventory of their abilities.

What about your command of English? For the secretary, incorrect grammar or punctuation leads to extra time in retyping letters . . . possibly the loss of a job. For the student, it means lower grades. So take time out to review your grammar and punctuation rules until you can use them correctly without thinking.

How good is your typing? If your speed and accuracy are not what they should be, make up your mind right now to devote more time and concentration to typing.

And finally, your spelling? Are you one of the rare "born spellers?" Or are you one of the many "non-spellers?" If you think you fall into the first category, ask someone to test you on a list of spelling demons. Prove to yourself your ability or lack of ability to spell correctly. And remember, never guess at spelling. Learn to use your dictionary if you aren't sure.

Cp 14

1 Before studying the next principle, let's review the marks of punctuation you have already learned to use to represent sounds. Review the rules, study the words, and practice the words.

Final "ing" and "thing":

getting		**anything**	
something		**wrappings**	
avoiding		**nothing**	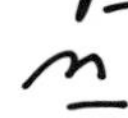

Final "ed":

followed		**remitted**	
valued		**skilled**	
looked		**rushed**	

Medial and final "nt" and "ment":

wanted	u=	**don't**	do-
judgment	jj-	**presently**	pz-l
prints	p--	**printing**	p=

Medial and final "nd":

depend	dp—	**rendered**	r—/
commandant	k— —	**friendship**	f—ʃ
background	bkgr—	**trends**	tr— —

Final "ss" and "ness":

countless	kul'	**happiness**	hpe'
addresses	aD''	**distress**	dS'
confess	kf'	**newness**	nu'

Final "ssness":

recklessness	rcl''	**ruthlessness**	rll''
helplessness	hpl''	**hopelessness**	hopl''

Final "er" and "ter":

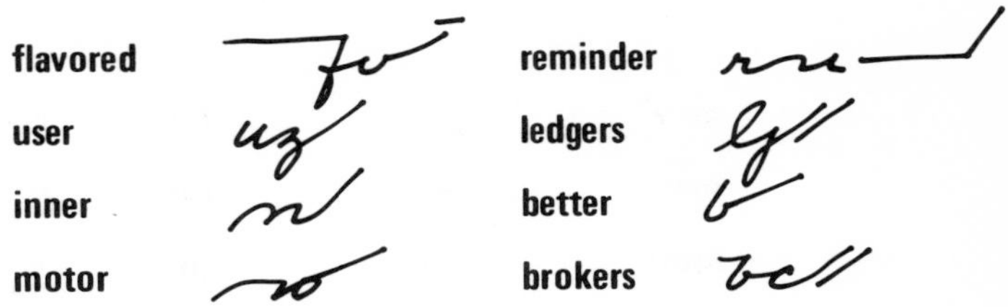

Initial "combination-r":

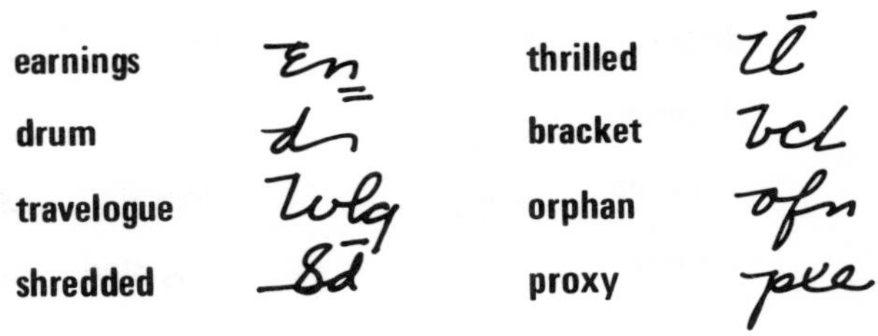

earnings
drum
travelogue
shredded
thrilled
bracket
orphan
proxy

Initial "combination-l":

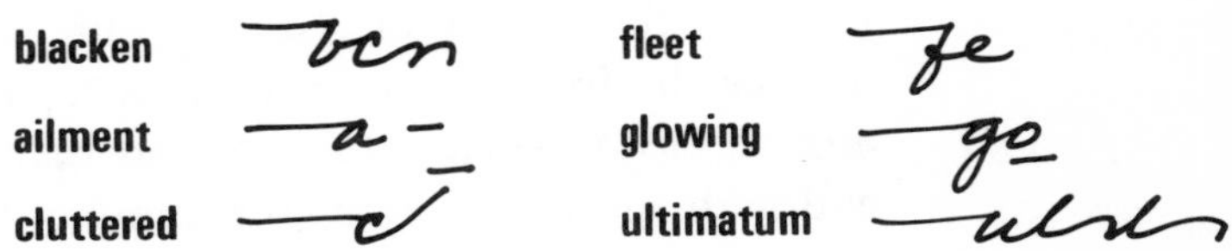

Here is another sound that is represented by a punctuation mark.

For the initial and final sound of "st" write a comma (,).

Study these words and practice them:

just	best
most	cost
must	costs
first	insists
fast	listings
trusting	highest
largest	lists
request	coast
adjusted	suggests
biggest	suggested
tests	guests

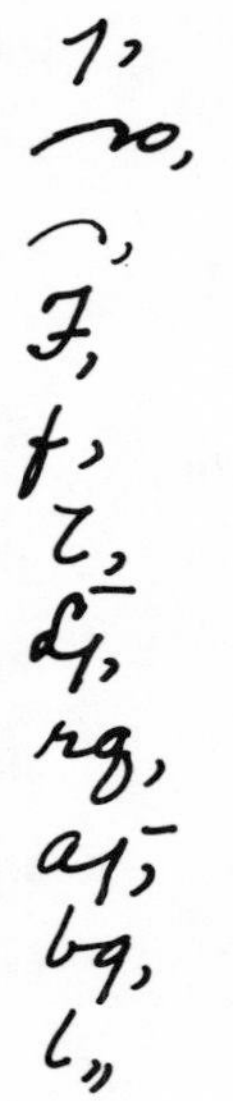

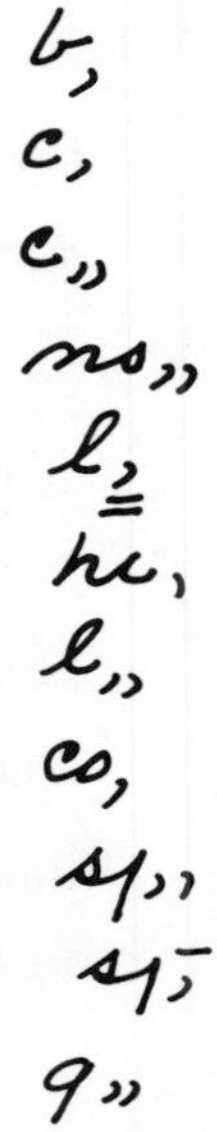

Note that the rule instructs you to write a comma to indicate the **sound** of "st." In this connection, pronounce the following pairs of words: *past, passed; mist, missed; baste, based.* You can hear that these words all end with the same sound—the sound of "st." Therefore, since you write a comma for the sound of "st," *passed* is written 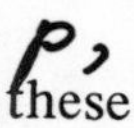 ; *missed*  ; *based* 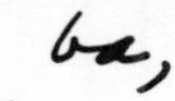.

Study these words and practice them:

expressed	introduced
reduced	released

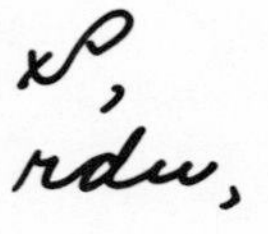

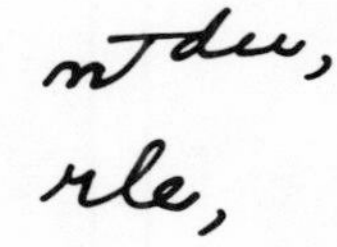

discussed		**promised**	
addressed		**increased**	

Note that *reduced, introduced, released,* and *increased* all contain long vowels preceding the for "st." Remember, a long vowel sound is always written before a punctuation mark.

This rule states that a comma is also to be written for the **initial** sound of "st." To avoid confusion this initial comma must be joined to the rest of the outline. For ease in writing it will be raised above the line  . Thus: *steps*  ; *style*  ; *stand*  .

Study these words and practice them:

state		**studied**	
students		**still**	
station		**statement**	
steel		**standing**	
stay		**step**	

The rule above instructs you to write a comma for the initial and final sound of "st." But what if this sound is in the **middle** of a word? The next rule explains this.

For the sound of medial "st," write  .

In other words, instead of writing a comma for "st" as you do at the beginning or end of a word, you simply write *s* for this sound when it occurs in the middle of a word.

Study these words and practice them:

assistant	ass-	**testament**	ts-
statistics	)tscs	**investments**	nvs--
system	ss)	**instead**	nsd
domestic	d-sc	**install**	nsal
justly	jsl	**installation**	nsl/
mistake	-sc	**institute**	nstu

The following words illustrate how the handling of the initial and final sounds of "st" differs from the medial sound of "st."

Study these words and practice them:

post	po,	**costs**	c,,
posts	po,,	**costly**	csl
posting	po,_	**adjust**	a/,
posted	po,¯	**adjustments**	ajs--
postal	psl	**state**	2a
postage	ps/	**estate**	esa
invest	nv,	**assist**	as,
investment	nvs-	**assists**	as,,
investigate	nvsga	**assistants**	ass--
investigation	nvsg/	**stand**	2—
cost	c,	**newsstand**	nzs—

READING EXERCISE

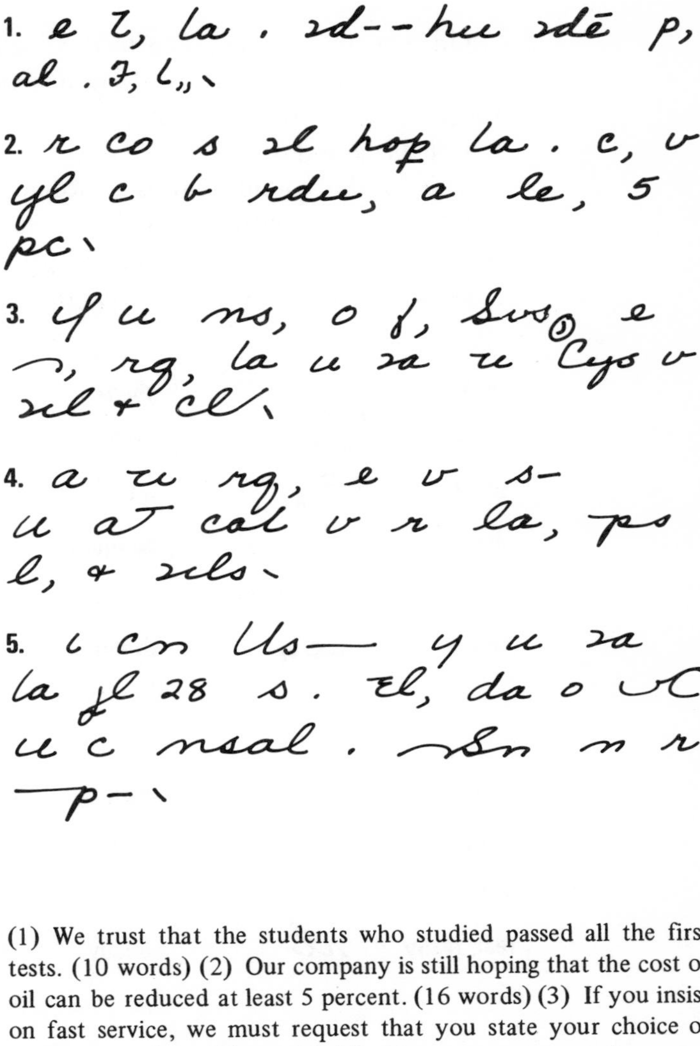

KEY (1) We trust that the students who studied passed all the first tests. (10 words) (2) Our company is still hoping that the cost of oil can be reduced at least 5 percent. (16 words) (3) If you insist on fast service, we must request that you state your choice of style and color. (16 words) (4) At your request we have sent you another catalog of our latest price list and styles. (18 words) (5) I cannot understand why you state that July 28 is the earliest date on which you can install the/ machine in our plant. (24 words)

2 Once again you are going to deal with a combination sound—the sound that is derived from the blending together of the sounds of "n" and "k" into "nk."

For the sound of "nk," write *q*.

This is the sound that is heard in the word *bank.* Since you are to write *q* for the sound of "nk," *bank* is written *bq* and, in the same way, *think* *lq*.

Study these words and practice them:

pink	*pq*	**thank**	*lq*
banked	*bq̄*	**tank**	*lq*
blank	*—bq*	**ink**	*iq*
delinquent	*dlq-*	**banquet**	*bql*
blanket	*—bql*	**frankly**	*fql*
shrink	*—Sq*	**thinking**	*lq̶*

BRIEF FORMS

stop	*so*	**small**	*sa*
extra	*X*	**country**	*c/*
extraordinary	*Xo*	**always**	*l*
real, really	*rl*	**already**	*lr*

ABBREVIATIONS

capital	*cap*	**federal**	*fed*
represent, representative	*rep*		
government	*gvt*		

READING EXERCISE

1. 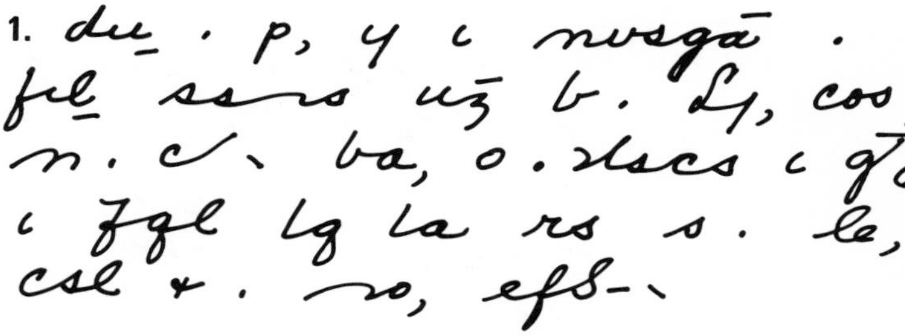

2. 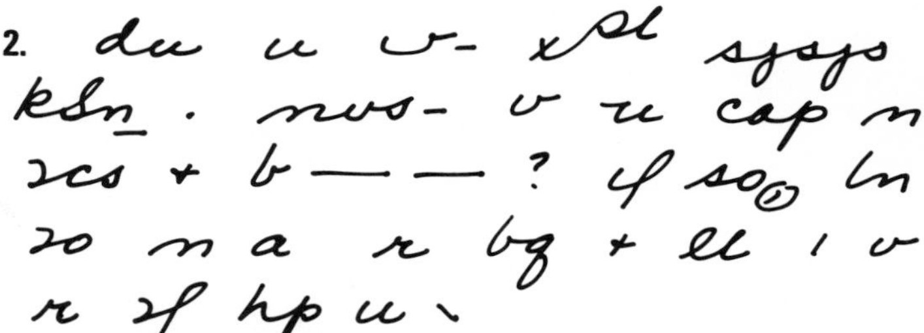

3. 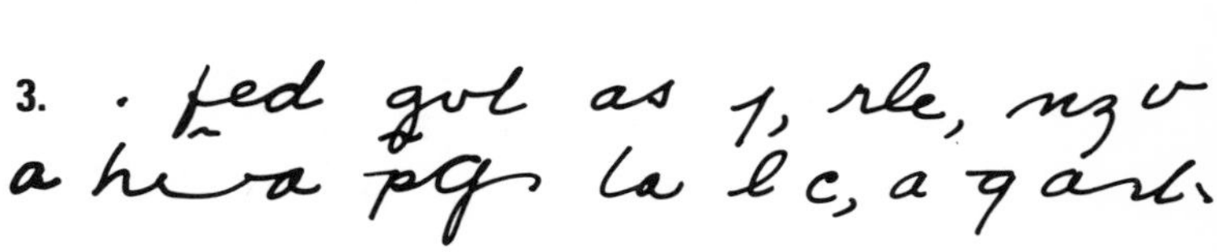

4. 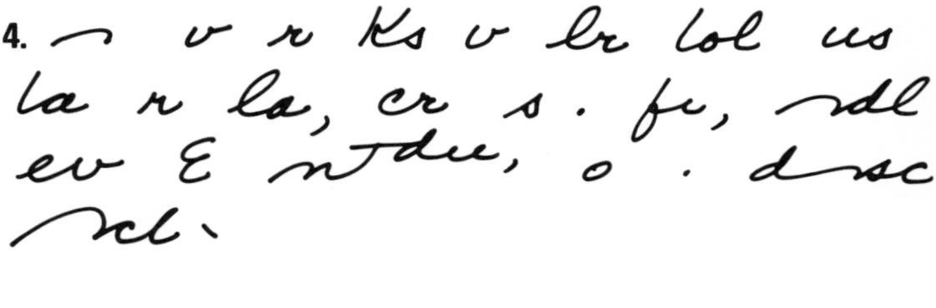

5. 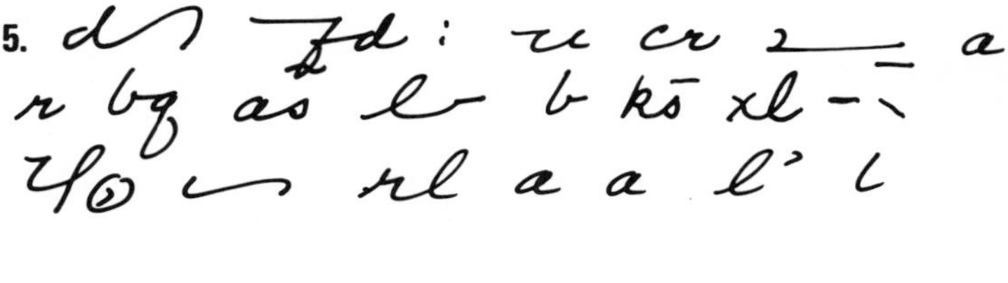

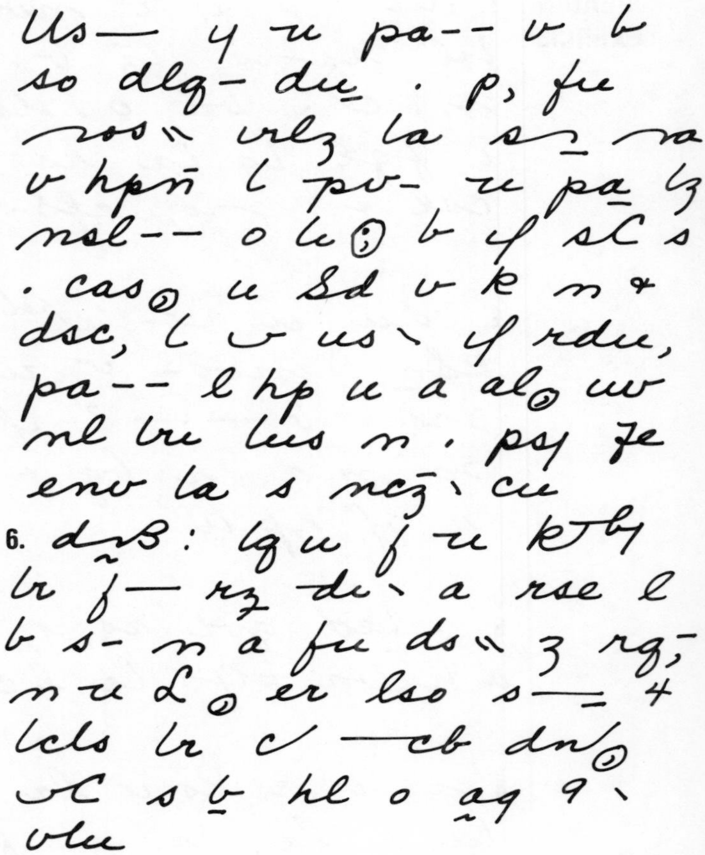

KEY (1) During the past year I investigated the filing systems used by the largest companies in the country./ Based on the statistics I gathered, I frankly think that ours is the least costly and the most efficient. (39 words) (2) Do you want expert suggestions concerning the investment of your capital in stocks and bonds? If so, then stop/ in at our bank and let one of our staff help you.

(29 words) (3) The Federal Government has just released news of a highway program that will cost a great amount. (18 words) (4) Many of our customers have already told us that our latest car is the finest model we have ever/ introduced on the domestic market. (27 words) (5) Dear Mr. Flood: Your credit standing at our bank has always been considered excellent. Therefore, I am really/ at a loss to understand why your payments have been so delinquent during the past few months. (P) I realize that/ something may have happened to prevent your paying these installments on time; but if such is the case, you should have come/ in and discussed it with us. If reduced payments will help you at all, you have only to write to us in the/ postage-free envelope that is enclosed. Cordially yours, (89 words) (6) Dear Member: Thank you for your contribution to our fund-raising drive. A receipt will be sent in a few days. (P) As/ requested in your letter, we are also sending four tickets to our country club dinner, which is being held/ on August 9. Very truly yours, (46 words)

3 To express round numbers 100 or above write as follows:

hundred  **thousand** 

million  **billion** 

Examples:

50,000 men 

two million women 

5,000 copies  **14 billion** 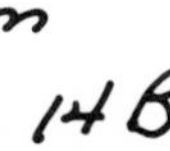

$123,000,000 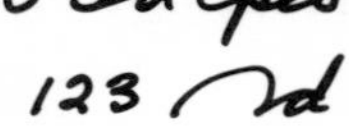 **700 books** 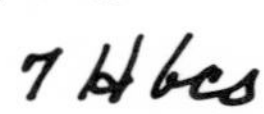

PHRASING Do you have the mistaken belief that phrasing is the key to shorthand speed? Then take heed.

Excessive phrasing may actually be slowing you down! If you pause for even a fraction of a second in writing a phrase, you have lost speed. A phrase is valuable only when it can be written without the slightest hesitation and can be read accurately. It will help you to remember this.

The Reading Exercises contain phrases such as *I will* (), *he is* (), *you can* (), *to know* (), and *to me* (). In addition to such combinations, it is often possible to omit one or more unimportant words in a common expression. Here are some examples:

nevertheless	
time to time	
more and more	
again and again	
now and then	
up to date	

Phrase only those combinations which come to you naturally when you are taking dictation—and only those which occur over and over again. If you have the feeling that you should be phrasing more, forget it! Concentrate on moving from one outline to another with no hesitation!

SUMMARY

STamp ,

1. Write a comma (,) for the initial and final sounds of "st."

drumSTick s

2. Write s for the medial sound of "st."

blaNK g

3. Write g for the sound of "nk."

READING EXERCISE

1. 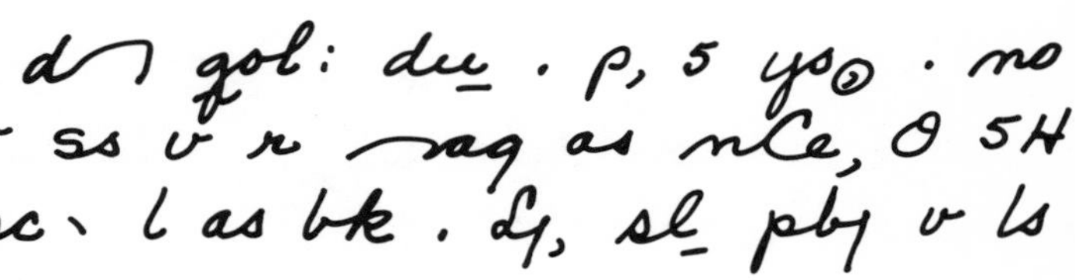

cu n. c/o + subs r k n a
. ra v ab a Id a d. ba, o
a rs- 2de e esra la a le,
a — m + — m 2dē. dscs
+ sjsjs cSū b r 2f v xSls l,
y" f ur lg v rc ne nvs--
n eT 2cs o gvl b—— e
s/, la u F, 2o a u
nzs— lpc p. la, cSu
v lh v pop raq. e no
la rd l l hp u nv,
u cap vzl. l sls f
/, 'd a cpe. ul

2. ds: las l b r cs l
du r ulso, l nvsga
+ sll al —cas gcl. l
as, us n rc f, pa-
o u —ca e —, F,
ns, la u da p a l,
So . esrā vlu v .
ālcls l, vn fr dSyu

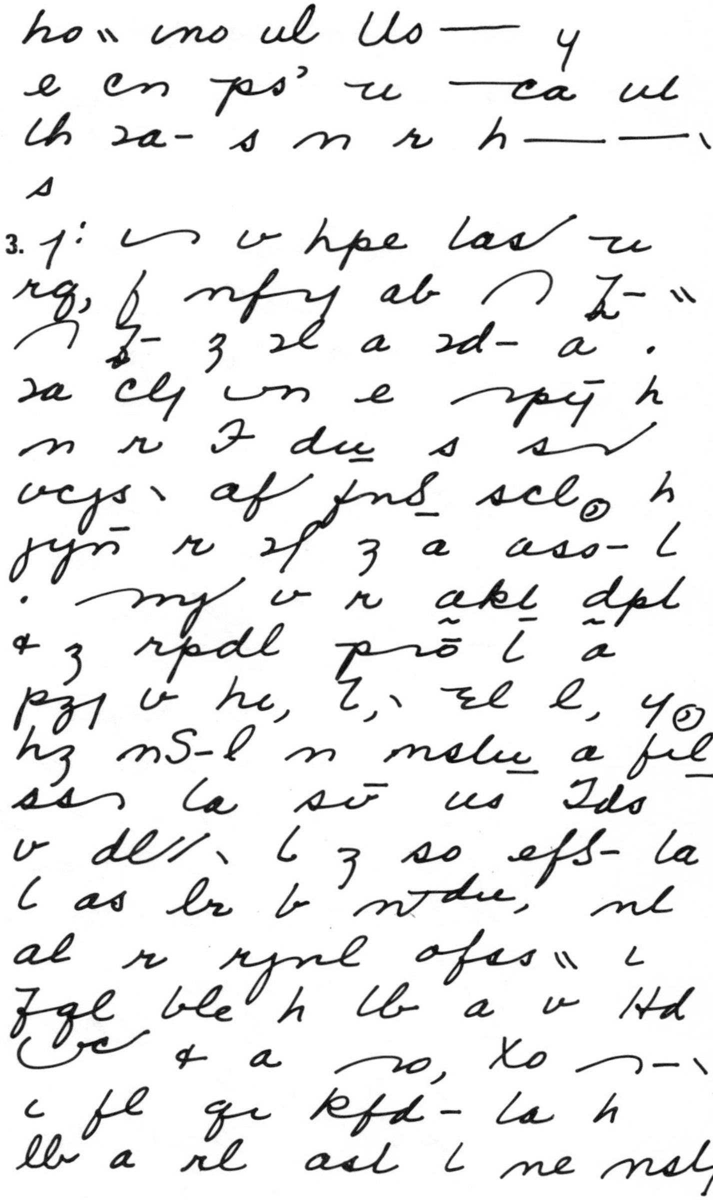

h reps\ su

4. d⌐ ~bq: ru gl. ro,
ou v u ol he ss? dz
l 2 p U ks- v-l us?
r, u Zq-l cl u Svs-
Lsc csl ajs--? ru
f, lpa hl pss eC y n
O lcp l osa psl?? y
ku lb dssaī vn uc
gl. b, he ss o. rcl
f a rlvl sra arl v
me?? cf ul fl ou.
bq Cd la s ncz el
s— 1 v r reps l u ho\
h l esra. c, v a kpel
nu nsly & l lso xpn
y l lb vl u vl l
dl v a co lc rs\ uvl

5. dK: z i zā n. L aD,
lu l, vk dl// Z co, l
co, r rSL la r nu
psc bql co= r sl
b ln E\\ n vu v lh

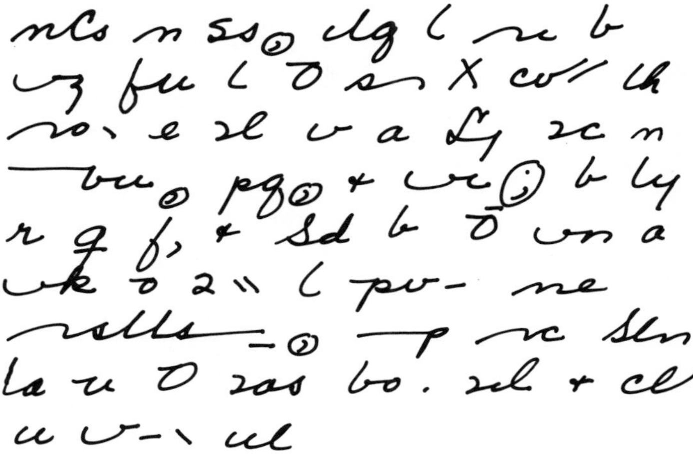

KEY (1) Dear Mr. Gold: During the past five years, the number of sales of our magazine has increased over 500/ percent. It has become the largest selling publication of its kind in the country, and subscriptions are coming/ in at the rate of about a thousand a day. Based on a recent study, we estimate that at least a/ million men and women studied the statistics and suggestions issued by our staff of experts last year. (P) If you/ are thinking of making any investments in either stocks or government bonds, we suggest that you first stop at/ your newsstand to pick up the latest issue of this very popular magazine. We know that reading it will/ help you invest your capital wisely. It sells for just $1 a copy. Yours truly, (136 words) (2) Dear Sir: It has always been our custom to do our utmost to investigate and settle all claims quickly. To/ assist us in making fast payment on your claim, we must first insist that you draw up a list showing the estimated/ value of the articles lost when fire destroyed your home. (P) I know you will understand why we cannot process/ your claim until this statement is in our hands. Sincerely, (70 words) (3) Gentlemen: I am very happy to answer your request for information about Mr. Front. (P) Mr. Front/ was still a student at the state college when we employed him in our firm during his summer vacations. After/ finishing school, he joined our staff as an assistant to the Manager of our Accounting Department and was/ rapidly promoted to a position of highest trust. Early last year, he was instrumental in instituting/ a filing system that saved us thousands of dollars. It was so efficient that it has already been/ introduced into all our regional offices. (P) I frankly believe him to be a very hard/ worker and a most extraordinary man. I feel quite confident that he will be a real asset to any institution/ he represents. Sincerely yours, (147 words) (4) Dear Mr. Blank: Are you getting the most out of your old heating system? Does it stand up under constant winter/ use? Must you frequently call your serviceman to make costly adjustments? Are you forced to pay higher prices each/ year in order to keep it operating properly? (P) Why continue to be dissatisfied when you can get/ the best heating system on the market for a relatively small amount of money? (P) If you will fill out the/ blank card that is enclosed, we will send one of our representatives to your home. He will estimate the cost of/ a completely new installation and will also explain why it will be worth your while to deal with a company/ like ours. Yours very truly, (125 words) (5) Dear Customer: As I stated in the letter addressed to you last week, dealers from coast to coast are reporting/ that our new plastic blanket covers are selling better than ever. (P) In view of this increase in sales, I think it/ might be wise for you to order some extra covers this month. We still have a large stock in blue, pink, and white; but they/ are going fast and should be ordered within a week or two. (P) To prevent any misunderstanding, please make certain/ that your order states both the style and color you want. Yours truly, (92 words)

Cp 15

1 In previous lessons, you learned that when a word ends in the sound of a long vowel followed by "t," "v," or "m," the long vowel is written to represent the resulting sound.

Review these rules. Then study the following words and practice them:

Words ending in "ate," "eet," "ite," "ote," and "ute."

date	*da*	**designated**	*dzgnā*
neat	*ne*	**completes**	*kpes*
bright	*bi*	**invited**	*nvī*
float	*fo*	**voting**	*vo*
fruit	*fu*	**computer**	*kpu*

Words ending in "ave," "eve," "ive," "ove," and "uve."

gave	ga	**concave**	kca
receive	rse	**achievement**	aCe-
alive	ali	**revival**	rvil
stove	so	**rover**	ro
groove	gu	**behoove**	bhu

Words ending in "ame," "eem," "ime," "ome," and "ume."

frame	fa	**same**	sa
stream	Se	**screaming**	sCe̲
rhyme	ri	**crime**	ci
chrome	co	**tome**	lo
tomb	lu	**doomed**	dū

You are now going to learn another family of words in which the long vowel will be used in the same way.

For the final sound of a long vowel and "r" write the long vowel to represent the resulting sound.

You can see how similar this rule is to the ones just reviewed regarding the sounds of a long vowel and "t," "v," or "m."

In the following words, notice that the long vowel is written to represent the complete sound of the long vowel + "r."

Study these words and practice them.

dear	de	**desire**	dzi
here	he	**desired**	dzī
hearing	he̲	**require**	rqi
engineer	nyne	**more**	—o
appear	ape	**nor**	no
inquire	nqi	**explore**	xpo
wire	ᴗi	**secure**	scu
wiring	ᴗi̲	**insured**	nSū
tire	ti	**brochure**	bSu

What of the sound of the vowel in the words *care* or *fair*? This is not the long "a" sound that is heard in *cape* or *fate,* and it is not the short sound of "a" that occurs in the words *cap* or *cat.* In other words, the pronunciation of *a* in *care* and *fair* lies midway between the long- and short-vowel sounds. For the purpose of this rule, however, this sound of "air" will be treated the same way as the other long-vowel sounds and "r."

Study these words and practice them:

fair	fa	**sharing**	Sa̲
care	ca	**fares**	fas
repair	rpa	**aware**	aᴗa
wear	ᴗa	**compared**	kpā
hardware	Hdᴗa	**preparing**	ppa̲

Of course, although this rule refers to the final sound of a long vowel + "r," it will be applied when a suffix is added to a root word that is written according to this rule.

Study these words and practice them:

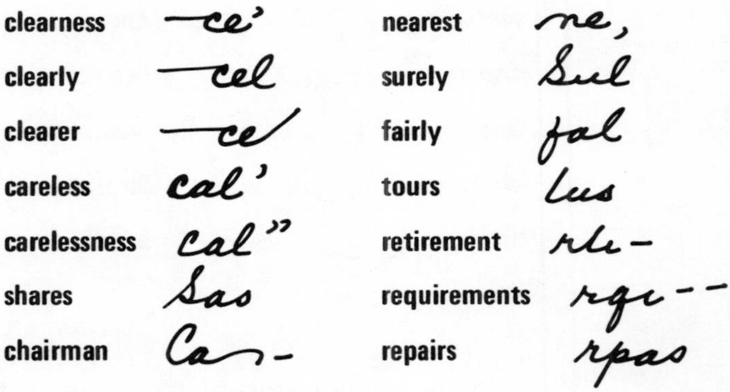

clearness
clearly
clearer
careless
carelessness
shares
chairman
nearest
surely
fairly
tours
retirement
requirements
repairs

Here's a hint to help you remember the four rules that concern the dropping of a consonant after a long vowel. In the early days of television, a well-known comedian was called Mr. TV. Remember the name. It will remind you that when a word ends in the sound of a long vowel + "m," "r," "t," or "v," only the vowel is written.

READING EXERCISE

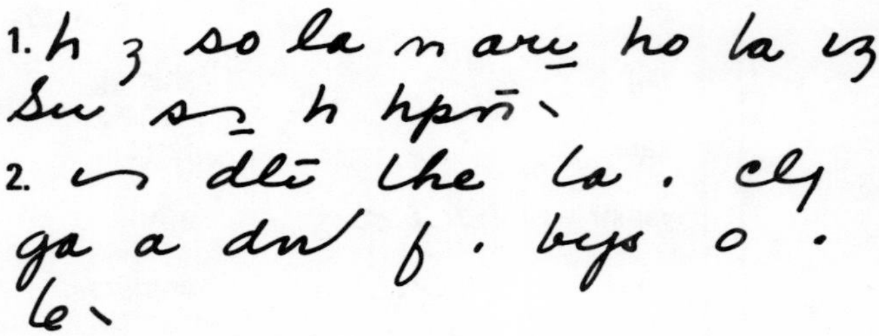

3. 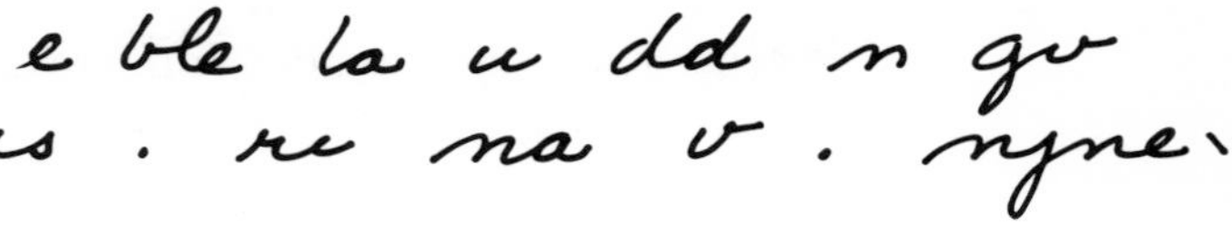

4. 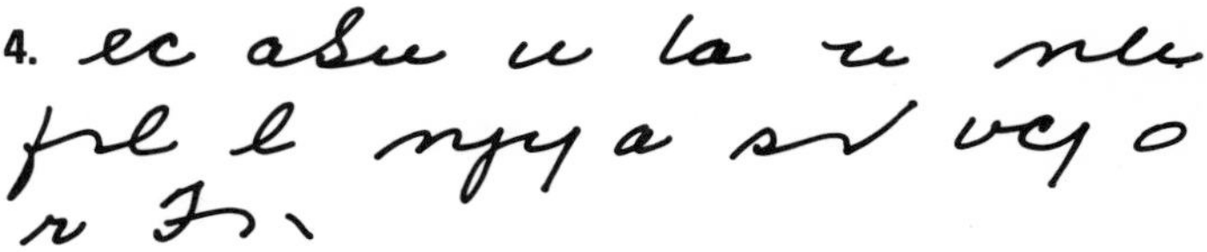

5. 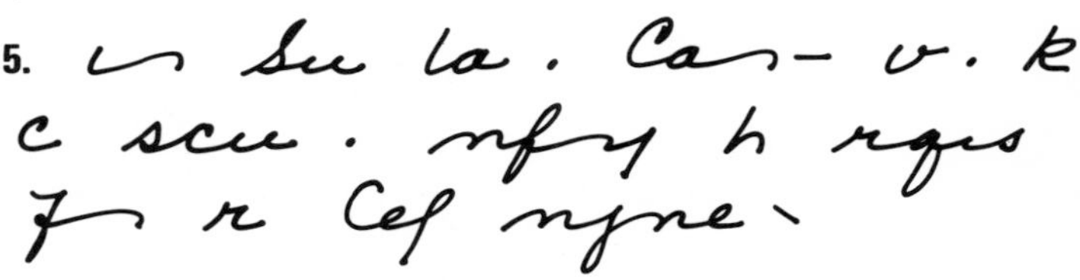

KEY (1) He was so late in arriving home that I was sure something had happened. (13 words) (2) I am delighted to hear that the college gave a dinner for the boys on the team. (15 words) (3) We believe that you did not give us the right name of the engineer. (13 words) (4) We can assure you that your entire family will enjoy a summer vacation on our farm. (17 words) (5) I am sure that the chairman of the committee can secure the information he requires from our chief engineer. (20 words)

2 Omit *n* before the sounds of "g," "j," and "ch."

This rule simply tells you that in such words as *young* or *single,* you will omit the *n* from the outline and write *young* 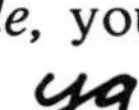 and *single* 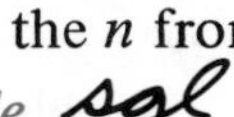.

Similarly, the *n* will be omitted before the sound of "j," and you will write *singe* 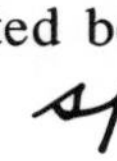 ; *arrangement* 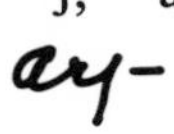 ; *exchange* 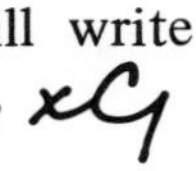 .

Finally, the rule refers to the sound of "n" before "ch" and, once again, you are to omit the *n*. Thus, *branch* bC ; *franchise* JCz .

Study these words and practice them:

luncheon	lCn	**ranch**	rC
thing	lq	**wrong**	rq
long	lq	**strongly**	Sgl
youngsters	yqSs	**among**	a-q
passenger	psj	**strangely**	Sjl
arrange	arj	**arranged**	ar$\overline{j}$

Note: The outlines for the words *strength* and *length* are derived from the words *strong* Sq and *long* lq ; therefore *strength* Sgl and *length* lgl .

Before going on to the next rule, let's review something you have already learned. You know that for the initial sound of "pl," you write —p as in *plan* —pn and *play* —pa . You also know that for the sound of medial "pl," you write p as in *duplicate* dpca and *apply* api . Similarly, for the sound of initial "bl," you write —b as in *blue* —bu ; but for medial "bl," you write b as in *problem* pb- .

Many of the "combination-l" sounds occur at the ends of words, but the only ones that are used with high frequency are the "bl" and "pl." The next rule deals with these sounds at the ends of words.

For the sounds of final "bul" and "blee," write b ; for the sounds of final "pul" and "plee," write p .

Let's start with the sounds in the words *able, available,* and *possible.* Each of these words contains the final sound of "bul" and, since you are to write b for this sound, you write *able* ab ; *available* avlb ; *possible* psb .

The first part of the rule also instructs you to write b for the final sound of "blee." Therefore, *reasonably* rznb ; *possibly* psb .

Study these words and practice them:

valuable	vlub	**trouble**	Tb
double	db	**reliable**	rlib
enable	nab	**favorable**	fvb
suitable	sub	**favorably**	fvb
profitably	pflb	**reasonable**	rznb

The second part of the rule states that p is to be written for the final sound of "pul" or "plee."

Study these words and practice them:

example	xmp	**simple**	smp
people	pp	**simply**	smp
couple	cp	**examples**	xmps

READING EXERCISE

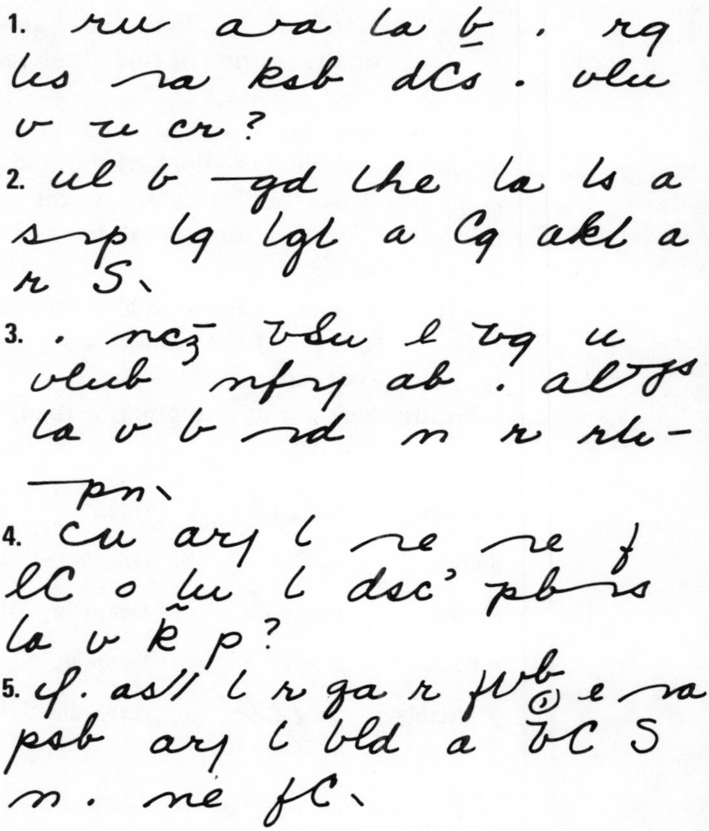

KEY (1) Are you aware that buying the wrong tires may considerably decrease the value of your car? (17 words) (2) You will be glad to hear that it is a simple thing to get a charge account at our store. (16 words) (3) The enclosed brochure will bring you valuable information about the alterations that have been made in/ our retirement plan. (24 words) (4) Can you arrange to meet me for lunch on Tuesday to discuss problems that have come up? (15 words) (5) If the answers to our questionnaire are favorable, we may possibly arrange to build a branch store in the near future. (20 words)

3 BRIEF FORMS

open	op	result	rsl
opinion	opn	important	ip
life	lf	between	bl
prove	pv	subject	sj
difficult, difficulty	dfk	situation	sil
regular, regulation, regularly	reg		

ABBREVIATIONS

establish esl

Express time as follows:

2 o'clock	2°
10 o'clock	10°
10:30	10^{30}

SUMMARY

dOOR	o
ARE	a
ERE	e
IRE	i
URE	u

1. For the final sounds of "are," "ear," "ire," "ore," and "ure," write the long vowel and omit the r.

riNG g
NJ j
NCH c

2. Omit n before the sounds of "g," "j," and "ch."

taBLE b

3. Write b for the final sounds of "bul" and "blee."

aPPLE p

4. Write p for the final sounds of "pul" and "plee."

READING EXERCISE

1. d rs Sg: ro + ro pp r bg l Us— h up ls f r chn lagr . b, edc avlb.

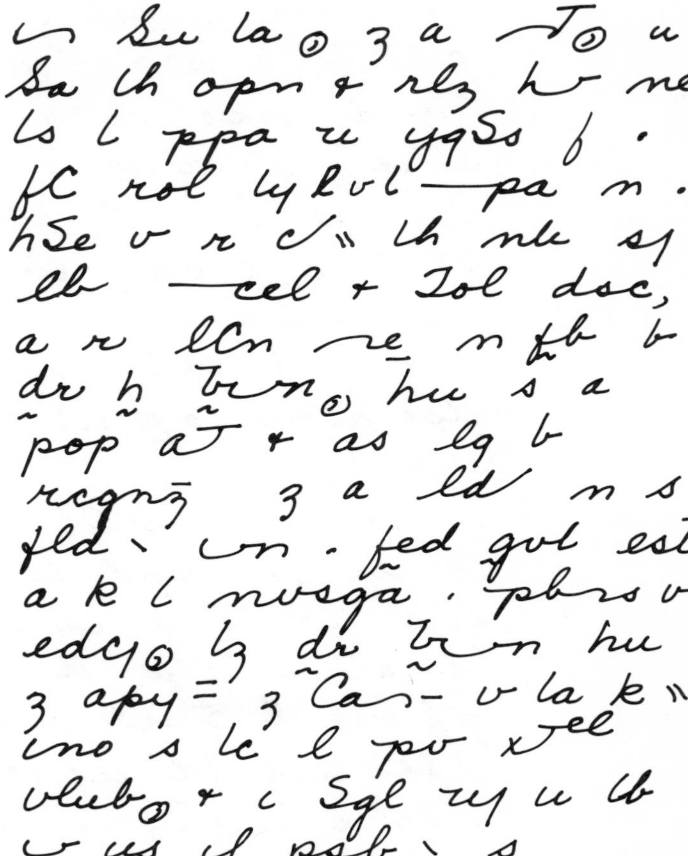

2.

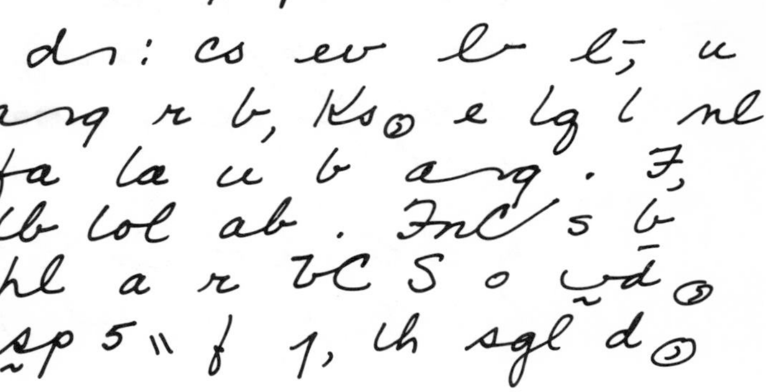

er g lrc l psb f u l pC
pess gs r reg x a . rs,
rznb pss n r hSe. f
xp a sl v 4 vlnl
Cas & a Lj rC lb vC
nsl c, 250d lb sol f
nl 175d, envc u ttc
avj v lh opl. rB r
dos rn op ul 9° E vn.
su

3. nd pl: ugl lnf u
la er n ppā lsn a FC,
age- v u a lh li. efl
la sC a age-d n pv
pflb & d nel rsl n a
dfk sil bl us & r lcl
dl/, hE uf ud ca
l h—l r li v Hdra
n . reg nm ed b
hpe lrc . nec arj--.
uvl

4. dK: h lq r e rqī
l va bf e he gs u?

4 rol za-- v br gn ou
lu◎ b uv nT s- us u
Cc no rln lus" er n
ab l va ne lq/ + v
sc̄ r aTne l bq su
aq u f pa- f. S- v
lnb s n rsē b. e—
v lh vk \ ul

5. dn yq: ino ur avala
. cr uv j, aqī reps a
Lj nvs- \ ino◎ lo◎ la ul
lql dzb ldu E uc l
gl. b, psb oSj" he r
sn snp yl up lgs uc
du la l nab u l
db. lf v u cr + nSu
la ll gv u n ys v
nyb◎ Tb Je Sos \ (1) bq
u Cr l a rlub Sp.
no- s_ ses lb rq \ do-
va ul a sra ajs-bks
a Tf rpa jb \ (2) f
plsv ne cc r rqī◎

xc Su la ly r scū fs
a dp—b Ss \ (3) flo al
nScps n rGd l req
sznl Ccps \ (4) lq v us
In und a nu h o lub
r b— v q Sq hs + lubs
l n nl ad l . kfl v u
+ u psf//(1) b l lso gv u . ad
q-e v a saf Zp" hpe du \ c

6. d l dl: unl fs u rel
la r av nol Ss bl jn +
sp r lr ksb bv los v
l, y" — i Kc n asu
la lh lo nCs s du l .
X adv ev dn n lcl
vn pp//? if u rl ble
la ls(1) In i lq l nec
l nv; a vn gl pl v r
cap n lh va \ ul

7. d s fld: w rln lu sv
lus D u aly l . arl la
u sl o us U . Is v r
Kc \ z u no(1) cp sC a

sra arl op o r bcs
pos x~el dfk⊙ & ls cp
la u ~c pa- n fu bf
. e— v . ~o" y n
s— us a Cc vl lh L
s bf u? vlu

8. d Z— : Sd Lj zel cos
b sj l k~l b . fed gvl?
Sd . gvl esl ~ax pss
la ~a b Cq f zel?? s~
pp sub l . opn la sC
k~l s abs nec f . bnf
v . pb & la ld gl k~bu
l . ek~c efv: c\
h~E⊙ Sln reps v . gvl
& . zel cos fl la lz regs
d n pv sal & d nl
rsl n dfk sils" bo
sds v lh g r fu dsc,
n . C- iSu v . ~ag e
pb\ . ~ag l- sls
rpdl⊙ & e sj, la u zo
a u nzs— vl cpes
r zl avlb\ su

KEY (1) Dear Mrs. Strong: More and more people are beginning to understand how important it is for our children to/ acquire the best education available. I am sure that, as a mother, you share this opinion and/ realize how necessary it is to prepare your youngsters for the future role they will have to play in the/ history of our country. (P) This entire subject will be clearly and thoroughly discussed at our luncheon meeting in/ February by Dr. H. Brown, who is a popular author and has long been recognized as a leader/ in his field. When the Federal Government established a committee to investigate the problems of/ education, it was Dr. Brown who was appointed as chairman of that committee. (P) I know his talk will prove/ extremely valuable, and I strongly urge you to be with us if possible. Sincerely, (156 words) (2) Dear Madam: Because we have always listed you among our best customers, we think it only fair that you be/ among the first to be told about the furniture sale being held at our branch store on Wednesday, September 5./ (P) For just this single day, we are going to make it possible for you to purchase pieces from our regular/ stock at the most reasonable prices in our history. For example, a set of four walnut chairs and a/ large matching table, which normally costs $250, will be sold for only/ $175. (P) We invite you/to take advantage of this opportunity. Remember, our doors remain/ open until nine o'clock every evening. Sincerely yours, (136 words) (3) My dear Mr. Place: I regret to inform you that we are not prepared to sign a franchise agreement with you/ at this time. We feel that such an agreement would not prove profitable and would merely result in a difficult/ situation between us and our local dealers. (P) However, if you would care to handle our line of hardware/ in the regular manner, we would be happy to make the necessary arrangements. Yours very truly, (80 words) (4) Dear Customer: How long are we required to wait before we hear from you? Four monthly statements have already gone/ out to you, but you have neither sent us your check nor written to us. (P) We are not able to wait any longer/ and have asked our attorney to bring suit against you if payment for the shipment of lumber is not received by/ the end of this week. Yours truly, (65 words) (5) Dear Mr. Young: I know you are aware that the car you have just acquired represents a large investment. I know,/ too, that you will think it desirable to do everything you can to get the best possible operation./ (P) Here are some simple yet important things you can do that will enable you to double the life of your car/ and insure that it will give you many years of enjoyable, trouble-free service. 1. Bring your car to a/ reliable shop the moment something seems to be wrong. Don't wait until a small adjustment becomes a major repair/ job. 2. If parts of any kind are required, make sure that they are secured from a dependable source. 3. Follow/ all instructions in regard to regular seasonal checkups. 4. Think of us when you need a new tire or tube. Our/ brand of good strong tires and tubes will not only add to the comfort of you and your passengers, but will also give/ you the added guarantee of a safe trip. (P) Happy driving. Cordially, (173 words) (6) Dear Mr. Deal: I note from your report that our average monthly sales between June and September are already/ considerably above those of last year. (P) Am I correct in assuming that this extraordinary/ increase is due to the extra advertising we have done in local evening papers? If you really believe/ that it is, then I think it necessary to invest an even greater part of our capital in this/ way. Yours truly, (82 words) (7) Dear Mrs. Field: I have written to you several times directing your attention to the amount that you still/ owe us under the terms of our contract. As you know, keeping such a small amount open on our books proves extremely/ difficult; and it is important that you make payment in full before the end of the month. (P) Why not send us/ a check while this letter is before you? Very truly yours, (70 words) (8) Dear Friend: Should large steel companies be subject to control by the Federal Government? Should the Government/ establish maximum prices that may be charged for steel? (P) Some people subscribe to the opinion that such control is/ absolutely necessary for the benefit of the public and that it would greatly contribute to the/ economic life of the country. However, certain representatives of the Government and the steel/ companies feel that these regulations would not prove satisfactory and would only result in difficult/ situations. (P) Both sides of this question are fully discussed in the current issue of the magazine we publish./ The magazine always sells rapidly, and we suggest that you stop at your newsstand while copies are still available./ Sincerely yours, (144 words)

Cp 16

1 Let's start this lesson with a review of the marks of punctuation that you have learned in previous lessons.

1. **UNDERSCORE: For "ing" or "thing" that is added to a word:** getting *g$\underline{t}$* ; something *$\underline{s}$* .
2. **OVERSCORE: For "ed" that is added to form the past tense of a word:** named *nā* ; required *rqī* .
3. **HYPHEN: For the medial and final sounds of "nt" or "ment":** went *w-* ; statement *,a-* .
4. **DASH: For the medial and final sound of "nd":** depend *dp—* ; handle *h—l* .
5. **APOSTROPHE: For the final ss and ness:** discuss *dsc'* ; happiness *hpe'*.
6. **QUOTATION MARK: For the final ssness:** fearlessness *fel"*; hopelessness *hopl"*.
7. **COMMA: For the initial and final sounds of "st":** first *F,* ; discussed *dsc,* ; step *,p* .

8. SLANT (joined): For the final sounds of "er" and "ter":
bigger bg/ ; after af/ .

Study these words and practice them:

printing	p=	**nothing**	n_
recommending	rk—=	**anything**	ne_
addressing	aD'_	**lasting**	l,_
wanted	u=	**depended**	dp—=
invested	nv;	**altered**	al/
mistaken	⌒scn	**reduced**	rdu,
largest	Lj,	**listings**	l,=
chapters	Cp//	**encounter**	nk/
distress	dS'	**errorless**	El'
shapelessness	Spl"	**crossroad**	csrd
resist	rz,	**stabilization**	sblz)
steadily	sdl	**statements**	sa--
resumed	rzū	**grandmother**	g— —/
outstanding	ous—=	**commander**	k—/

You are now going to learn to use another mark of punctuation to represent a sound.

For the final sound of "tee" write) .

Ordinarily, this mark of punctuation) is called a right parenthesis; but because this is rather a long name, it will be referred to as a **blend**.

Remember, you always write a long vowel sound before a mark of punctuation. Note *duty* and *beauty*.

Study these words and practice them:

city	s)	**duty**	du)
safety	sf)	**duties**	du))
maturity	⌒du)	**quantity**	g–)
university	unVs)	**authority**	aT)
liberty	lB)	**county**	k)
community	kn)	**quantities**	g–))
facilities	fsl))	**quality**	gl)
beauty	bu)	**locality**	lcl)
party	P)	**activities**	acv))

Notice in the following words that you retain the root outline and simply add a blend) for the addition of the sound of "tee": *possible* psb ; *possibility* psb) ; *able* ab ; *ability* ab) ; *disability* dsab); *necessary* nec ; *necessity* nec); *public* pb ; *publicity* pb) ; *popular* pop ; *popularity* pop).

READING EXERCISE

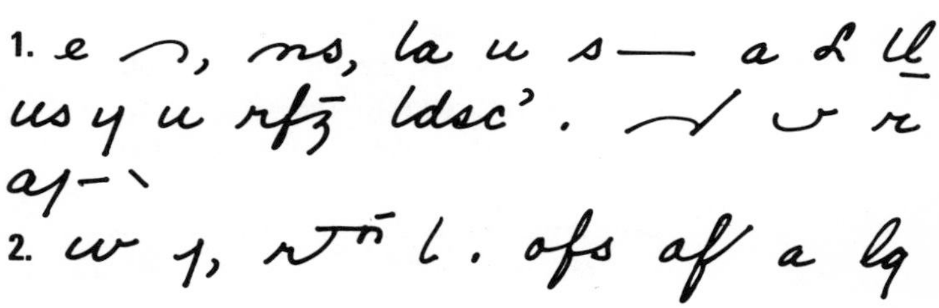

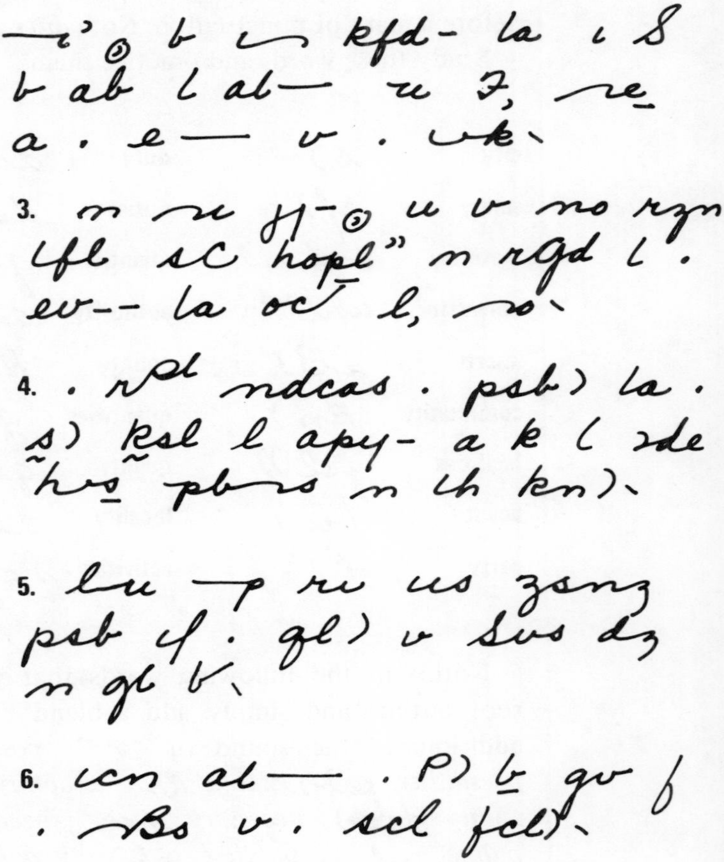

KEY (1) We must insist that you send a letter telling us why you refused to discuss the matter with our agent. (20 words) (2) I have just returned to the office after a long illness, but I am confident that I shall be able to/ attend your first meeting at the end of the week. (29 words) (3) In my judgment, you have no reason to feel such hopelessness in regard to the events that occurred last month. (19 words) (4) The report indicates the possibility that the City Council will appoint a committee to study/ the housing problems in this community. (28 words) (5) Will you please write us as soon as possible if the quality of service does not get better. (17 words) (6) I cannot attend the party being given for the members of the school faculty. (16 words)

2 Before going on to the next rule, let's review two rules which were in chapters you have already covered. You will recall that *made* is written md and *graze* gz, in accordance with the rule that stated that you are to drop the long vowel when it is followed by the sound of "d" or "z." Thus: *raid* rd; *raise* rz; *seed* sd; *seize* sz; *wide* wd; *wise* wz; *rode* rd; *rose* rz; *feud* fd; *fuse* fz.

The rule which you are now going to learn deals with another group of words in which you will also omit the long vowel and write the consonant sound that follows it.

For the sounds of "ane," "ene," "one," and "une" write n; for the sound of "ine" write in.

You can see that once again you are going to drop the long vowel and write the consonant sound that follows it except for long *i* + *n*.

Study these words and practice them:

gain	gn	**means**	mns
main	mn	**lonely**	lnl
cleaned	cn	**phone**	fn

green	gn	**noon**	nn
dean	dn	**plain**	—pn
seen	sn	**mean**	⌒mn
soon	sn	**grain**	gn
shown	Sn	**zone**	zn
screening	sCn̲	**trained**	Tn̄

Notice that this rule refers to the sounds of "ane," "een," "one," and "une," but it does **not** include the sound of "ine" that is heard in such words as *sign* and *design.* For this sound of "ine," you will write in no matter how many syllables are in the word.

Study these words and practice them:

sign	sin	**incline**	ncin
design	dzin	**assigned**	asin̄
assignment	asin-	**combined**	Kbin̄
decline	dcin	**inclined**	ncin̄
resign	rzin	**designed**	dzin̄

To summarize: When a word contains the sound of a long vowel and "d," "z," or "n," write the consonant and drop the vowel—except for the sound of "ine," for which you write both *i* and *n*. It may be helpful for you to remember the outline for the clue word *design* dzin. As you look at this outline, say the rule—drop all vowels before *d, z,* and *n,* except for the long *i* before *n*.

One further point before leaving this rule. According to the rule, you write *chain*  . However, in the words ***change, range,*** and ***strange,*** an additional rule must be applied—the omission of *n* before *j*. Thus: *change*  ; *changes*  ; *range*  ; *strange*  .

In each of these words you omitted the long *a* before *n* and then you omitted *n* before the sound of "j."

For the initial sound of "im" write  ; for the initial sound of "un" write  .

Study these words and practice them:

imprinted		**unless**	
imperative		**unfortunately**	
impose		**undoubtedly**	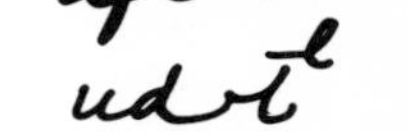
impossible		**unemployment**	
impossibility		**unable**	
imitate		**unhappy**	
imitation		**unwise**	
unpaid		**unlikely**	
unskilled		**unfair**	

Note that the root word is not changed when adding prefixes or suffixes **except** when the suffix rule includes the vowel such as the **vowel + "shun"** shown in the word *imitation.* Since  includes the whole sound of "ashun," the final *a* in the root word *imitate* is included in the sound represented by  .

READING EXERCISE

1. 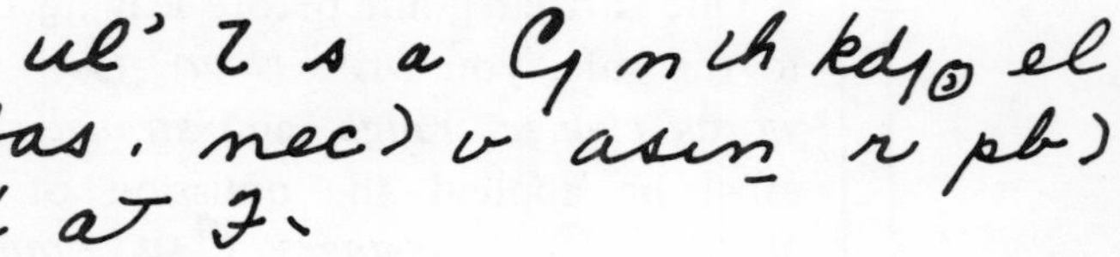

2. 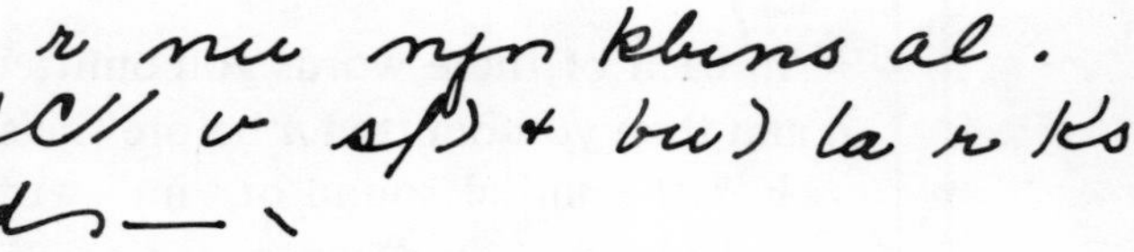

3. 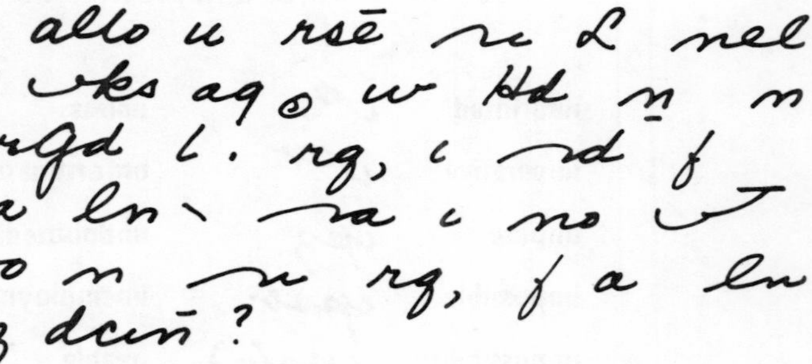

4. 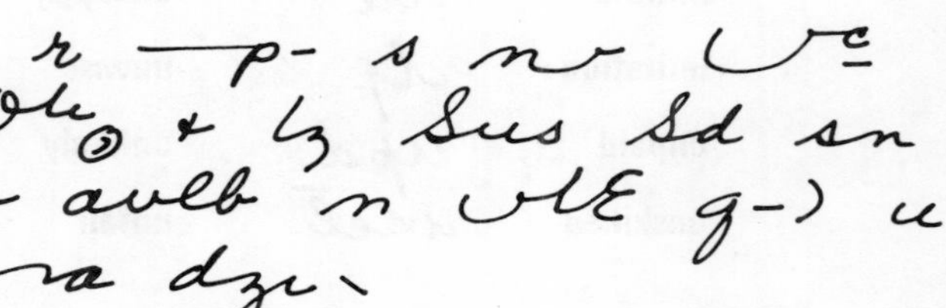

5. 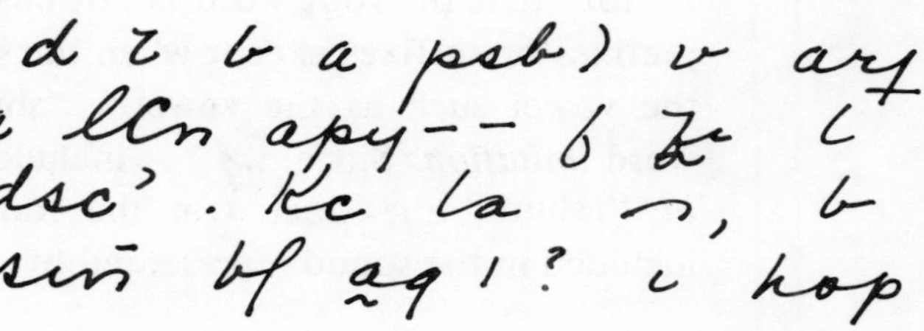

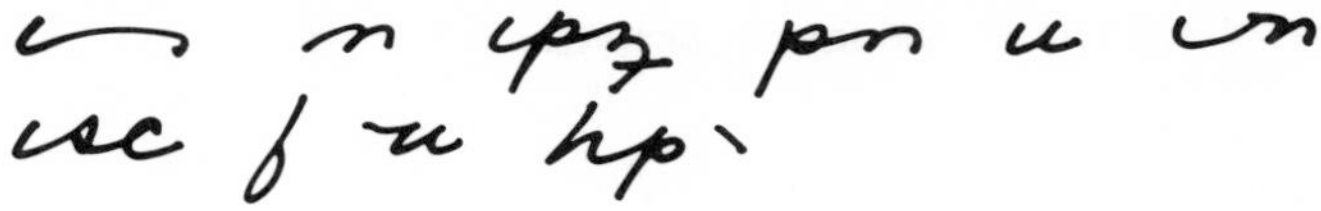

KEY (1) Unless there is a change in this condition, we will face the necessity of assigning our/ publicity to another firm. (26 words) (2) Our new engine combines all the features of safety and beauty that our customers demand. (16 words) (3) Although you received my letter nearly two weeks ago, I have heard nothing in regard to the request I made/ for a loan. May I know whether or not my request for a loan was declined? (34 words) (4) Our plant is now working overtime, and these shoes should soon be available in whatever quantity you may desire. (20 words) (5) Would there be a possibility of arranging a luncheon appointment for Friday to discuss the contract/ that must be signed before August 1? I hope I am not imposing upon you when I ask for your help. (39 words)

3 BRIEF FORMS

whole hl

develop dv

organize, organization og

immediate, immediately ida

particular, particularly p

success, successful, successfully suc

acknowledge ak

almost lmo

ABBREVIATIONS **volume** vol

ounce oz

pair pr

SUMMARY ____________________

parTY)

1. Write) **for the final sound of "tee."**

____

phONE n
ANE
ENE
UNE

2. For the sounds of "ane," "ene," "one," and "une," drop the vowel and write n **.**

____

sIGN in

3. Write in **for the sound of "ine."**

IMage 

4. Write  **for the initial sound of "im."**

UNtie 

5. Write  **for the initial sound of "un."**

READING EXERCISE

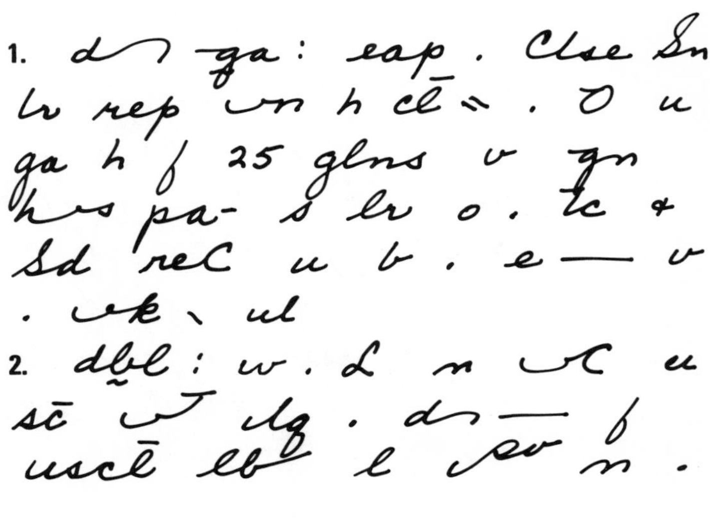

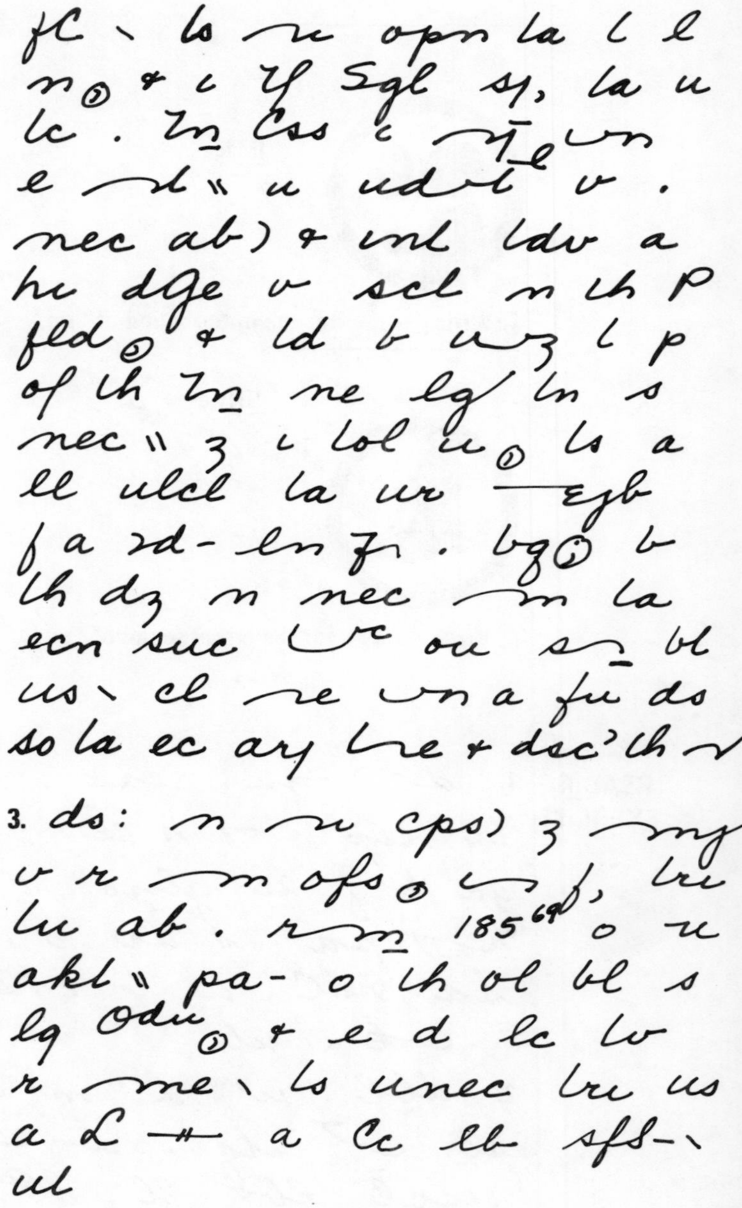

4. 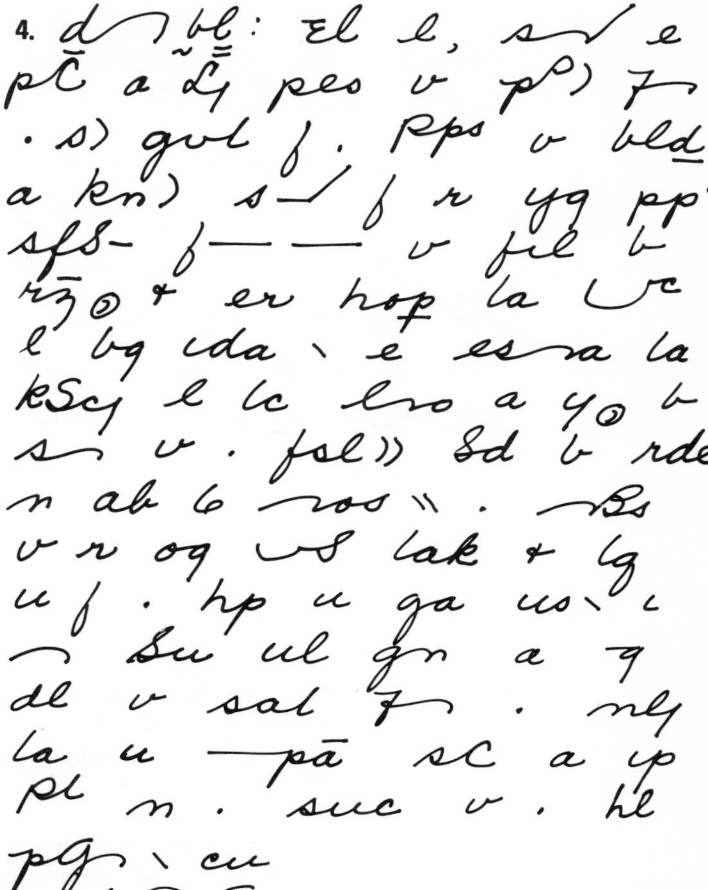

5. 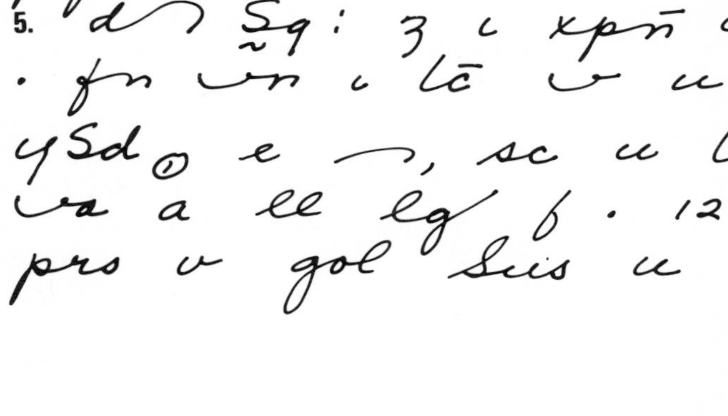

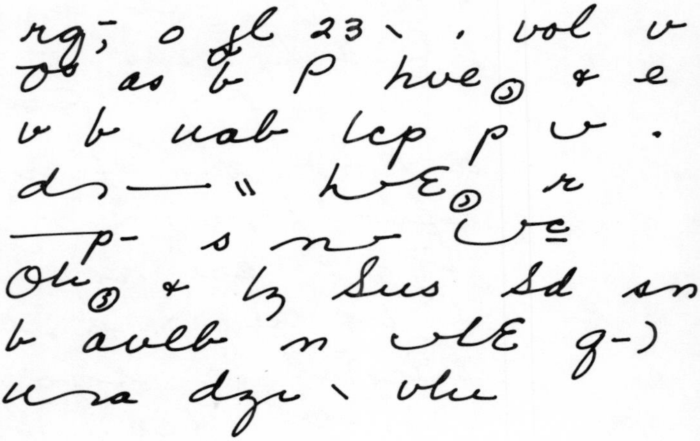

KEY (1) Dear Mr. Gray: We appreciate the courtesy shown to our representative when he called. (P) The order you/ gave him for 25 gallons of green house paint is already on the truck and should reach you by the end of the/ week. Yours truly, (42 words) (2) Dear Bill: I have the letter in which you asked whether I think the demand for unskilled labor will improve in the/ future. It is my opinion that it will not, and I therefore strongly suggest that you take the training courses/ I mentioned when we met. (P) You undoubtedly have the necessary ability and intelligence to develop/ a high degree of skill in this particular field, and it would be unwise to put off this training any/ longer than is necessary. (P) As I told you, it is a little unlikely that you are eligible/ for a student loan from the bank; but this does not necessarily mean that we cannot successfully work out/ something between us. Call me within a few days so that we can arrange to meet and discuss this matter. Sincerely,/ (140 words) (3) Dear Sir: In my capacity as manager of our main office, I am forced to write to you about the remaining/ $185.69 on your account. (P) Payment on this old bill is long/ overdue, and we would like to have our money. It is unnecessary to write us a letter–a check will be/ sufficient. Yours truly, (64 words) (4) Dear Mr. Billings: Early last summer we purchased a large piece of property from the city government for/ the purpose of building a community center for our young people. Sufficient funds have finally been raised,/ and we are hoping that work will begin immediately. We estimate that construction will take almost a/ year, but some of the facilities should be ready in about six months. (P) The members of our organization/ wish to acknowledge and thank you for the help you gave us. I am sure you will gain a great deal of satisfaction/ from the knowledge that you played such an important part in the success of the whole program. Cordially yours, (118 words) (5) Dear Mr. Strong: As I explained on the phone when I talked with you yesterday, we must ask you to wait a little/ longer for the 12 pairs of gold shoes you requested on July 23. The volume of orders has been/ particularly heavy, and we have been unable to keep up with the demand. (P) However, our plant is now/ working overtime; and these shoes should soon be available in whatever quantity you may desire. Very/ truly yours, (81 words)

17

1 In Chapter Thirteen you learned to use the letter *x* for the sounds of "aks," "eks," "iks," "oks," and "uks." At this time you learned a simplified method for writing this letter that would allow you to continue smoothly and quickly to the next letter without interruption.

The letter *x* is now going to be used for another series of sounds.

In words of more than one syllable, write for the medial and final sounds of "us," "usly," "shus," "shusly," "shul," "shully," "nshul," "nshully."

Let's examine this rule carefully. It states that *x* is to be written for the sounds of "us" and "usly." Therefore, *obvious* and *obviously* are written . In the same way, *generous* and *generously* 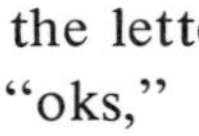; *previous* and *previously* 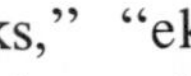.

Study these words and practice them:

campus 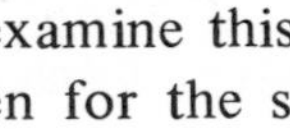 **numerous** 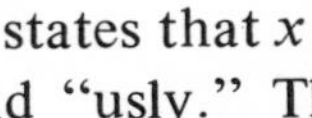

surplus	Spx	**tremendous**	Tm—x
bonus	bnx	**tremendously**	Tm—x
bonuses	bnxs	**famous**	fax
religious	rlgx	**famously**	fax

This rule does not apply to one-syllable words such as *thus* ls and *bus* bs.

The rule also tells you to write *x* for the sounds of "shus" and "shusly." Therefore, you write *anxious* and *anxiously* agx.

Study these words and practice them:

conscious	kx	**delicious**	dlx
consciously	kx	**deliciously**	dlx
ambitious	—bx	**precious**	px
gracious	gx	**graciously**	gx

This rule also instructs you to write *x* for the sounds of "shul" and "shully." Thus *beneficial* bnfx; *commercial* and *commercially* Kx.

Study these words and practice them:

partial	px	**social**	sx
partially	px	**socially**	sx
official	ofx	**officials**	ofxs
officially	ofx	**judicial**	jdx

And finally, the rule refers to the sounds of "nshul" and "nshully," and you are instructed to write *x* for these sounds. Observe how this is done in the following words.

Study these words and practice them:

confidential	kfdx	**financial**	fnx
confidentially	kfdx	**financially**	fnx
essential	esx	**credentials**	cdxs
essentially	esx	**residential**	rzdx

READING EXERCISE

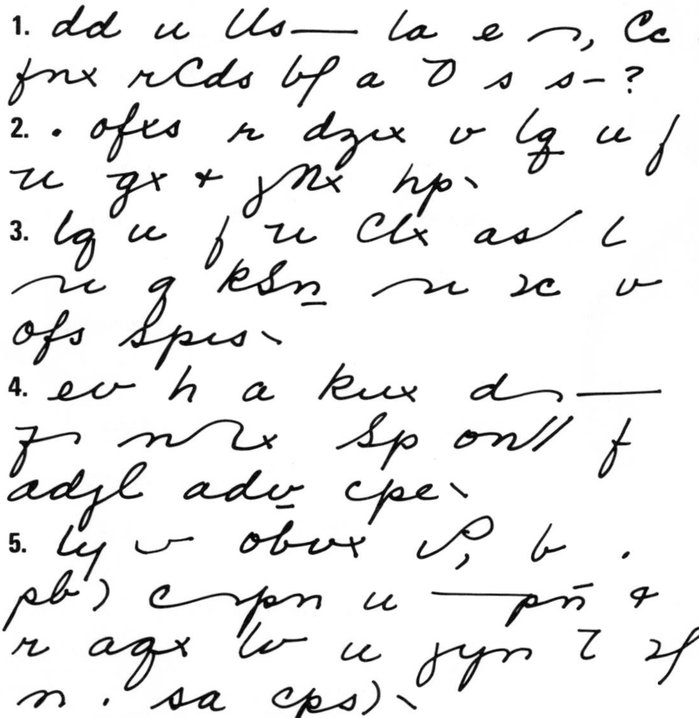

KEY (1) Did you understand that we must check the financial records before an order is sent? (16 words) (2) The officials are desirous of thanking you for your gracious and generous help. (16 words) (3) Thank you for your courteous answer to my question concerning my stock of office supplies. (16 words) (4) We have had a continuous demand from numerous shop owners for additional advertising copy. (20 words) (5) They were obviously impressed by the publicity campaign you planned and are anxious to have you join their staff/ in the same capacity. (25 words)

2 For the medial and final sound of a vowel followed by "ry" write y.

In other words, you are to write *y* for the sounds of "ary," "ery," "iry," "ory," and "ury." In this series of sounds, the *y* has the sound of long *e*. Observe how this rule is followed in these words.

Study these words and practice them:

salary	sly	**sorry**	sy
temporary	tPy	**hurry**	hy
stationery	2y	**territory**	Tly
worry	wy	**inventory**	nv-y
inquiry	nqy	**weary**	wy
voluntary	vl-y	**carry**	cy
machinery	mSny	**library**	lBy
ordinary	odny	**memory**	mmy

Notice that the rule states that you are to write *y* also for the **medial** sounds of "ary," "ery," "iry," "ory," and "ury."

Study these words and practice them:

material		**series**	
period	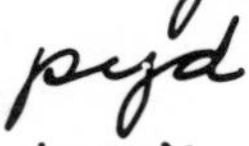	**serious**	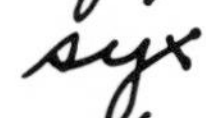
various		**interior**	
editorial		**territorial**	

For the sound of "sp" write a small printed  .

You have learned to print a **capital** *S* for the sound of "str." This rule instructs you to write a **small** printed *s* for the sound of "sp" whenever it occurs in a word.

Study these words and practice them:

speed	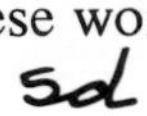	**speak**	
spend		**spare**	
hospital		**inspection**	
prospective		**specifications**	
specific		**grasping**	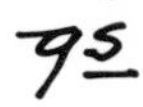
clasped	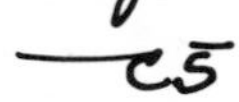	**special**	
speech		**especially**	

You have learned to write a hyphen on the initial letter of a word for the initial "combination-r" sound and a dash for the initial "combination-l" sound. Apply these two principles to  for the initial "spr" and "spl." Thus spread 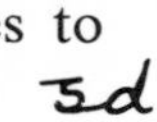 and splice 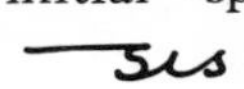 .

READING EXERCISE

1. 

2. 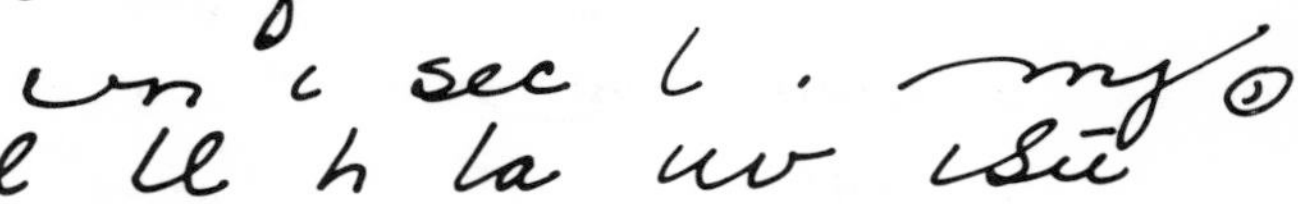

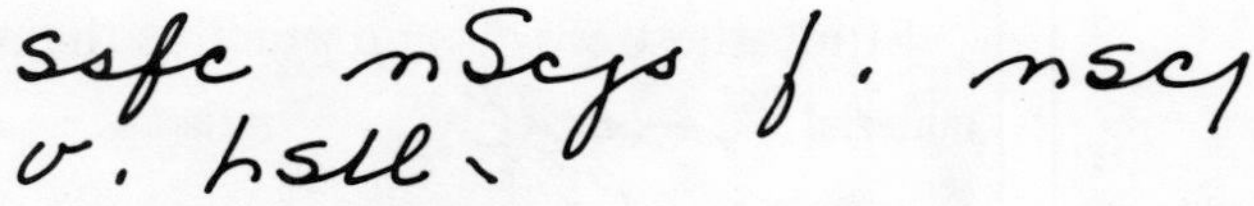

3. 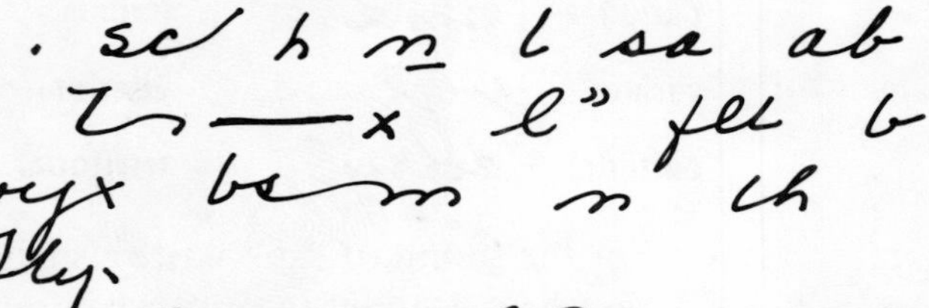

4. 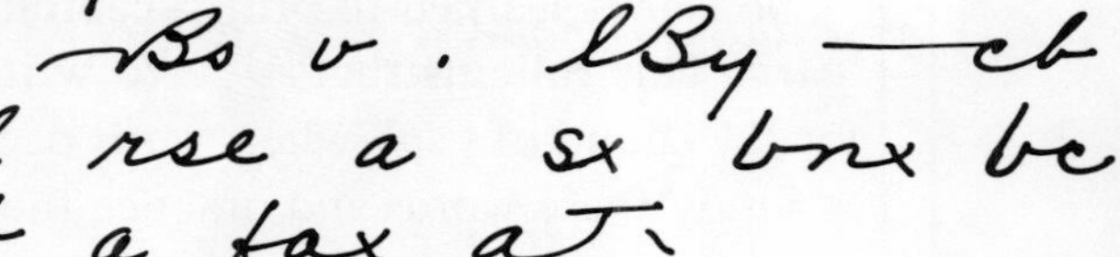

5. 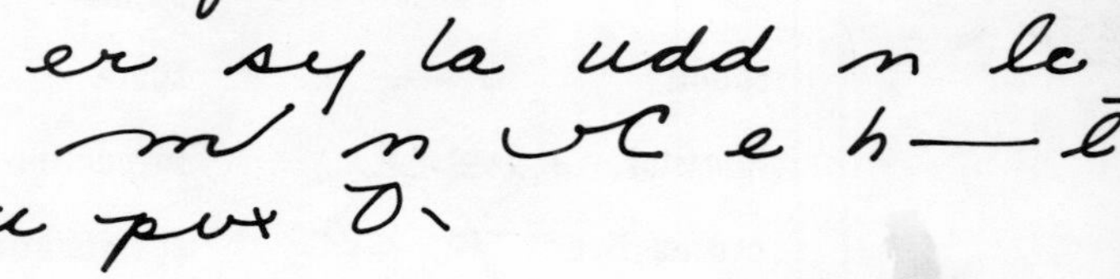

KEY (1) How much must I spend for the spare tire for my car? (9 words) (2) When I speak to the manager, I will tell him that you have issued specific instructions for the inspection/ of the hospital. (25 words) (3) The speaker had nothing to say about the tremendous losses felt by various businessmen in this/ territory. (21 words) (4) Members of the Library Club will receive a special bonus book by a famous author. (16 words) (5) We are sorry that you did not like the manner in which we handled your previous order. (16 words)

3 BRIEF FORMS

thought		**poor**	
around		**idea**	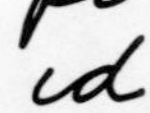
world		**object**	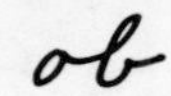

usual, usually	x	initial, initially	ix
probable, probably	pb	definite, definitely	dfn

ABBREVIATIONS

minute	mn	warehouse	whs
junior	jr	senior	sr
manufacture	mfr	independent	ind
signature	sig	America, American	a
approximate, approximately	apx		

SUMMARY

octopUS x
SHUS
SHUL
NSHUL

1. Write x for the medial and final sounds of "us," "usly," "shus," "shusly," "shul," "shully," "nshul," and "nshully."

chERRY y
ARY
IRY
ORY
URY

2. Write y for the medial and final sounds of a vowel + "ry."

SPoon S

3. Write a small printed S for the sound of "sp."

ARE YOU USING YOUR SHORTHAND PAD EFFICIENTLY?

Have you stopped to think about how you are using your notebook? Are you slowing yourself down by not using it properly? Well, it's a fact: Proper use of your notebook will decidedly improve your dictation and transcription efficiency! Check the list of hints below. Be sure you are following each one carefully.

1. Use a standard 6- by 9-inch steno pad that has a line printed down the middle of the page dividing it into two columns.
2. Write in columns rather than across the whole page.
3. As you begin writing, use the thumb and index finger of your left hand to slowly move the sheet upward. This minimizes arm movement and brings the page into position for flipping, so that you can begin writing on the next page with no loss of time.
4. Form the habit of starting each day's dictation by writing the date at the bottom of the page.
5. Place a rubber band around the cover of your pad and slip your finished notes under it, so that you can immediately open your pad at the proper place for taking dictation.

6. **Always draw a diagonal line through each letter as soon as it has been transcribed.**
7. **Indicate the end of a letter by drawing a horizontal line before starting the next letter.**
8. **Edit your notes carefully before you transcribe them.**

READING EXERCISE

1.

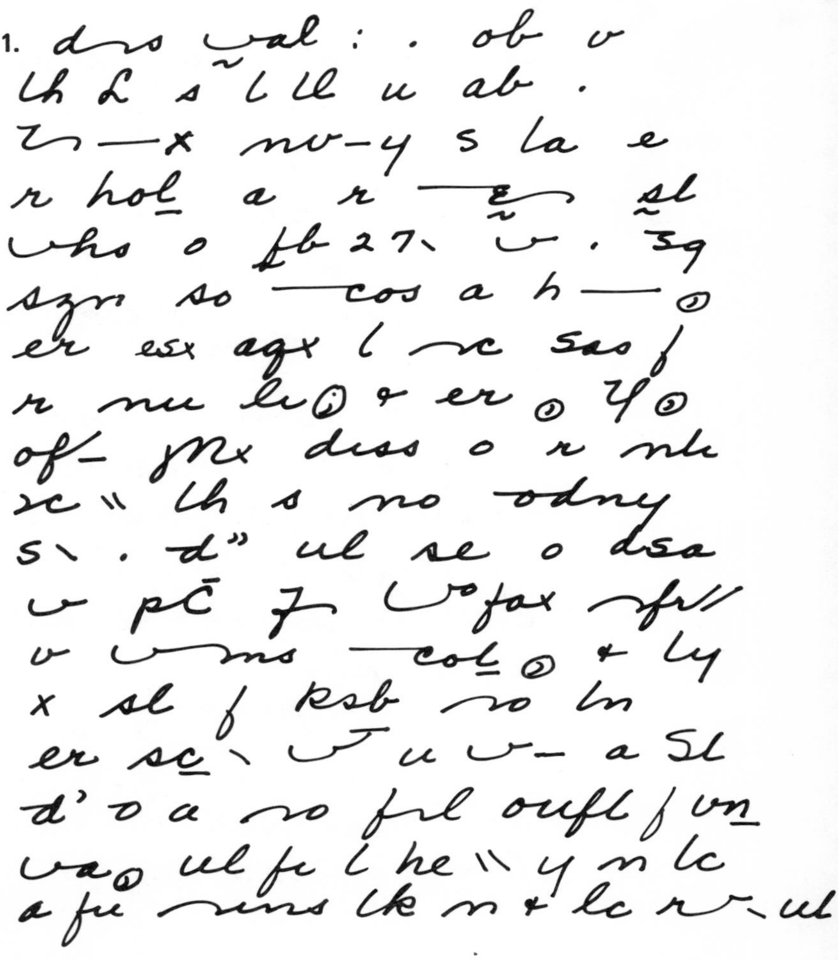

2. d) bgs: w p, sn . vnd
Sva ñd b u k o . po
gl) lb fr— n Sln rdse
cy n vyx lcl So" lgs
v u Cgs r x el syx ⊙ &
i Sgl ry u l sec v u
a me bf u du ne dfn
ab u id lpb u fe \ cfl
Su la hl b ncm l
age la pby v lh rsl
d pb rsl n lgl acy
ag u" —p ll re
no sl u dsd ldu\
vlu

3. ds: vn i soc v u
o nv 3⊙ vd l gi
—pn la lz abs esx f
. rlyl e ō lb dē no
la ln ja 13\ usd l d
lc a pyd v apx 2 ros
lc lh P S-" ls nv
ja 6⊙ & er bq l vy cs
ev rsē nl px S- o lh
O\ 3 i lol u⊙ a dla

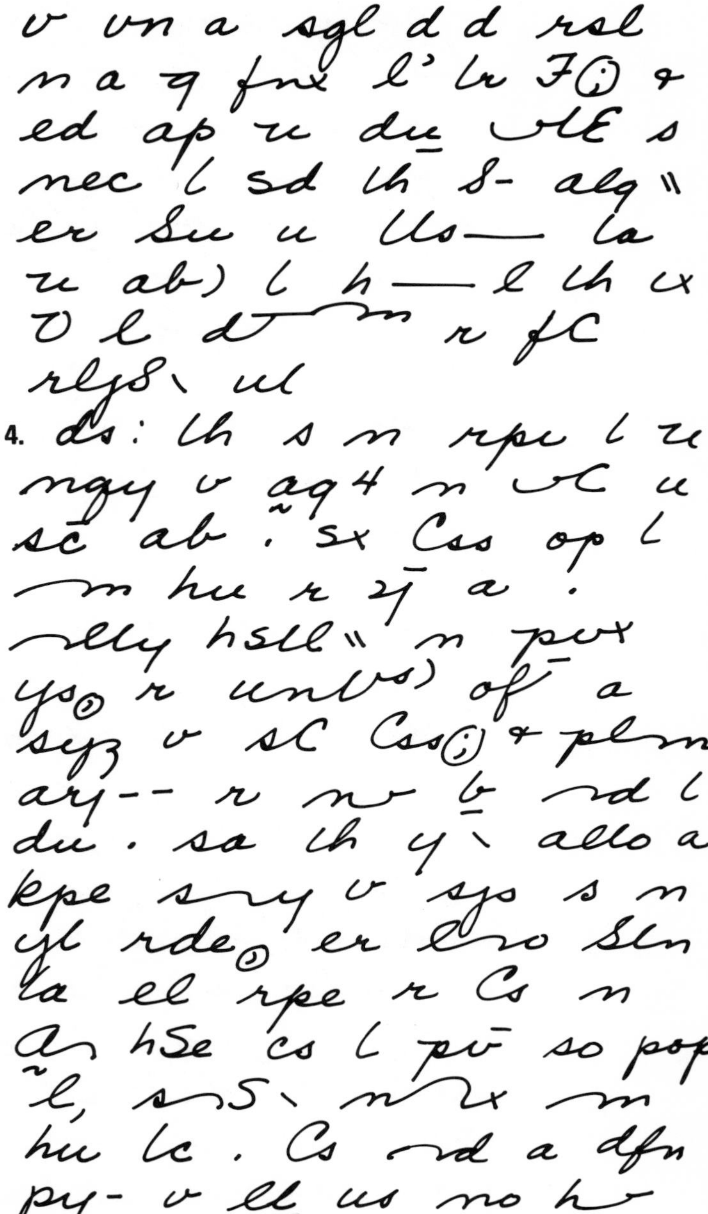

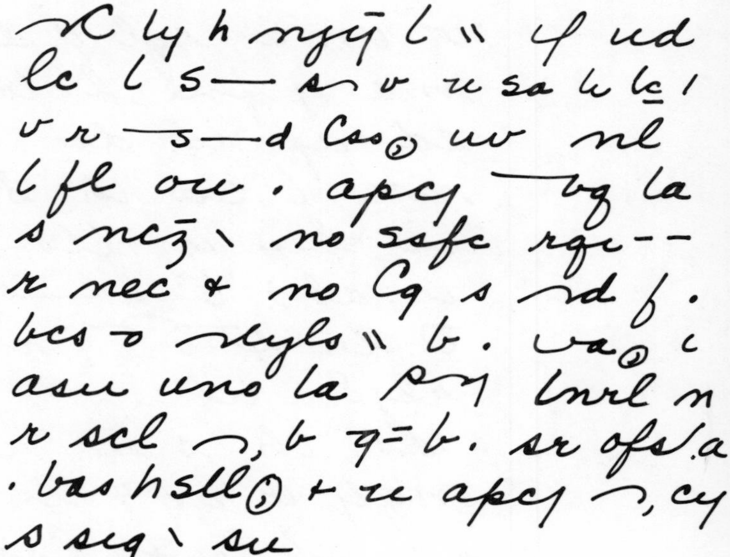

5.

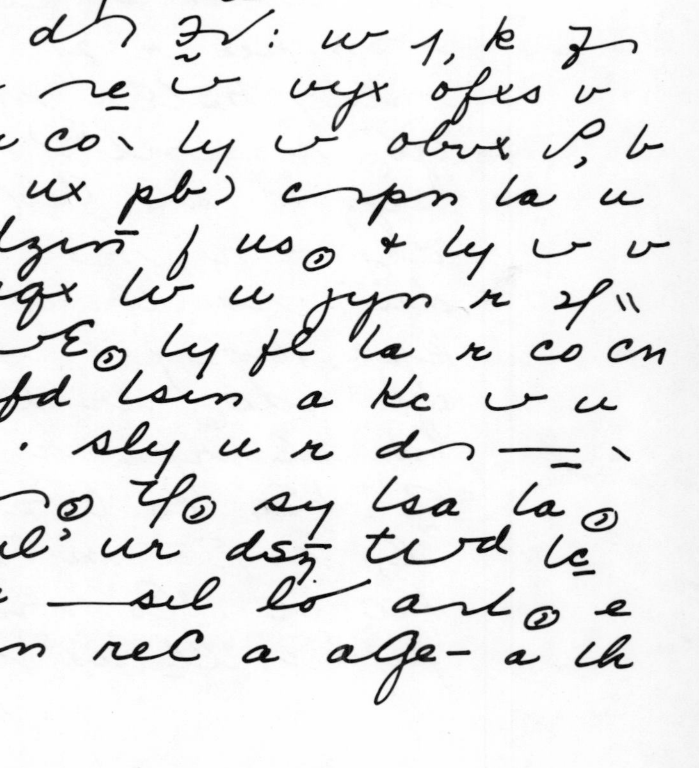

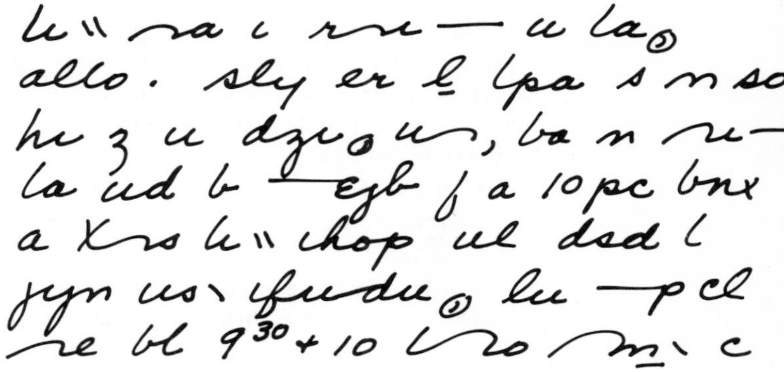

KEY (1) Dear Mrs. Wall: The object of this letter is to tell you about the tremendous inventory sale that we/ are holding at our Elm Street warehouse on February 27. With the spring season so close at hand, we/ are especially anxious to make space for our new line; and we are, therefore, offering generous discounts on/ our entire stock. (P) This is no ordinary sale. The dresses you will see on display were purchased from world-famous/ manufacturers of women's clothing, and they usually sell for considerably more than we are asking./ Whether you want a sport dress or a more formal outfit for evening wear, you will find it here. (P) Why not take/ a few minutes to come in and look around. Yours truly, (130 words) (2) Dear Mr. Banks: I have just seen the independent survey made by your committee on the poor quality to/ be found in certain merchandise carried in various local stores. (P) I think some of your charges are extremely/ serious, and I strongly urge you to speak with your attorney before you do anything definite about/ your idea to publish your findings. I feel sure that he will be inclined to agree that publication of this/ report would probably result in legal action against you. (P) Please let me know what you decide to do. Very/ truly yours, (102 words) (3) Dear Sir: When I spoke with you on November 3, I made it quite plain that it was absolutely essential for/ the material we ordered to be delivered no later than January 13. You said it would take/ a period of approximately two months to make this particular shipment. (P) It is now January/ 6, and we are beginning to worry because we have received only partial shipment on this order. As

I/ told you, a delay of even a single day would result in a great financial loss to our firm; and we would/ appreciate your doing whatever is necessary to speed this shipment along. (P) We are sure you understand/ that your ability to handle this initial order will determine our future relationship. Yours/ truly, (141 words) (4) Dear Sir: This is in reply to your inquiry of August 4 in which you asked about the special courses open/ to men who are stationed at the military hospital. (P) In previous years, our university offered/ a series of such courses; and preliminary arrangements are now being made to do the same this year./ Although a complete summary of subjects is not yet ready, we are almost certain that we will repeat our/ course in American history because it proved so popular last semester. Numerous men who took the/ course made a definite point of letting us know how much they had enjoyed it. (P) If you would like to spend some of your/ spare time taking one of our splendid courses, you have only to fill out the application blank that is enclosed./ No specific requirements are necessary and no charge is made for the books or materials. (P) By the way, I/ assume you know that permission to enroll in our school must be granted by the senior officer at the base/ hospital; and your application must carry his signature. Sincerely yours, (194 words) (5) Dear Mr. Farmer: I have just come from a meeting with various officials of our company. They were obviously/ impressed by the unusual publicity campaign that you designed for us, and they were very anxious/ to have you join our staff. (P) However, they feel that our company cannot afford to sign a contract with you/ for the salary you are demanding. I am, therefore, sorry to say that, unless you are disposed toward taking/ a slightly lower amount, we cannot reach an agreement at this time. (P) May I remind you that, although the/ salary we are willing to pay is not so high as you desire, you must bear in mind that you would be eligible/ for a 10 percent bonus at Christmas time. (P) I hope you will decide to join us. If you do, will you please call/ me between 9:30 and 10:00 tomorrow morning. Cordially, (151 words)

Cp/ 18

1 For the sounds of "nse" and "nsy" write a disjoined slant.

You have learned that the final sounds of "er" and "ter" are represented by a slant that is joined to the letter or mark of punctuation that precedes it. In the present rule, however, you are instructed to write a *disjoined* slant—which simply means that it will **not** be joined to the letter or mark of punctuation that goes before it.

The word *assure,* as you know, is written aSu. If the sound of "nse" is added to this word to form *assurance,* you write a disjoined slant at the end of the outline: *assurance* aSu/. In the same way, the word *rely* is rli and you write *reliance* rli/.

Study these words and practice them:

balance	bl/	**license**	ls/
announce	a~/	**allowance**	al~/
assistance	ass/	**since**	s/

insurance	nSu/	**correspondence**	Cs—/
convinced	kvT̄	**accordance**	aCd/
entrance	nT/	**expense**	xp/
remittance	rmt/	**response**	rs/
convenience	kvn/	**financing**	fn/̲
confidence	kfd/	**experience**	xpy/
distance	ds/	**preference**	‾pf/

How will you form the plurals of these words? You will simply follow the rule for any outline that ends in a mark of punctuation and double the slant—as in *senses* s// ; *responses* rs//.

This sound of "nse" may also occur in the middle of a word. When it does, you will follow the same rule and write a disjoined slant.

Study these words and practice them:

responsible	rs/b	**principle**	p/p
sponsored	sV̄	**announcement**	an/-

This rule also states that the disjoined slant will be used to represent the sound of "nsy"—the sound that is heard in *agency* or *fancy*. Thus: *agency* aj/ ; *fancy* f/ ; *emergency* emj/; *efficiency* efS/ .

READING EXERCISE 1. s/ w h no rs/ l u L ɵ cl go . akl l a rs/b aj/ ˋ

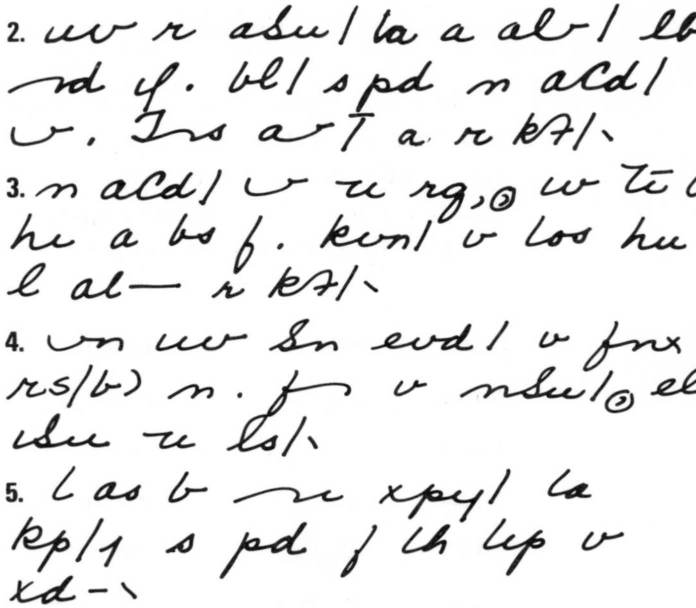

KEY (1) Since I have had no response to my letter, I will give the account to a responsible agency. (19 words) (2) You have our assurance that an allowance will be made if the balance is paid in accordance with the terms/ announced at our conference. (25 words) (3) In accordance with your request, I have tried to hire a bus for the convenience of those who will attend our/ conference. (21 words) (4) When you have shown evidence of financial responsibility in the form of insurance, we will issue/ your license. (22 words) (5) It has been my experience that compensation is paid for this type of accident. (16 words)

2 You have omitted letters that are lightly pronounced such as the *h* in "wh." The next rule is a continuation of this practice.

Omit *t* after the sounds of "k," "p," "f," "x"; omit *pt* after *m.*

This rule teaches you how to handle such words as *act, instruct,* and *district*—words in which the sound of "k" is followed by *t*. Therefore, in compliance with the rule, you omit the *t* from the outline.

Study these words and practice them:

acts	acs	**district**	dSc
instruct	nSc	**expect**	xpc
inspected	nsc̄	**factory**	fcy
project	pjc	**protect**	plc
affect	afc	**practical**	pccl
neglected	ngc̄	**practically**	pccl
respect	rSc	**conflict**	kfc
connected	kc̄	**exactly**	xcl
products	pdcs	**contact**	klc
fact	fc	**effect**	efc
practice	pcs	**selected**	slc̄
exact	xc	**conducting**	kd<u>c</u>

Similarly, you are instructed to eliminate *t* after the sounds of "p," "f," and "x."

Study these words and practice them:

except	xp	**left**	lf

adopt		**gift**	
accepting		**next**	
acceptable		**text**	
accept		**draft**	
kept		**swiftly**	
context		**pretext**	

The second part of this rule instructs you in the handling of such words as *attempt* and *prompt.* Both the *p* and *t* are omitted and the outline ends with *m*.

Study these words and practice them:

prompt		**attempt**	
exempt		**attempted**	

You have learned to capitalize letters to represent the "combination-r" sounds in the middle of words as well as to indicate the medial "vowel + r." Examples: *library* 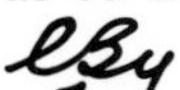 ; *regret* 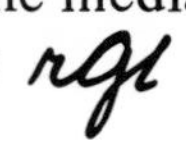 ; *personal* 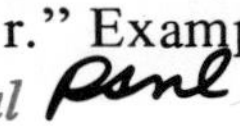 ; *thorough* 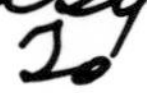 .

There are situations, however, where this capitalization procedure cannot be followed.

When the nature of an outline is such that the capitalization rule cannot be applied, write *r* for the medial sound of a vowel + "r."

You know that *chat* is  and *shot* is  . You also know that when the sound of a vowel plus "r" occurs in the middle of a word, you capitalize the preceding letter. But what if the letter preceding these sounds is already capitalized—for example: *chart* or *short?* The present rule says that you will simply write *r*.

Study these words and practice them:

shortly	Srtl	**charter**	Cr/
sharp	Srp	**church**	CrC
short	Srt	**chart**	Crt
shortage	Srtj	**natural**	nCrl
shorthand	Srth—	**naturally**	nCrl

In the same way, since you cannot apply the capitalization rule to such words as *standard* or *central*, you will write *standard* 2— nd and *central* s—nl .

READING EXERCISE

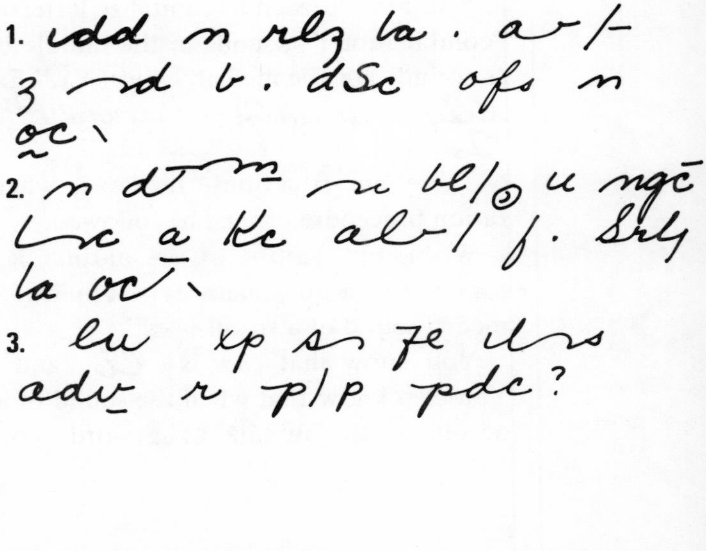

4. . mo, nCrl tq tdu s tst p a s-nl kCrl grp.

5. pm aly Sd b gv l . isu v Crl/.

KEY (1) I did not realize that the announcement was made by the district office in October. (16 words) (2) In determining my balance, you neglected to make a correct allowance for the shortage that occurred. (19 words) (3) Will you accept some free items advertising our principal product? (13 words) (4) The most natural thing to do is to set up a central control group. (13 words) (5) Prompt attention should be given to the issuing of charters. (13 words)

3 BRIEF FORMS

without	wo	**whom**	hm
collect	cc	**known**	no
sample	sa	**conclusion**	kcl
once, circumstance	c/	**individual, individually**	ndv
describe, description	des		

ABBREVIATIONS

post office	po	**memorandum**	mo
figure	fg	**inch**	in
page	p	**total**	tol
parcel post	pp		

SUMMARY

fe**NCE** /
NSY

1. Write a disjoined slant for the sounds of "nse" and "nsy."

gi**FT** t
KT c
PT p
XT x
MPT

2. Omit t after the sounds of "k," "p," "f," and "x"; omit pt after m.

ch**UR**ch r

3. When the capitalization rule cannot be applied to indicate the medial sound of a vowel + r, write r for this sound.

READING EXERCISE

1. rd) — an : c s/el rgl . fc la u ~S- dd n rel

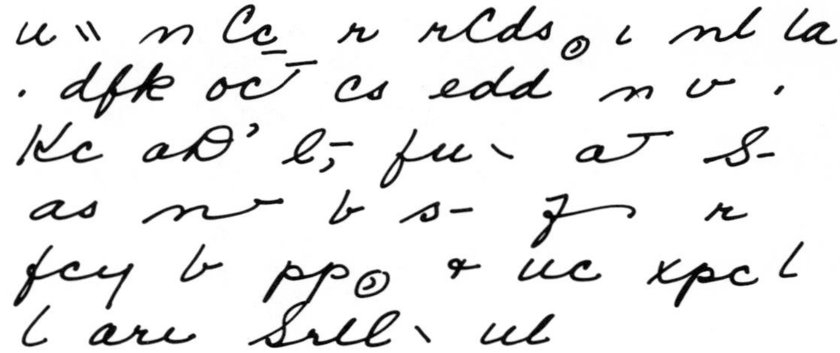

2. 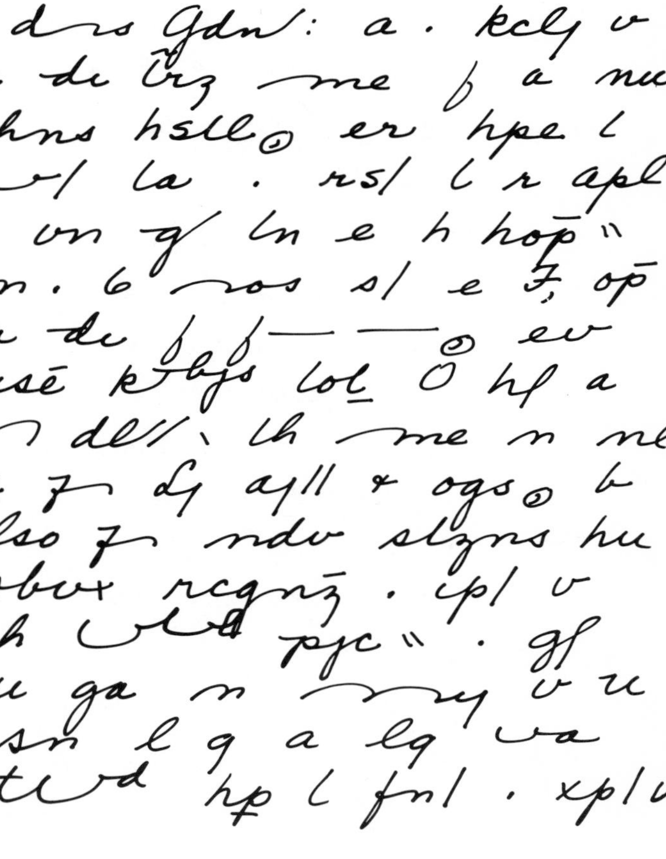

bld lh — s — d hsll, uSd fl v
pd v. assl uv gv " lq u
c/ aq f u ca hp + ksj, s

3. dsi' gv: n u L v pn
q u ō 10 lyds v 18 un fBc deō
n r cal o p 21" hE u
ngc lndca . xc Sd v
bu la u v-O + el
Y n als lfl lh ō ul
uv klc us ab. cl u
dzi, ul

4. ds psi: cz v gd lrd
. reso u lf f e o lh,
lqu ids r x el pccl +
Sd pv v suc" z u sp
il als lklc ss v.
m kc v. ajl u j
+ l se lf l s ne C/
v arj a k7l f nx vk,
c

5. ds lq: . po as p, ar T
a Srp nCs n. ras f
nSul o al pcjs la r

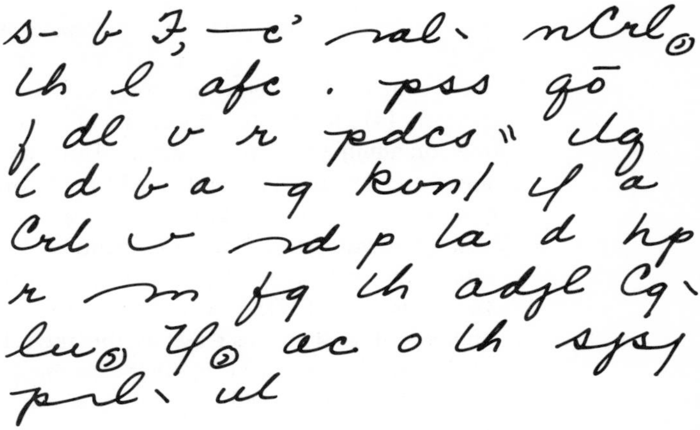

KEY (1) My dear Mr. Allen: I sincerely regret the fact that your shipment did not reach you. (P) In checking our records, I note/ that the difficulty occurred because we did not have the correct address listed for you. Another shipment/ has now been sent from our factory by parcel post, and you can expect it to arrive shortly. Yours truly,/ (60 words) (2) Dear Mrs. Gardner: At the conclusion of our drive to raise money for a new children's hospital, we are happy/ to announce that the response to our appeal was even greater than we had hoped. (P) In the six months since we first/ opened our drive for funds, we have received contributions totaling over half a million dollars. This money not/ only came from large agencies and organizations, but also from individual citizens who/ obviously recognized the importance of this worthwhile project. (P) The gift you gave in memory of your son will/ go a long way toward helping to finance the expense of building this splendid hospital. You should feel very proud/ of the assistance you have given. (P) Thank you once again for your kind help and consideration. Sincerely, (139 words) (3) My dear Miss Rivers: In your letter of June 9, you ordered 10 yards of 18-inch fabric described in our/ catalog on page 21. (P) However, you neglected to indicate the exact shade of blue that you want; and/ we will, therefore, not attempt to fill this order until you have contacted us about the color you desire./ Yours truly, (62 words) (4) Dear Mr. Price: I was very glad to read the memorandum you left for me on Thursday. I think your ideas/ are extremely practical and should prove very successful. (P) As you suggested, I will attempt to contact/ some of the men connected with the agency you mentioned and will see if there is any chance of arranging/ a conference for next week. Cordially, (67 words) (5) Dear Mr. Long: The post office has just announced a sharp increase in the rates for insurance on all packages/ that are sent by first-class mail. Naturally, this will affect the prices quoted for delivery of our products/. (P) I think it would be a great convenience if a chart were made up that would help our men figure this additional/ charge. Will you, therefore, act on this suggestion promptly. Yours truly, (71 words)

READING AND EDITING NOTES

In a short time now, you will successfully complete your theory in shorthand. Then you'll move on into an interesting phase of your training. An employer will expect accurate, rapid transcription to be one of your skills. Now is the time to easily develop that accuracy and speed. You can in this way: After you take dictation, sit down with your notes and follow these suggestions–

1. **Learn to read your notes in phrases rather than word by word. You will automatically choose the right words in context and will eliminate many errors. In the beginning, the phrases you read will be short ones; but practice will make it possible for you to read sentences as a whole.**
2. **Correct any necessary outlines and make any necessary deletions or additions.**

3. **Insert punctuation marks, placing a circle around each one. Some students prefer using a red pen to do this.**
4. **If a sentence doesn't seem to make sense, add or delete words as necessary.**
5. **Spell out proper names.**
6. **Check all numbers and dates for accuracy.**
7. **Use the dictionary to check the spelling of all words about which you are doubtful.**

These are all very basic rules. If you follow them, your rate of transcription and its accuracy will decidedly improve.

19

1 You have learned many rules for handling many suffixes. Here are some examples:

overscore for final "ed"

underscore for final "ing" and "thing"

joined slant for final "er" and "ter"

 **for final "bul" and "blee"**

 **for final "pul" and "ple"**

 **for final "lee"**

 **for final "ness"**

 **for final "ssness"**

 for final "tee"

 **for final "ther"**

For the suffixes "ful" and "fully" and for the final sound of "fy," write  .

Study these words and practice them:

careful	caf	**respectfully**	rscf
useful	usf	**beautifully**	blf
hopeful*	hopf	**notify**	nlf
wonderful	u— rf	**qualify**	glf
carefully	caf	**justified**	jsf̄
respectful	rscf	**colorful**	clf
beautiful	blf	**colorfully**	clf
fearfully	fef	**specify**	ssf
qualified	glf̄	**simplified**	sipf̄

*Note that the long vowel is retained in this word to avoid conflict with the outline for the word *helpful* hpf.

You learned that *t* is omitted after the sounds "k," "p," "f," and "x." Thus, *fact* fc ; *gift* gf ; *next* nx.

The following rule is similar to this and deals with the dropping of *d* when it comes before certain sounds.

Omit *d* before "m" and "v."

Study these words and practice them:

admit	a~l	**advisory**	avzy
admittance	a~l/	**advised**	avz̄

admission	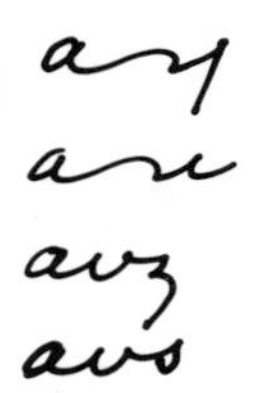	**advisable**	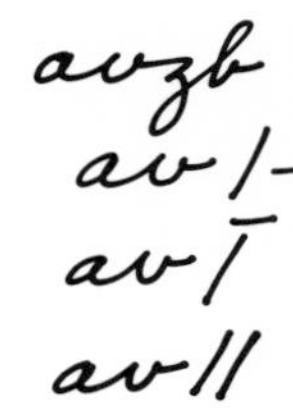
admire		**advancement**	
advise		**advanced***	
advice		**advances**	

*Although *advanced* has the sound of "st," use the overscore with the disjoined slant rather than the comma.

READING EXERCISE

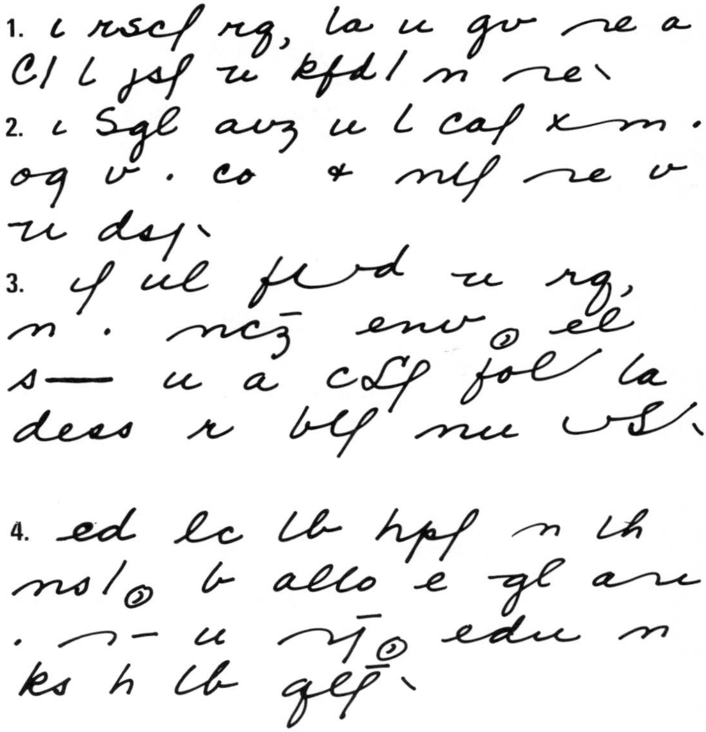

5. 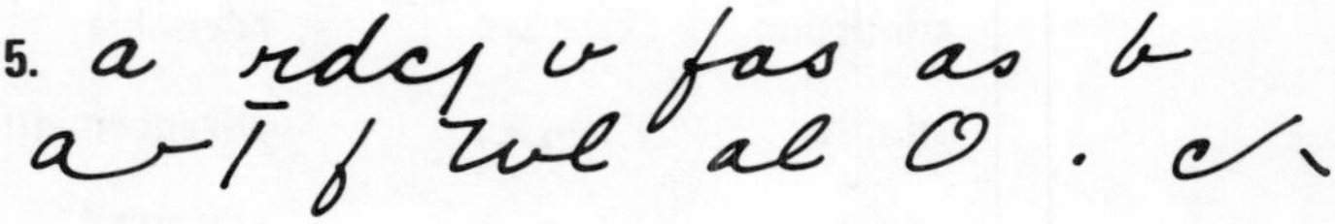

KEY (1) I respectfully request that you give me a chance to justify your confidence in me. (16 words) (2) I strongly advise you to carefully examine the organization of the company and notify/ me of your decision. (24 words) (3) If you will forward your request in the enclosed envelope, we will send you a colorful folder that describes/ our beautiful new washer. (27 words) (4) We would like to be helpful in this instance, but although we greatly admire the man you mentioned, we do not/ consider him to be qualified. (28 words) (5) A reduction of fares has been announced for travel all over the country. (14 words)

2 For the sounds of "inter" and "enter," write a capital  .

You have learned to write *n* for *in* and for the sound of "en," so this rule will be easy to remember.

Study these words and practice them:

enter		**interstate**	
entertainment		**interrupt**	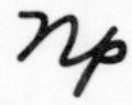
interested	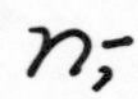	**uninteresting**	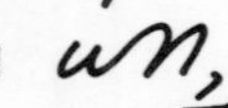
entered		**internal**	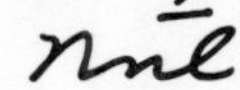
entering	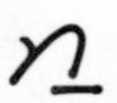	**interests**	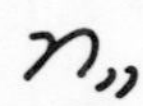
international	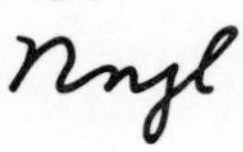	**interesting**	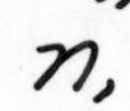

Notice that this rule refers specifically to the sounds of "inter" and "enter"—**not** to "intra," "intri," or "intro." These latter sounds, you will recall, were incorporated into the rule dealing with the writing of capital *T* for medial "tr" in such words as *intrastate* nTsa; *intricate* nTcl; *introduce* nTds; *introduction* nTdcy.

You have learned to write a disjoined slant to represent the sounds of "nse" and "nsy" in such words as *insurance* nsu/ and *agency* ay/. In the following rule, you will learn that s/ also represents a certain sound.

For the sounds of "self" and "selves," write s/.

Study these words and practice them:

self	s/	**yourself**	us/
self-interest	s/n,	**itself**	ts/
myself	-us/	**himself**	hs/
herself	Hs/	**self-addressed**	s/aD,

You are also instructed to write s/ for the sound of "selves." In other words, it is not necessary to double the mark of punctuation to indicate the formation of a plural. Thus, *themselves* ls/ and *ourselves* rs/. The only exception to this is the word *yourselves* which is written us// to avoid conflict with *yourself* us/. In all other examples of this rule, there can be no confusion because words in this group exist only in the singular or plural form—never both. For example, -us/ can only be read as *myself* because there is no such word *myselves.* Similarly, you will know that rs/ is *ourselves* because there is no singular form for this word.

READING EXERCISE

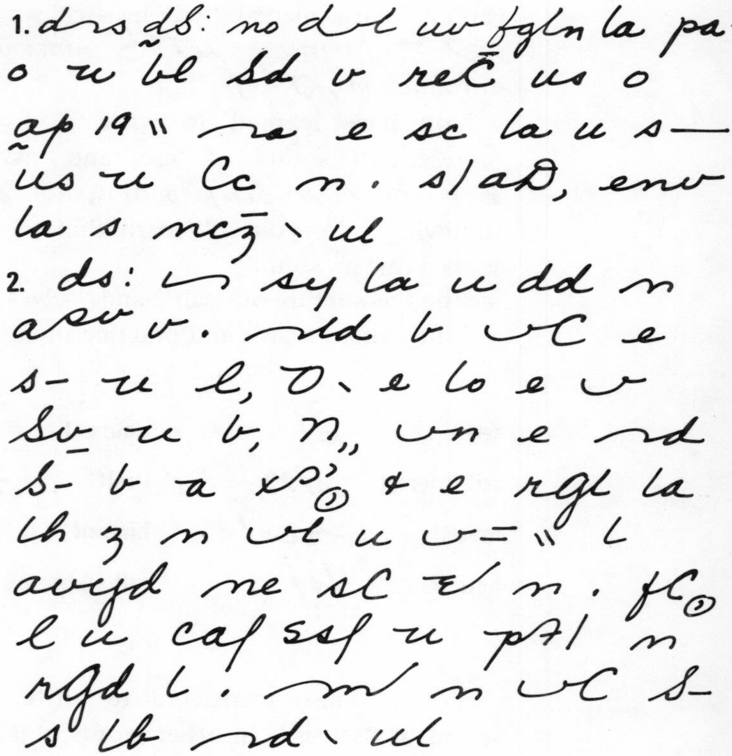

KEY (1) Dear Mrs. Dash: No doubt you have forgotten that payment on your bill should have reached us on April 19. (P) May we/ ask that you send us your check in the self-addressed envelope that is enclosed. Yours truly, (35 words) (2) Dear Sir: I am sorry that you did not approve of the method by which we sent your last order. We thought we were/ serving your best interests when we made shipment by air express, and we regret that this was not what you wanted. (P) To/ avoid any such error in the future, will you carefully specify your preference in regard to/ the manner in which shipment is to be made. Yours truly, (70 words)

3

BRIEF FORMS

move	mv	auto	a
perhaps	pps	throughout	Tuo
entitle	ntl		

ABBREVIATIONS

mile	mi	north	N
railroad	rr	south	S
railway	ry	east	E
mortgage	mtg	west	W
associate	asso	feet, foot	ft

SUMMARY

painFUL
FULLY
FY
f

1. Write f for the final sounds of "ful," "fully," and "fy."

aDMit 

2. Omit d before m and v.

INTERchange 
ENTER

3. Write  for the sounds of "enter" and "inter."

mySELF 

4. Write  for the sounds of "self" and "selves."

READING EXERCISE 1. 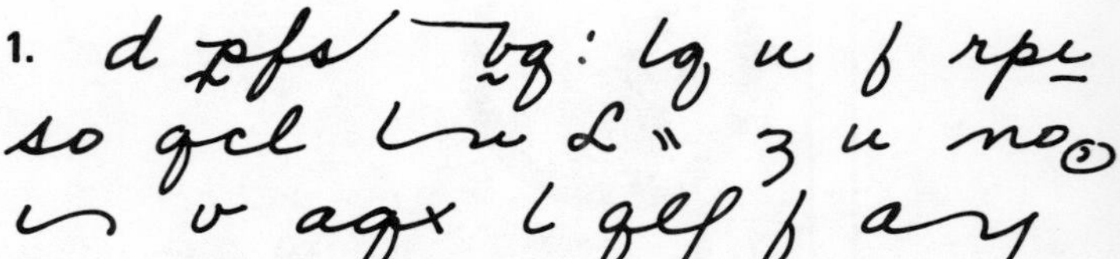

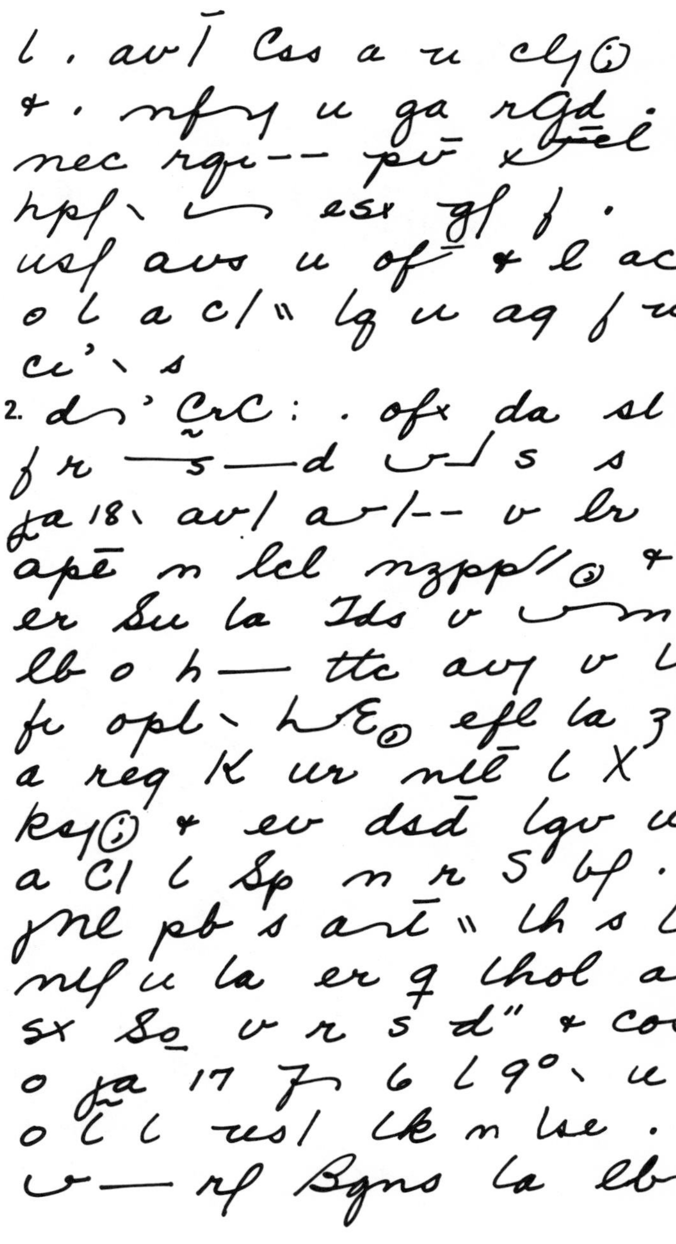

avlb lu \ cu

3. d) hal: n aCd/ v
u nScjs w nsc u la,
cal caf ; + u sy lsa la
idu n Sa u opn \ allo
c asl la. Osl apel s
qi cdf c f— no,
v. lyl x l un, \
Fgl ido- fl ll akps
enf l jsf. q xpl nolo
np l lq \ lq F la.
gl) v. pp s v po +
dz n kp l .x2— rds v
. co la dd . p= " h c b
n Cq v lh pjc usl
id v ns, la. jb b
dn aq ; + id n v aGe
l xp l \ ul

4. d) dvs: id lc ttc
a ro- ttl u h sC
w njj u assoj v
u Tuo. ys \ w l ko
usl fCnl lw U so

—csl w u⊙ + ι 7ul
rGl la uv dsd̄ Lv
ru ofss l aT s)\\ . rep
w hs ul b dl̲ n u
nu lcj as lr xP, s
dzr lb z hpf z psb⊙ +
ls Sln la h l du
wlE h c lb usf lu n
E wa\ s

5. d7 b̃r: w lc̄ a s7
pP)) ñ wC u ra b N;
z a psb sr f u nu—p-\
l v lz pP)) s ab 5 rus
N v. s) +. T lrs a Srl
ds/ l. W\ bo r lcā
wn a H fl v. mhra
+ wn a fu rus v .
rr\\ ι Us— la . k) 7̃,
c̃o hols . rlgo lh l—
+ s/, la u klc ls f
T nfy\\ a L flos
gv̄ dlE dess v . pP))\
ul

KEY (1) Dear Professor Blank: Thank you for replying so quickly to my letter. (P) As you know, I am very anxious to/ qualify for admission to the advanced courses at your college; and the information you gave regarding/ the necessary requirements proved extremely helpful. I am especially grateful for the useful advice/ you offered and will act on it at once. (P) Thank you again for your kindness. Sincerely, (75 words) (2) Dear Miss Church: The official date set for our splendid winter sale is January 18. Advance announcements/ have already appeared in local newspapers, and we are sure that thousands of women will be on hand to take/ advantage of this fine opportunity. However, we feel that as a regular customer you are/ entitled to extra consideration; and we have decided to give you a chance to shop in our store before/ the general public is admitted. (P) This is to notify you that we are going to hold a special showing/ of our sale dresses and coats on January 17 from six to nine o'clock. You owe it to yourself/ to come in to see the wonderful bargains that will be available to you. Cordially yours, (137 words) (3) My dear Mr. Hall: In accordance with your instructions, I have inspected your latest catalog carefully;/ and I am sorry to say that I do not share your opinion. Although I admit that the overall appearance/ is quite colorful, I found most of the material extremely uninteresting. Frankly, I don't feel/ it will accomplish enough to justify the great expense involved in putting it together. I think further/ that the quality of the paper is very poor and does not come up to the usual standards of the company/ that did the printing. (P) Had I been in charge of this project myself, I would have insisted that the job be done/ again; and I would not have agreed to accept it. Yours truly, (131 words) (4) Dear Mr. Davis: I would like to take a moment to tell you how much I have enjoyed my association/ with you throughout the years. I have always considered myself fortunate to have worked so closely with you, and I truly/ regret that you have decided to move your offices to another city. (P) The representative/ with whom you will be dealing in your new location has already expressed his desire to be as helpful as/ possible, and I am certain that he will do whatever he can to be useful to you in every way./ Sincerely, (103 words) (5) Dear Mr.

Bright: I have looked at some properties in which you may be interested as a possible site for/ your new plant. One of these properties is about five miles north of the city and the other lies a short distance/ to the west. Both are located within a hundred feet of the main highway and within a few miles of the railroad./ (P) I understand that the County Trust Company holds the mortgage on this land and suggest that you contact them/ for further information. (P) A letter follows giving detailed descriptions of the properties. Yours truly, (97 words)

Cp 20

1 Let's examine some words in which two vowels occur together but have only **one** sound. For example, *lease, tail, built.* In these words, the sound of only one vowel is heard. However, there are some words in which two vowels occur together—**both** of which are pronounced: *actual, fuel, graduate, ruin.* It is to this latter group of vowel sounds that this next rule applies.

When a word contains two medial **pronounced** consecutive vowels, only the first vowel sound is written.

Study these words and practice them:

annual	aul	**actual**	acCul
mutual	-Cul	**dual**	dul
fuel	ful	**ruin**	run
gradual	gdul	**trial**	Tul
poet	pol	**manual**	-mul
diameter	du-	**diet**	dul

When a word ends in two pronounced consecutive vowel sounds, only the final vowel sound is written.

Study these words and practice them:

create	ca	**graduate**	gda
radio	rdo	**area**	aa
media	⌒da	**audio**	ado
mediate	⌒da	**cameo**	c⌒o

Here is a summary of the various rules concerned with the writing and/or omission of vowels.

1. **Write all initial and final vowels:** edge ej ; data dla ; value vlu ; item i⌒ .
2. **Omit all medial short vowels:** sell sl ; check Cc .
3. **Omit long vowels in words of more than one syllable unless covered by a specific rule:** music ⌒zc ; prevail pvl .
4. **When "ing" or "ed" are added to a root word that contains a long vowel, retain the vowel:** sealing sel ; reached reC .
5. **When the root word outline ends in a vowel, retain the vowel when a suffix is added:** reliable rlib ; lightly lil ; happiest hpe, ; evaluation evluj; myself ⌒s/; fairness fa' ; compliance Kpi/; gaiety ga) .
6. **When a long vowel is followed by a sound that is represented by a mark of punctuation, retain this long vowel in the outline:** variety vri) ; science si/ ; client ci– ; remind r⌒—; acquaint aga–.

7. **When a word contains two pronounced consecutive vowels, the first vowel is written:** ruin *run* ; gradual *gdul* ; poet *pol* .
8. **When an outline ends in a vowel, write the final vowel and omit any vowel that precedes it:** graduate *gda* ; create *ca* .

There is one sound in our language that has no alphabetic representation—the sound of "zh" heard in *visual, casual, treasure.* It is to this sound that the following rule applies.

For the sound of "zh," write *z* .

Study these words and practice them:

casual	czul	**visual**	vzul
casualty	czul)	**treasury**	tzy
pleasurable	pZb	**treasurer**	tZ
leisurely	lZl	**measuring**	mz/-
pleasure	pz/	**enclosure**	ncz/
treasure	tz/	**seizure**	sz/
enclosures	ncz//	**measured**	mz/-
measures	mz//	**treasured**	tz/-

Note the words *pleasure* pz/ and *pleasurable* pZb. In *pleasure* the sound of "er" is final and is represented by a joined slant. In *pleasurable* the sound of "er" becomes medial so it is indicated by capitalizing the *z* which is the letter that precedes the sound.

The same would be true for *treasure* Tz/ and *treasurer* TZ/ . But look at the word *treasury* Tzy . The sound of "er" in this word is included in the sound "ery" which is represented by y . When you break this word down, you have "tr," "zh," and "ery" sounds.

READING EXERCISE

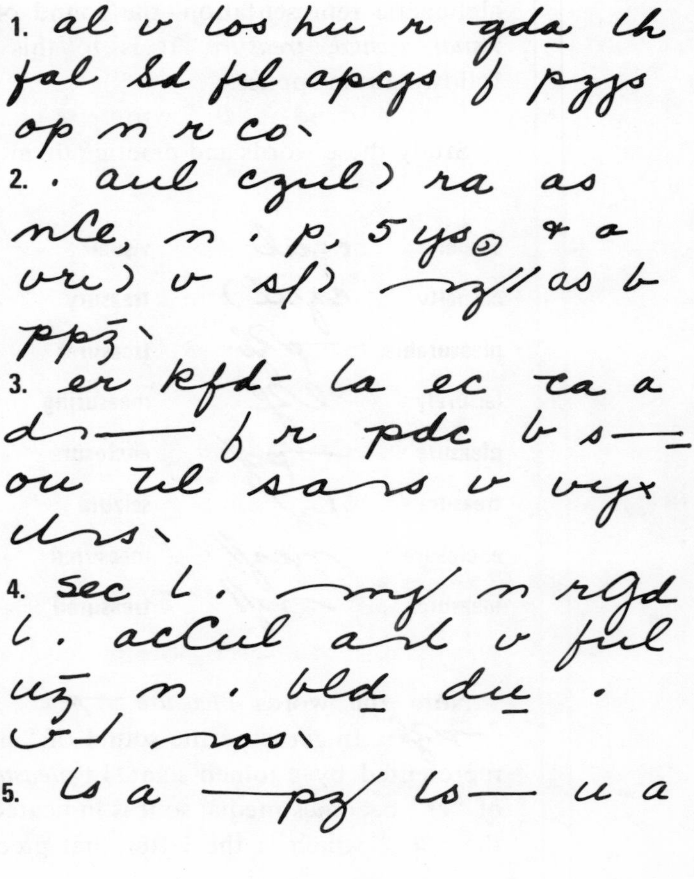

Sx 2 lb gf slc, v r
fax C3\

KEY (1) All of those who are graduating this fall should file applications for positions open in our company. (20 words) (2) The annual casualty rate has/increased in the past five years, and a variety of safety measures has/been proposed. (22 words) (3) We are confident that we can create a demand for our product by sending out trial samples of various/ items. (22 words) (4) Speak to the manager in regard to the actual amount of fuel used in the building during the winter/ months. (21 words) (5) It is a pleasure to send you a special two-pound gift selection of our famous cheese. (16 words)

2 For the sound of "sub," write *s* .
Study these words and practice them:

submitted	smt̄	**subsequently**	ssq-l
substantial	ssx	**substitute**	sstu
subsistence	sss/	**subtract**	str
submit	smt	**substantially**	ssx
subsequent	ssq-	**substitution**	ssl,
subway	swa	**submitting**	smt̲

For the sound of "trans," write Z .
Study these words and practice them:

transaction	transferred
transmission	transportation
transcription	transit
transcript	transfer
transport	transferring

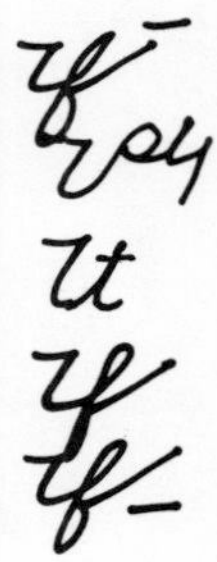

READING EXERCISE

1. 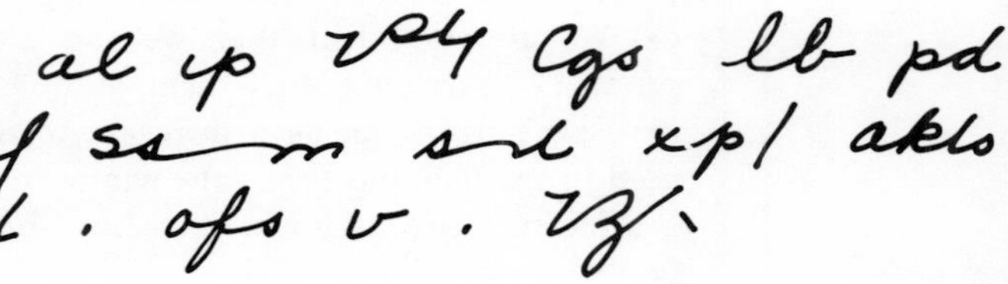

2. 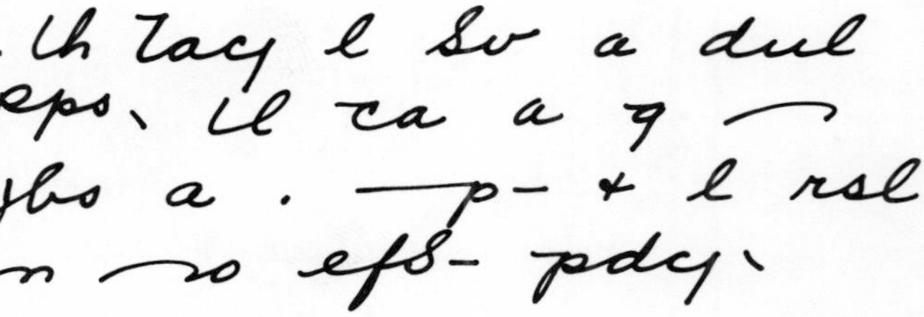

3. 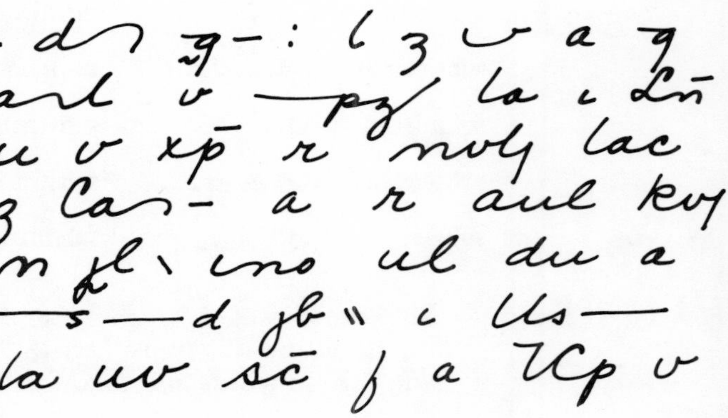

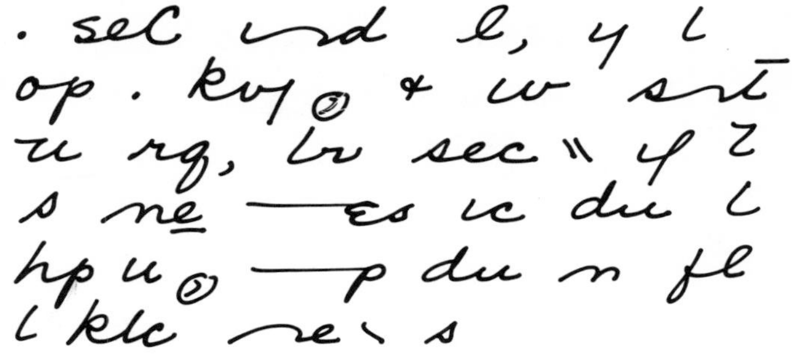

KEY (1) All important transportation charges will be paid if salesmen submit expense accounts to the office of the/ treasurer. (22 words) (2) This transaction will serve a dual purpose. It will create a great many jobs at the plant and will result in/ more efficient production. (27 words) (3) Dear Mr. Grant: It was with a great amount of pleasure that I learned you have accepted our invitation to/ act as chairman at our annual convention in July. I know you will do a splendid job. (P) I understand/ that you have asked for a transcript of the speech I made last year to open the convention, and I have submitted/ your request to our Secretary. (P) If there is anything else I can do to help you, please do not fail to contact/ me. Sincerely, (83 words)

3

BRIEF FORMS

declare	dec
pull	pu
pupil	pup

ABBREVIATIONS

miscellaneous	msc	**bureau**	Bu
pound	lb	**corporation**	corp

superintendent	*supt*	**square**	*sq*
administrate, administration	*ad*		

SUMMARY

L<u>IO</u>n *i*

1. **When a word contains two medial pronounced consecutive vowels, write only the first vowel.**

rad<u>IO</u> *o*

2. **When a word contains two final pronounced consecutive vowels, write only the final vowel.**

trea<u>S</u>ure *3*

3. **Write** *3* **for the sound of "zh."**

SUBmarine *s*

4. Write *s* for the sound of "sub."

TRANSpose *T*

5. Write *T* for the sound of "trans."

READING EXERCISE

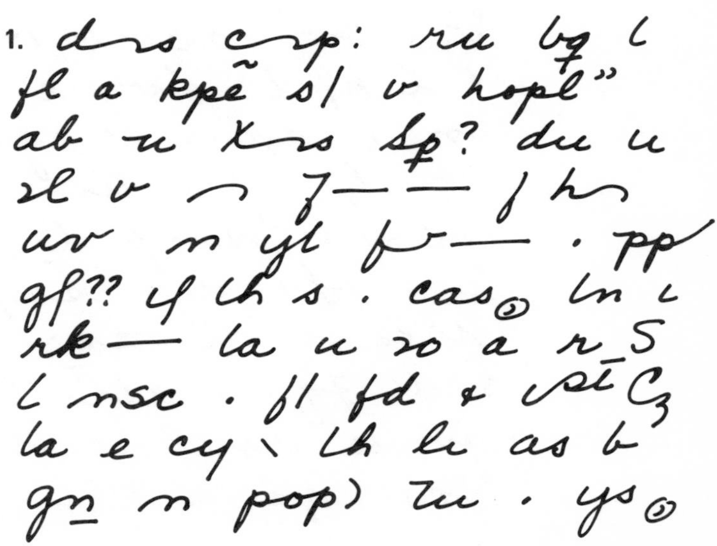

+ nel o u Xrs l, l
lk a 1 o 2 lb Tz/ C,
—d p v r dlx pdcs»
er un ez uc dsl v
al bs + sa TPY ⊙ + r
dos rm op E ud + sl
vn ul 10° \ y n k n +
pa e— l u Sp pbrs\ ul
2. ds' sra: . Bu v Nnl
afas as a T. pQ v
a y pcC la u u
fu hpl fus n u ar gvl
—c"\ lh Srl fl l
gv u pups a —ce/ id
v. — acv» v. Bu
+ l hpl dv a q N,
n. ads v gvl aj//
v lh lup» uc oblns lh
fls b srp D u rq,
l. ofs v. supl v
scls n u aa\ cu
3. d Zq: . alC Crl l
gv u vzul evd/ v.
fcs iga u KSn . xcs

Sū b r corp dū . p,
18 ys\ z uc se⊙ Z z nl
a gdul rz n. aul
dvd— — pd lr xchol//
n. F, 10 ys⊙ b n.
pyd s/ ln⊙ r xc as dt
n olu v a ssg- nls
n. sz v. dvd— —
dec \\ z fr z. fC s kSn⊙
er nvlō n nsc
Tacys la l ca vn no
ssx pfls f us\ f lh
rzn⊙ idu n hzla l avz u
lb r xczasaf nbs-f u sv\ us
4. nds: lh s n rs/l. L e
rsē F, u n vC u nd
ngy rGd r Cgs f lpru
r-ls\\ ecn go a 2— rd
ra a lh lu cs — fc//
r kō n d m—. acCul
c,\ f xp⊙ e nd lno
h — Sns ul v-⊙
. lgl v lu nvlō⊙ +
v u rqi mul o

elctc lprul" uf ul spe
th nfys o. ncz Cd.
el b hpe lgv u a xc
ps f r r-l Sos. ul
5. d [illegible] r: w j, h a
lq kvsy v. P + Zz/
v r co ab. rGib sel
n vC e nv fe rsl.
zu no. ev b lz a q
[illegible] v r pyes l vyx
cos n. s) la of lBl
aul nCss n sly. frs v
hll nSul/. X vcj bnes. + J
fnx bnfs" ls obvx la s
[illegible], b dn cda. f th rzn.
vn cl a sx re v.
Bd v D// f Zi. ap 5. a
3[15]" n. mlu. du
rvu. l, v usc sjsjs la
s ncz so la una gv re
u opn vn e re. ul
6. d) vi: r F sagx
lw u Zf u bs l us. + er

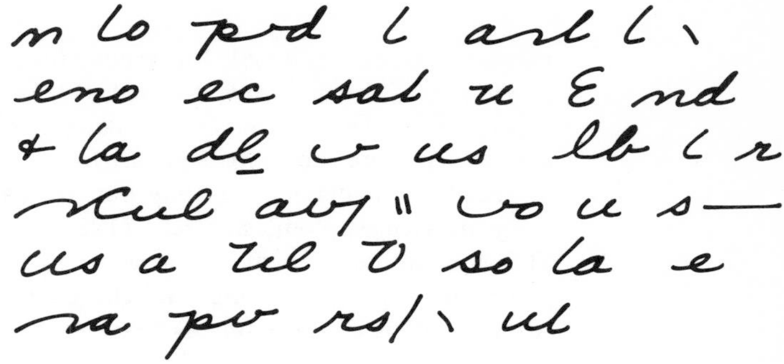

KEY (1) Dear Mrs. Camp: Are you beginning to feel a complete sense of hopelessness about your Christmas shopping? Do you/ still have many friends for whom you have not yet found the proper gift? (P) If this is the case, then I recommend that you/ stop at our store to inspect the fancy food and imported cheese that we carry. This line has been gaining in/ popularity through the years, and anyone on your Christmas list will welcome a one- or two-pound treasure chest made/ up of our delicious products. (P) We are within easy walking distance of all bus and subway transportation,/ and our doors remain open every Wednesday and Saturday evening until ten o'clock. Why not come in and/ put an end to your shopping problems. Yours truly, (128 words) (2) Dear Miss Small: The Bureau of Internal Affairs has announced the preparation of a motion picture that you/ might find helpful for use in your American Government classes. This short film will give your pupils a clearer/ idea of the many activities of the Bureau and will help to develop a greater interest/ in the administration of government agencies of this type. (P) You can obtain this film by simply directing/ your request to the Office of the Superintendent of Schools in your area. Cordially yours, (98 words) (3) Dear Frank: The attached chart will give you visual evidence of the facts I gave you concerning the stocks issued/ by our corporation during the past 18 years. As you can see, there was only a gradual rise in the/ annual dividends paid to our stockholders in the first 10 years; but in the period since then, our/ stock has doubled in value with a subsequent increase in the size of the dividends declared. (P) As far as the/ future is concerned, we are involved in miscellaneous transactions that will create even more substantial/ profits for us. For this reason, I do not hesitate to advise you to buy our stock as a safe investment/ for your savings. Yours sincerely, (125 words) (4) My dear Sir: This is in response to the letter we received from you in which you made inquiry regarding our/ charges for typewriter rentals. (P) We cannot quote a standard rate at this time because many factors are considered/ in determining the actual cost. For example, we need to know how many machines you will want, the/ length of time involved, and whether you require manual or electric typewriters. (P) If you will supply this/ information on the enclosed card, we will be happy to give you an exact price for our rental service. Yours truly,/ (100 words) (5) Dear Mr. March: I have just had a long conversation with the President and Treasurer of our company/ about the regrettable situation in which we now find ourselves. As you know, we have been losing a great/ many of our employees to various companies in the city that offer liberal annual/ increases in salary, forms of health insurance, extra vacation bonuses, and other financial benefits./ (P) It is obvious that something must be done immediately. For this reason, I am calling a special/ meeting of the Board of Directors for Friday, April 5, at 3:15. (P) In the meantime, would you review the/ list of miscellaneous suggestions that is enclosed so that you may give me your opinion when we meet. Yours/ truly, (141 words) (6) My dear Mr. White: Our firm is anxious to have you transfer your business to us, and we are not too proud to admit/ it. We know we can satisfy your every need and that dealing with us will be to our mutual/ advantage. (P) Won't you send us a trial order so that we may prove ourselves. Yours truly, (55 words)

SUMMARY OF PRINCIPLES

WRITING VOWELS

1. Write long vowels in one-syllable words: *goal* **gol** ; *huge* **huj** ; *wife* **wf** ; *league* **leg** .
2. Write **initial** and **final** short vowels: *asset* **ast** ; *egg* **eg** ; *ice* **is** ; *quota* **goa** ; *editor* **edr** ; *formula* **frla**.
3. When a word **ends** in the sound "ate," "eet," "ite," "ote," or "ute," write the vowel and omit the *t:* *date* **da** ; *meet* **me** ; *light* **li** ; *vote* **vo** ; *suit* **su** .
4. When a word **ends** in the sound of "ave," "eve," "ive," "ove," or "uve," write the vowel and omit the *v:* *gave* **ga** ; *leave* **le** ; *arrive* **ari** ; *drove* **do** ; *groove* **gu** .
5. When a word **ends** in the sound of "ame," "eem," "ime," "ome," or "ume," write the vowel and omit the *m:* *same* **sa** ; *extreme* **xte** ; *lifetime* **lfti** ; *home* **ho** ; *presume* **pzu** .
6. When a word **ends** in the sound of "air," "eer," "ire," "ore," or "ure," write the vowel and omit the *r:* *repair* **rpa** ; *appear* **ape** ; *acquire* **aqi** ;

explore xpo ; *insure* nbu .

7. When "ing" or "ed" is added to an outline that contains a long vowel, retain the vowel in the outline: *hoping* hop ; *teaching* leC ; *filed* fil .
8. When the outline of a root word **begins** or **ends** in a vowel, retain that vowel when a prefix or suffix is added to it: *high* hi ; *highly* hil ; *true* tu ; *truly* tul ; *pay* pa ; *payroll* parl; *renew* rnu ; *renewal* rnul ; *react* rac ; *reelect* relc ; *reopen* rop .
9. When a long vowel is followed by a mark of punctuation, retain the vowel: *moment* mo- ; *truant* tu- ; *duty* du) ; *consumer* ksu/ .
10. Write ol for the sound of "old": *golden* goln ; *boulder* bol/ ; *folder* fol/ .
11. Write i for the **initial** sound of "im": *imitate* ila ; *impossibility* ipsb) .
12. Write u for the **initial** sound of "un": *undoubtedly* udt ; *unfortunately* ufCnll .
13. Write in for the sound of "ine": *combine* kbin ; *consignee* ksine .
14. When a word contains two **medial pronounced** consecutive vowels, write the first vowel only: *trial* til ; *annual* aul ; *diameter* di/ .
15. When a word contains two **final pronounced** consecutive vowels, write the last vowel only: *create* ca ; *graduate* gda .
16. Write al for the **final** sound of "all": *install* nsal ; *football* ftbal .
17. Write a for the **initial** and **final** sound of "aw": *all* al ; *alter* al/ ; *law* la ; *saw* sa .

OMITTING VOWELS

1. Omit all **medial** short vowels: *citizenship* slznS; *finish* fnS; *yellow* ylo; *knowledge* nlj.
2. Omit all **medial** long vowels in words of more than one syllable: *obtain* obtn; *procedure* psj; *belief* blf.
3. Write c for the **medial** and **final** sounds of "ake": *make* ⌢c; *lakeside* lcsd; *taking* tc.
4. Omit the vowel and write d for the **medial** and **final** sounds of "ade," "ede," "ide," "ode," and "ude": *made* ⌢d; *cede* sd; *side* sd; *reload* rld *crudely* Cdl.
5. Omit the vowel and write z for the **medial** and **final** sounds of "aze," "eze," "ize," "oze," and "uze": *phase* fz; *reason* rzn; *wisely* uzl; *chosen* Czn; *chooses* Czs.
6. Write ⌢ for the prefix "em": *emphatic* ⌢flc; *emblem* ⌢bl; *employer* ⌢py.
7. Omit the vowel and write *n* for the sounds of "ane," "ene," "one," and "une": *train* Tn; *seen* sn; *loan* ln; *soon* sn.
8. Write y for the **medial** or **final** sound of a vowel + "ry": *various* vyx; *machinery* ⌢Sny; *inquiry* nqy; *territory* Tly; *hurry* hy.
9. Write n for the prefix "en": *enclosure* ncz; *endure* ndu; *engine* njn.
10. When a word contains two medial **pronounced consecutive** vowels, omit the second vowel: *trial* Til; *annual* aul; *diameter* dm/.
11. When a word contains two final **pronounced consecutive** vowels, omit the first vowel: *create* Ca; *graduate* gda.

12. Write **l** for the final sound of "lee": *efficiently* **efS-l** ; *originally* **ojnl** ; *early* **El** .

13. Write **j** for the **medial** or **final** sounds of a vowel + "shun": *qualifications* **qlfcjs** ; *completion* **kpj** ; *competition* **kptj** ; *promotions* **pmjs** .

14. Write a **)** for the **final** sound of "tee": *duty* **du)** ; *quantities* **q-))** ; *ability* **ab)** ; *authority* **aT)** .

COMBINATION SOUNDS

1. Write **ᵕ** for the sound of "wh": *what* **ᵕl** ; *when* **ᵕn** ; *which* **ᵕC** .
2. Write **C** for the sound of "ch": *attachment* **alC-** ; *chiefly* **Cfl** ; *much* **mC** ; *nature* **nC** .
3. Write **S** for the sound of "sh": *issuing* **iSu** ; *insurance* **nSu/** ; *sufficient* **sfS-** .
4. Write **ᵕ** for the **medial** and **final** sounds of "ow": *allowance* **alᵕ/** ; *doubt* **dᵕl** ; *now* **nᵕ** .
5. Write **l** for the sound of "th": *them* **ln** ; *method* **mld** ; *health* **hll** .
6. Write a hyphen on the **initial** letter of an outline to indicate the initial "combination-r" sounds: *broke* **b̄oc** ; *crashed* **c̄S** ; *dropped* **d̄p** ; *free* **f̄e** ; *group* **ḡup** ; *privilege* **p̄vlj** ; *travel* **t̄vl** ; *through* **t̄u** ; *argue* **āgu** ; *earn* **Ēn** ; *or* **ō** ; *urge* **ūj** ; *shred* **S̄d** .

   To express a **medial** "combination-r" sound, capitalize the letter that precedes the *r* and omit the *r* from the outline: *fabric* **fBc** ; *increase* **nCs** ;

refresh rFS ; *agreement* agr- ; *approach* aPC ; *attractive* atrcv .

7. Write y for the sound of "oi": *appointment* apy-- ; *oil* yl ; *toy* ty .
8. Write g for the sound of "kw": *frequently* Fg-l ; *acquainted* aga= ; *quit* gl ; *quite* gi *adequate* adgl.
9. Write a dash on the **initial** letter of an outline to indicate the **initial** "combination-l" sounds: *block* —bc ; *clients* —ci-- ; *element* —E- ; *flight* —fi ; *glad* —gd ; *ill* —i ; *plan* —pn ; *slow* —so ; *ultimate* —ulml ; *alibi* —ab ; *else* —es .

   When the "combination-l" sound is **medial**, omit the *l* and write the letter that precedes it: *application* apcj .
10. Write a comma (,) for the **initial** and **final** sound of "st": *largest* lj, ; *listings* l2= ; *introduced* ntdu, ; *study* ,de ; *stands* ,— .
11. Write s for the **medial** sound of "st": *mistake* msc ; *instead* nsd.
12. Write g for the sound of "nk": *frankly* Fgl ; *thinking* tg .
13. Write b for the final sounds of "bul" and "blee": *able* ab ; *favorably* fvb .
14. Write p for the final sounds of "pul" and "plee": *simple* smp ; *simply* smp.
15. Write a small printed S for the sound of "sp": *spend* S— ; *respect* rSc ; *grasp* gS .
16. Write a disjoined slant for the sounds of "nse" and "nsy": *expense* xp/ ; *responsible* rs/b ; *fancy* f/ .

17. Write z for the sound of "zh": *treasure* tz/ ; *treasury* tzy .
18. Write a capital printed S for the sound of "str": *distribute* dSbu.
19. Write a dash (–) for **medial** or **final** "nd": *recommend* rk— ; *brand* b— .
20. Write s for "sub": *submit* sl.
21. Write t for "trans": *transfer* tf .

PUNCTUATION MARKS

1. Use an underscore to indicate the addition of "ing" or "thing" to a word: *getting* gt̲ ; *recommending* rk—̲ ; *anything* ne̲ .
2. Use an overscore to indicate the addition of "ed" to form a past tense: *added* ad̄ ; *occurred* oc/̄ ; *wanted* w-̄ ; *mended* m—̄ ; *announced* a-/̄ .
3. Use a hyphen for the **medial** and **final** sounds of "nt" and "ment": *resident* rzd- ; *didn't* dd- ; *judgment* jj- ; *rental* r-l .
4. Use a joined slant to indicate the **final** sounds of "er" and "ter": *favor* fv/ ; *feature* fc/ ; *officers* ofs// ; *errors* e// ; *center* s-/ .
5. Use a dash for the sound of "nd": *recommend* rk— ; *brand* b— .
6. Use an apostrophe to indicate a **final** *ss* and *ness*: *regardless* rgdl' ; *addresses* aD" ; *illness* —l' .
7. Use a quotation mark to indicate a **final** "ssness": *hopelessness* hopl" ; *helplessness* hpl" .
8. Use a comma to indicate the **initial** and **final** sounds of "st": *largest* lj, ; *listings* l,̲ ;

introduced ntdu, ; *study* sde ; *stands* s— .

9. Use a blend ( )) to indicate the final sound of "tee": *duty* du) ; *abilities* ab)) .
10. Use a disjoined slant to indicate the sounds of "nse" and "nsy": *expense* xp/ ; *responsible* rs/b ; *fancy* f/ ; and s/ for *self* and *selves*: *selfish* s/8 ; *myself* ms/ ; *themselves* ms/ .

CAPITALIZATION

1. To express a **medial** "combination-r" sound, capitalize the letter that precedes the *r* and omit the *r* from the outline: *fabric* fBc ; *increase* nCs ; *refresh* rFS ; *agreement* aGe- .
2. To express the **medial** vowel and *r*, capitalize the outline that precedes the sound: *liberally* lBl ; *report* rPt ; *accordingly* aCdg ; *modern* mDn ; *furniture* FnC ; *regard* rGd ; *certainly* Stnl ; *determine* dTm ; *converse* kVs ; *reserved* rZv ; *thorough* To .
3. For the final sound of "ther" write a capital *t*: *author* aT ; *farther* frT .
4. Write C for the sound of "ch": *cheap* Cep ; *reach* reC .
5. Write S for the sound of "sh": *issue* iSu ; *rush* rS .
6. Write N for the sounds of "enter" and "inter": *entertain* Ntn ; *interest* N, .

MISCELLANEOUS

1. Write s to form plurals of outlines ending in a letter of the alphabet: *groups* gups ; *today's* tds ; *joins* jyns .

2. Repeat the punctuation mark to form plurals of outlines ending in punctuation marks: *mailings* mal= ; *events* ev-- ; *abilities* ab)) ; *expenses* xp// ; *invests* nv,,.
3. Write c for the sound of "k": *cashier* cSe ; *keynote* cenl; *booklet* bcll; *walk* wc.
4. Write v for **medial** and **final** "tiv": *effective* efcv ; *tentative* t-v ; *positively* pzvl.
5. Write k for the sounds of "com," "con," and "coun": *combination* kbnj ; *convenient* kvn- ; *counters* k//.
6. Write S for the sounds of "str," "star," "ster," and "stor": *distribute* dSbu ; *start* St ; *registered* rjS̄ ; *story* Se.
7. Write x for the sounds of "aks," "eks," "iks," "oks," and "uks": *accident* xd- ; *extent* xt- ; *fix* fx ; *box* bx ; *deluxe* dlx.
8. Write j for the sounds of **medial** and **final** "shun," vowel + "shun," and "nshun": *national* njl ; *invitations* nvtjs ; *attention* atj.
9. Omit *n* before the sounds of "g," "j," and "ch": *bring* bg ; *length* lgl ; *exchange* xCj ; *ranch* rC.
10. Write x for **medial** and **final** sounds of "us," "usly," "shus," "shusly," "shul," "shully," "nshul," and "nshully" in words of more than one syllable: *bonus* bnx ; *officially* ofx ; *anxious* agx ; *financially* fnx.
11. Omit *t* after the sounds of "k," "p," "f," and "x" and omit *pt* after "m": *act* ac ; *except* xp ; *draft* df ; *next* nx ; *prompt* pr.
12. Omit *d* before "m" and "v": *admit* aml ; *advance* av/.

13. Write *f* for "ful," "fully," and the final sound of "fy": *carefully* caf ; *beautiful* blf ; *notify* nlf.

WRITING SPECIFIC SOUNDS IN DIFFERENT POSITIONS

1. Write a hyphen on the **initial** letter of an outline to indicate the **initial** "combination-r" sound; capitalize the letter that precedes this sound in a **medial** position: *brick* bc ; *fabric* fBc ; *crease* ces ; *increase* nCs ; *drama* dra ; *melodrama* mDra ; *fresh* fS ; *refresh* rFS ; *gram* gm ; *program* pgm ; *print* p- ; *reprint* rP- .
2. Write a dash on the **initial** letter of an outline to indicate the **initial** "combination-l" sound; omit the *l* and write the letter that precedes the **medial** "combination-l" sound: *block* bc ; *glad* gd ; *plan* pn ; *apply* apc ; *duplicate* dpca .
3. **Initial** "er" is indicated E ; **final** "er" and "ter" are indicated with a joined slant; and **medial** "vowel + r" is indicated by capitalizing the letter that precedes the sound: *earn* En ; *cover* cv ; *after* af .

SUMMARY OF BRIEF FORMS

about	ab	as	z
above	bv	ask	sc
acknowledge	ak	at	a
advantage	avj	auto	A
again, st	ag	be	b
almost	lmo	because	cs
already	lr	been	b
also	lso	began	bg
always	l⌣	begin	bg
am	⌒	benefit	bnf
an	a	between	bl
appreciate	ap	billion	B
are	r	both	bo
around	r⌣	business	bs

busy	bz
but	b
buy	b
by	b
call	cl
came	k
can	c
cents	c
charge	Cg
circumstance	c/
collect	cc
come	k
committee	k
conclusion	kclj
consider	ks
continue	ku
contract	Kc
correct	Kc
country	c/
customer	K
deal	dl
declare	dec
definite, ly	dfn
deliver	dl
delivery	dl
describe	des
description	des
develop	dv
difficult	dfk
difficulty	dfk
direct	D
dollar, s	d
during	du̲
easy	ez
entitle	ntl
even	vn
evening	vn̲
ever	E
every	E
extra	X
extraordinary	Xo
fail	fl
feel	fl
field	fld
find	fi
fine	fi

fire	fr	important	ip
firm	F	in	n
for	f	individual, ly	ndv
full	fu	initial, ly	ix
fully	fu	is	s
future	fC	it	t
given	gv	keep	cp
go	g	kind	ci
good	g	known	no
great	g	letter	L
had	h	life	lf
has	as	like	lc
have	v	line	li
he	h	little	ll
held	hl	man	⌒-
help	hp	many	⌒
him	h	member	⌒B
his	s	million	⌒
hole	hl	move	⌒v
hour	r	necessarily	nec
hundred	H	necessary	nec
idea	id	not	n
immediate, ly	ida	note	nt

object	ob	publish	pb
of	v	pull	pu
on	o	pupil	pup
once	c/	purchase	pC
only	nl	put	p
open	op	real, ly	rl
opinion	opn	regular, ly	reg
opportunity	opl	regulation	reg
order	O	result	rsl
organization	og	sale	s
organize	og	sample	sa
other	J	satisfaction	sal
our	r	satisfactory	sal
out	ou	satisfy	sal
over	O	save	sv
particular, ly	P	school	scl
perhaps	pps	several	sv
please	p	shall	S
poor	po	she	S
price	ps	ship	S
probable, ly	pb	situation	sil
prove	pv	small	sa
public	pb	stop	so

Word	Outline	Word	Outline
subject	sj	usual, ly	x
success	suc	very	v
successful, ly	suc	was	z
that	la	we	e
the	.	well	l
their	T	were	w
there	T	where	wr
they	ly	while	wl
this	lh	whole	hl
those	los	whom	hm
thought	lo	why	y
thousand	Td	will	l
throughout	Tuo	with	w
to	l	without	wo
too	lo	woman	wm-
under	ul	world	wo
until	ul	would	d
up	p	your	u
upon	pn		

SUMMARY OF STANDARD ABBREVIATIONS

absolute, ly	abs
administrate	adm
administration	adm
advertise	adv
America, n	Am
amount	amt
and	&
approximate, ly	apx
associate	asso
avenue	ave
average	av
boulevard	blvd
bureau	Bu
capital	cap
catalog	cat
certificate	cert
certify	cert
child	ch
children	chn
Christmas	Xms
company	co
corporation	corp
credit	cr
day	d
department	dpt
discount	dis
doctor	dr
East	E

envelope env
establish est
federal fed
feet ft
figure fig
foot ft
government govt
inch in
independent ind
intelligence intl
intelligent, ly intl
invoice inv
junior jr
magazine mag
manufacture mfr
maximum max
memorandum memo
merchandise mdse
mile mi
minimum min
month mo
minute min
miscellaneous misc

mortgage mtg
North N
number no
ounce oz
page p
pair pr
parcel post pp
percent pc
place pl
popular pop
post office po
pound lb
president P
question q
railroad rr
railway ry
represent rep
representative rep
room rm
second sec
secretary sec
senior sr
signature sig

South	S	**total**	lol
square	sq	**vice-president**	VP
street	sl	**volume**	vol
subscribe	sub	**warehouse**	⌣hs
subscription	sub	**week**	⌣k
superintendent	supl	**West**	⌣̄
telephone	lel	**year**	y

SUMMARY OF GEOGRAPHICAL TERMS

THE UNITED STATES

Alabama (AL)
Alaska (AK)
Arizona (AZ)
Arkansas (AR)
California (CA)
Colorado (CO)
Connecticut (CT)
Delaware (DE)
District of Columbia (DC)
Florida (FL)
Georgia (GA)
Hawaii (HI)
Idaho (ID)
Illinois (IL)

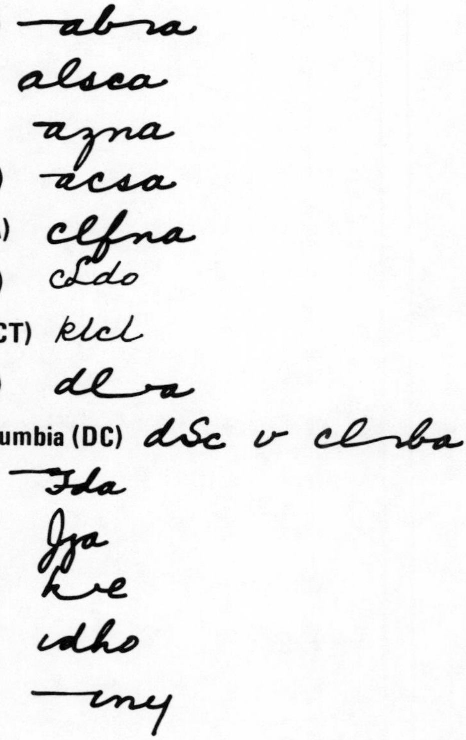

Indiana (IN)	ndena
Iowa (IA)	ia
Kansas (KS)	czs
Kentucky (KY)	c-ce
Louisiana (LA)	lzena
Maine (ME)	mn
Maryland (MD)	Ml—
Massachusetts (MA)	msCsls
Michigan (MI)	mSgn
Minnesota (MN)	mnsla
Mississippi (MS)	msspe
Missouri (MO)	mzy
Montana (MT)	m-na
Nebraska (NB)	nBsca
Nevada (NV)	nvda
New Hampshire (NH)	nu hmS
New Jersey (NJ)	nu Jze
New Mexico (NM)	nu mxco
New York (NY)	nu Yc
North Carolina (NC)	N Clina
North Dakota (ND)	N dcla
Ohio (OH)	oho
Oklahoma (OK)	ochma

Oregon (OR)	ogn
Pennsylvania (PA)	p/lvna
Rhode Island (RI)	rd l—
South Carolina (SC)	S Clina
South Dakota (SD)	S dcla
Tennessee (TN)	tnse
Texas (TX)	txs
Utah (UT)	ula
Vermont (VT)	V—
Virginia (VA)	Vjna
Washington (WA)	◡Sgln
West Virginia (WV)	◡ Vjna
Wisconsin (WI)	◡sksn
Wyoming (WY)	◡iq

AMERICAN CITIES

Akron	aCn
Albany	albne
Albuquerque	—abCce
Amarillo	⌒lo
Annapolis	apls
Atlanta	atl-a
Augusta	agsa
Austin	asn

Baltimore	bl-o
Baton Rouge	bln ruz
Birmingham	Bghm
Bismarck	bzrc
Boise	byze
Boston	bsn
Bridgeport	bjpl
Buffalo	bflo
Cambridge	kBj
Camden	c-dn
Carson City	Csn s)
Charleston	Crlsn
Chattanooga	Clnga
Cheyenne	Sin
Chicago	Scq
Cincinnati	snsn)
Cleveland	—cvl—
Columbia	cl-ba
Columbus	cl-bx
Concord	kCd
Dallas	dls
Dayton	dln
Denver	dnv

Des Moines
Detroit
Dover
El Paso
Erie
Evansville
Flint
Fort Wayne
Fort Worth
Frankfort
Gary
Grand Rapids
Greensboro
Harrisburg
Hartford
Helena
Honolulu
Houston
Indianapolis
Jacksonville
Jefferson City
Jersey City
Juneau

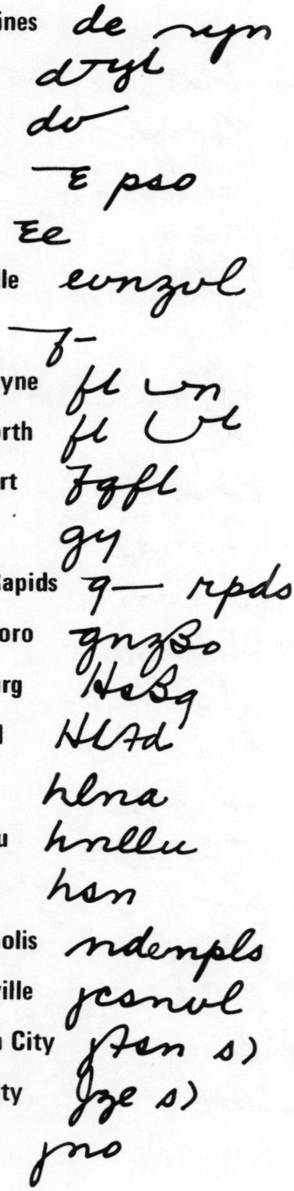

Kansas City
Lansing
Lincoln
Little Rock
Long Beach
Los Angeles
Louisville
Madison
Memphis
Miami
Milwaukee
Minneapolis
Montgomery
Montpelier
Nashville
Newark
New Haven
New Orleans
New York
Norfolk
Oakland
Oklahoma City
Olympia

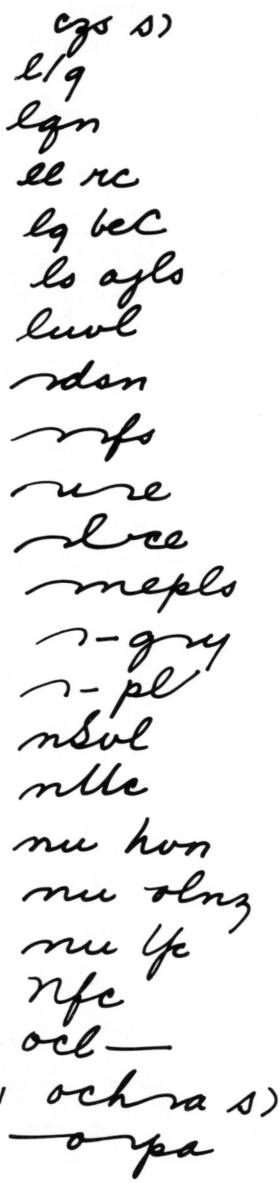

Omaha	oha
Paterson	pTn
Philadelphia	fldlfa
Phoenix	fnx
Pierre	pa
Pittsburgh	plsBq
Portland	pll—
Providence	pvd/
Raleigh	rl
Richmond	rC—
Rochester	rCS
Sacramento	sC-o
St. Louis	sa- lus
St. Paul	sa- pal
St. Petersburg	sa- pTZBq
Salem	sl
Salt Lake City	sll lc s)
San Antonio	sn alno
San Diego	sn deq
San Francisco	sn frnssco
San Jose	sn hza
Santa Fe	s-a fa
Savannah	svna

Seattle	sell
Shreveport	Svsl
South Bend	S b—
Spokane	Sc
Springfield	Sgfld
Syracuse	Scz
Tacoma	lcma
Tallahassee	llhse
Toledo	lldo
Trenton	T-n
Tucson	lsn
Tulsa	llsa
Washington	vSgln
Wichita	vCla
Worcester	vS
Yonkers	yg/
Youngstown	ygzl-n

CANADIAN PROVINCES AND TERRITORIES

Alberta	aBla
British Columbia	Bls clmba
Manitoba	mlba
New Brunswick	nu bnzvc
Newfoundland	nf— l—

Northwest Territory	nw Try
Nova Scotia	nva scSa
Ontario	o-yo
Prince Edward Island	p/ edwd l—
Quebec	qbc
Saskatchewan	sscCn
Yukon Territory	uk Try

CANADIAN CITIES

Alma	—a a
Amherst	—H,
Arvida	avda
Barrie	by
Belleville	blvl
Brampton	b—m
Brandon	b—n
Brantford	b-Fd
Brockville	bcvl
Calgary	clgy
Cap-de-la-Madeleine	cpdl-dln
Charlottetown	Srltt-n
Chicoutimi	Scl-e
Cornwall	Cn-al
Cote-St.-Michel	clsa-Sl

Dartmouth

Drummondville

Edmonton

Edmundston

Fairville

Flin Flon

Forest Hill

Ft. William

Ft. William-Pt. Arthur

Fredericton

Galt

Glace Bay

Granby

Guelph

Halifax

Hamilton

Hull

Jacques-Cartier

Jasper-Place

Joliette

Jonquiere

Kenogami

Kenora

Kingston	cgsn
Kirkland Lake	Ccl— lc
Kitchener	cCn
Lachine	lSn
LaSalle	lsl
La Tuque	la luc
Lauzon	lzn
Laval-des-Rapides	lvldrpd
Leaside	lsd
Lethbridge	lLBj
Lindsay	l—ze
London	l—n
Long Branch	lg bC
Magog	—gg
Medicine Hat	—dsn hl
Mimico	——co
Moncton	—gn
Montreal	—Tal
Moose Jaw	ms ja
Nanaimo	nn—o
New Toronto	nu T-o
New Westminster	nu ⌣—mS
Niagara Falls	nuGa fals

North Bay n ba
North Vancouver n vncv
Orillia ola
Oshawa oSa
Ottawa oLa
Owen Sound on s-
Pembroke pBc
Penticton p-cn
Peterborough pTBo
Pointe-aux-Trembles p- -o-b
Pointe-Claire p- ca
Portage la Praire plzlpy
Port Alberni pl aBne
Port Arthur pl aT
Port Colborne pl clBn
Prince Albert pl aBl
Prince George pl jj
Prince Rupert pl rpl
Quebec qbc
Red Deer rd de
Regina rjina
Rimouski r-sce
Riverside rVsd

St. Boniface	sa- bnfs
St. Catharines	sa- cTnz
St. Hyacinthe	sa- hisnl
St. James	sa- jmz
St. Jean	sa- zn
St. Jerome	sn zo
St. John's	sa- jnz
St. Lambert	sa- lBt
St. Laurent	snLn
St. Michel	snSl
St. Thomas	sa- Lms
Ste. Foy	sa- fy
Sarnia	Sna
Saskatoon	ssctn
Sault Sainte Marie	su sa- Me
Shawinigan Falls	Swngn fals
Sherbrooke	SrBc
Sillery	sly
Sorel	Sl
Stratford	StTfd
Sudbury	sdby
Swift Current	swf C-
Sydney	sdne

Thetford Mines

Timmins

Toronto

Trail

Trenton

Trois-Rivieres

Truro

Valleyfield

Vancouver

Verdun

Victoria

Victoriaville

Ville-Jaques-Cartier

Waterloo

Welland

Whitehorse

Windsor

Winnipeg

Woodstock

Index

P

R

S

T

U

V

Brief Forms

1 ab	2 bv	3 ak	4 avj	5 ag	6 lro	7 lr	8 lso	9 l⌣	10 ⌒
11 a	12 ap	13 r	14 r⌣	15 3	16 sc	17 A	18 b	19 cs	20 bq
21 bnf	22 bl	23 bo	24 bs	25 bz	26 cl	27 k	28 c	29 Cq	30 c/
31 cc	32 kcly	33 ks	34 ku	35 Kc	36 c⌣	37 K	38 dl	39 dec	40 dfn
41 des	42 dv	43 dfk	44 D	45 d	46 du (underlined)	47 ez	48 nll	49 vn	50 vn (underlined)
51 E	52 X	53 Xo	54 fl	55 fld	56 fe	57 fr	58 F	59 f	60 fu
61 fC	62 gv	63 g	64 g (crossed)	65 h	66 as	67 v	68 hl	69 hp	70 s
71 id	72 ida	73 ip	74 n	75 ndv	76 ix	77 l	78 cp	79 ci	80 no
81 l	82 lf	83 lc	84 li	85 ll	86 ⌒-	87 ⌒B	88 ⌣v	89 nec	90 nl
91 ob	92 o	93 nl	94 op	95 opn	96 opl	97 O	98 og	99 I	100 ou
101 O	102 P	103 pps	104 -p	105 po	106 ps	107 -pb	108 -pv	109 pb	110 pu
111 pup	112 pC	113 p	114 rl	115 req	116 rsl	117 s	118 sa	119 sal	120 sv
121 scl	122 S	123 sil	124 sra	125 ro	126 sj	127 suc	128 la	129 .	130 z
131 ly	132 th	133 los	134 lo	135 Tuo	136 U	137 ul	138 pn	139 x	140 e
141 l	142 ⌣	143 ur	144 ul	145 hs	146 y	147 ⌣o	148 ⌣-	149 l⌣o	150 u
151	152	153	154	155	156	157	158	159	160